This should be
$65-

THE CONFEDERACY'S FIGHTING CHAPLAIN

THE CONFEDERACY'S FIGHTING CHAPLAIN
Father John B. Bannon

Phillip Thomas Tucker

The University of Alabama Press
Tuscaloosa & London

Copyright © 1992
The University of Alabama Press
Tuscaloosa, Alabama 35487–0380
All rights reserved
Manufactured in the United States of America

designed by zig zeigler

∞

The paper on which this book is printed meets the minimum requirements of American National Standard for Information Science-Permanence of Paper for Printed Library Materials, ANSI Z39.48-1984.

Library of Congress Cataloging-in-Publication Data

Tucker, Phillip Thomas, 1953–
    The Confederacy's fighting chaplain : Father John B. Bannon / Phillip Thomas Tucker.
        p.   cm.
    Includes bibliographical references and index.
    ISBN 0-8173-0573-4 (alk. paper)
    1. United States—History—Civil War, 1861–1865—Religious aspects. 2. Bannon, John B., 1829–1913. 3. Confederate States of America. Army—Chaplains—Biography. 4. Catholic Church—United States—Clergy—Biography. 5. Catholic Church—Ireland—Clergy—Biography. I. Title.
E635.B36T84 1992
973.7'79'092—dc20
[B]   91-24815

British Library Cataloguing-in-Publication Data available

FOR MY PARENTS

Will and Betty Tucker

CONTENTS

PREFACE

THE IMPORTANCE OF RELIGION and religious leaders in the Confederate experiment at nationhood has long been ignored by modern historians. Year after year, a standard, well-known cast of military commanders, events, and battles reappear in "new" works with monotonous regularity. Most of this indulgence has focused on the Eastern Theater. The rewriting of common topics in Civil War historiography has led to mythology, hero-worship, and a further glorification of the most popular aspects of the conflict while other subjects of greater importance have been doomed to obscurity. This limitation of perspective has helped to place some of the most significant religious personalities of the South deep into the shadows.

In addition, such negligence has been greater for those Confederate religious leaders and chaplains in the West. For example, perhaps no other man of God who struggled in behalf of the Confederacy so rightly deserved recognition far beyond his peers as the Reverend John B. Bannon. A historic anti-Southern, anti-Catholic, and anti-Western-Theater bias contributed to Father Bannon's obscurity.

The Reverend John Bannon was truly a Renaissance man. After a distinguished career as one of the leading religious leaders of St. Louis, Missouri, in the antebellum period, he became a chaplain-soldier of perhaps the finest combat unit on either side during the Civil War, the First Missouri Confederate Brigade. He conceived a brilliant strategy, serving as diplomat in a crucial initiative to gain recognition for the Confederacy from the Pope and thus to open the door to foreign recognition from France and Britain. He acted as a secret agent in Ireland during an all-important clandestine mission to stop the flood of Irish immigrants pouring into the Union Armies at a critical time (before the decisive campaigns of 1864), and his distinguished postwar career marked him as one of the most significant, religious leaders in Ireland.

Indeed, no other religious personality of the Confederacy accomplished so much and received so little recognition as Father Bannon. As the years from the war's end passed, so the obscurity of Bannon's role in the conflict grew. This book details how an Irish immigrant found the equality, respect, and recognition in Confederate service and society that had been absent in the United States before the war. His story—the Irishman who brought the Bible, unwavering commitment, and daring to both the battlefield and the diplomatic field—has been ignored for more than one-hundred thirty years.

At the war's critical midway point, the key mission to the Vatican offered yet another, and the best last chance to gain foreign recognition for the Confederacy. This aspect of Confederate diplomacy lays to rest the belief that the earlier Emancipation Proclamation and Confederate defeat at Antietam, Gettysburg, and Vicksburg were the final acts that ended all possibilities for foreign recognition. The Bannon mission to Ireland proved that the Confederacy had to win any foreign recognition through diplomacy and not through battlefield victories—a crucial reality after 1863 with military defeat almost inevitable. Like no one else in the Southern leadership, Father Bannon understood that religion could be utilized to help win the Confederacy's independence via foreign recognition.

Clearly, few men in the Confederacy played such a distinguished and versatile role during the Civil War as Father Bannon. His story brings to life forgotten aspects of Southern, Confederate military, Missouri, St. Louis, and Irish historiography.

This book emphasizes as well the role of one of the forgotten components of Southern society during the war—the Irish immigrants of the Confederacy. Bannon's story is also the story of the Missouri Irish Confederates, whose participation in the conflict has been neglected in much the same way as has the history of the First Missouri Confederate Brigade itself. Without doubt, Father Bannon stands as one of the Confederacy's most important religious and diplomatic personalities of the war.

I owe thanks to the generosity of scores of people, who contributed so much during the last decade. I owe special thanks to Dr. Leslie Anders. He encouraged and assisted countless times through the years. Much credit goes to Rev. William Barnaby Faherty, who inspired this work in too many ways to count. Continuing a noble tradition, Father Faherty today often conducts Mass at the church that Father Bannon built. Thanks also are due the History Department at St. Louis University and its chair, Dr. Martin G. Towey. Father Bannon would be proud to have known these two gentlemen of Irish ancestry, who are active today in the Catholic community of St. Louis. Much appreciation goes to Dr. Michael H. Gorn and Annette Gorn, who both patiently listened to many redundant stories of Father Bannon's exploits. In addition, I also must thank William and Sarah Fetherston, both natives of Ireland, for locating Father Bannon's grave without my solicitation, and for other assistance. Dr. Richard P. Hallion and Dr. Perry D. Jamieson provided invaluable advice and encouragement on many occasions. Many thanks go to the good people of the Missouri Historical Society, who never ceased in their efforts to assist. Most of all, I thank my parents, Will and Betty Tucker. Both took the time and effort to instill the value of history.

Phillip Thomas Tucker

THE CONFEDERACY'S FIGHTING CHAPLAIN

ONE An Irish Priest in America

THE REVEREND JOHN B. BANNON was "the most notable chaplain in [all] the Civil War."[1] Gen. Sterling Price praised him: "I have no hesitancy in saying that the greatest soldier I ever saw was Father Bannon." Serving as chaplain of the First Missouri Confederate Brigade from 1861 to 1863, Bannon earned a reputation as "the Catholic Priest who always went into battle." The Missouri Brigade compiled a more distinguished combat record than the most famous units on either side, including the North's Iron Brigade and the South's Stonewall Brigade.[2] Even though repeatedly suffering high losses, the unit always rebounded to face the next challenge, a record unlike that of many other commands.

More than any Brigade member, Father Bannon provided the moral influence necessary to keep the exiled Missourians together, and this tough moral fiber partly explains the Missouri Brigade's superior record. A strong connection exists between a military unit's performance and the quality of its military and spiritual leaders. Religion played a significant role in strengthening morale and discipline among the common soldiers.[3] In providing this key influence and repeatedly demonstrating battlefield heroics, Chaplain Bannon earned the title of the Confederacy's "fighting Chaplain."[4]

It is odd how one of the South's most distinguished religious personalities could remain clouded in obscurity, but both the South and Ireland forgot about Father Bannon. Anti-Catholic prejudice, Southern defeat, neglect of the Western war, and a little-known Missouri Confederate effort all conspired to place Bannon outside the mainstream of Civil War historiography. While his services to the Confederacy faded from memory with time, few men had made such diverse contributions—religious, military, and diplomatic—to the Confederate war effort.

Little in the Irishman's beginning seemed promising. Bannon was born on 29 December 1829 in the small community of Roosky, Ireland. His mother gave birth unexpectedly while on the way to visit her invalid sister in Dublin. He was raised in County Roscommon,[5] where the land was forested and covered with peat bogs. But little of this picturesque country in west-central Ireland near the Shannon River was owned by native Irishmen. As early as the seventeenth century, British rulers had forced the Irish Catholics off their native lands for English Protestants. Since many Emerald Islanders were excluded from owning property, Bannon's parents were probably among the landless, tenant farmers, sharing the plight of most Irish.[6] But not all of Bannon's relatives were among the common class, for his mother was an O'Farrell, and he was the grandson of Lord Henry Sanford Pageman Mahon. O'Farrell kinsmen held extensive properties around Strokestown, County Roscommon.[7]

During his formative years, Bannon witnessed the suffering of his people under British rule. In a deliberate destruction of much of Celtic heritage and culture, native language, religion, history, and tradition were replaced by those of the English. Bannon early learned of a central government's power to control a people in an exploitative mercantile system. After his family moved to Dublin, early life in the capital further taught Bannon about world geopolitics and realpolitik.[8] The plight of the Irish people turned Bannon toward God and religion.[9] He saw in Catholicism the best hope for the long-suffering Celts.

Formal education for Bannon came at a general school in Castleknock, Ireland. His family had dwindled to only a brother and father, after his mother's death. Bannon enrolled at the Royal College of St. Patrick at Maynooth in County Kildare on 27 August 1847. At the college's Rhetoric House, Bannon devoted his energies toward two years of grammar and humanities. He was brilliant in academics, demonstrating scholastic ability as a teen-ager.

Bannon then entered the toughest curriculum, embarking upon six hard years of studies in metaphysics, theology, rhetoric, logic, and natural philosophy. As in his earlier general education, Bannon quickly rose to the top. He wrote of having earned the honor of being "called to write the First-Class Piece in each of my classes every year during my course." At Maynooth he embraced the great love of his life, theology, and after three years of theology, he devoted himself forever to religion.[10] Religion seemed the best method to help his oppressed countrymen in spite of "a disinclination for preaching tho' none for teaching or foreign missions. My disinclination for preaching arises principally from dislike of all offices which bring me prominently before the public. This disinclination would not extend to preaching to the poor and humble."[11] Perpetuating Roman Catholicism, it seemed to him, preserved a native culture and religious heritage among his people.

While Bannon studied at Maynooth, the worst natural disaster in Irish history struck the Emerald Isle, the Potato Famine. Almost a million men, women, and children died when the potato crops between 1845 and 1847 were destroyed. To reap economic gains under the mercantilist policy, the British had turned agricultural lands into grazing pastures for sheep to support England's woolens industry. Wool was more important than food to Britons but not to the Irish. The destruction of the country's main staple caused hundreds of thousands more Irish to depart for America. The economic and social catastrophe thus precipitated increased anti-English sentiment and Irish nationalism, and in 1848, Ireland was rocked by the "young Ireland" rebellion.[12]

Bannon was ordained into the priesthood at Maynooth in May of 1853 and was the first priest ordained by Paul Cardinal Cullen. Then Bannon volunteered to leave the isle of his birth and go to America, where so many of his countrymen had gone, because a need for priests followed the flood of immigrants to the United States. He elected to serve at the Archdiocese of St. Louis, Missouri, a good choice. The archdiocese contained nearly ten thousand native Irish, one of the most sizable concentrations in America.[13]

After crossing the Atlantic Ocean and then taking a steamboat up the Mississippi River, Bannon arrived on the St. Louis levee in the late summer or fall of 1853.[14] He found a challenge: although America offered more economic opportunities than any other land in the world, the majority of newly arrived Irish in St. Louis remained poor. Most Irish, without money, assistance, or land, gathered in a Celtic ghetto on St. Louis' north side known as "Kerry Patch." Named for County Kerry in southwest Ireland, the ethnic community duplicated the impoverished conditions of the Green Isle.[15] The myth of America's equality quickly faded. Only African Americans, both slave and free, were more discriminated against than the Irish.

But Bannon's dream became reality in America. He immediately began work at the city's main Cathedral under the guidance of Archbishop Peter Richard Kenrick.[16] The decade 1830 to 1840 was one in which one of America's ugliest paradoxes occurred. During the Nativist movement native Americans, mostly Protestants, rioted against the recent immigrants of the Catholic faith in a social upheaval caused by anti-Catholic prejudice and the changing demographics of St. Louis. Not long after Bannon's arrival, more riots erupted against the Irish. Reaction against a perceived Papal plot to control the Mississippi Valley had sparked a chain of violence that culminated in Know-Nothingism in 1849.[17]

Bannon and many other St. Louis Irishmen never forgot the anti-Catholic hatred. The Jesuits' St. Louis University, Irish residences, and Catholic churches were attacked by Protestant mobs.[18] Hostility from all classes of Americans cut ties of allegiance that many Irishmen felt toward the United States. For men like Bannon, America seemed to have betrayed both the Irish and its own mission. The republic's utopian vision of the "City upon a Hill" had an ugly side for the Emerald Islanders in St. Louis.

While ethnic violence swept the Mississippi River port city, Bannon moved higher up in the church hierarchy by becoming assistant pastor of St. Louis' main Catholic Church. This Cathedral, the first cathedral west of the Mississippi, stood atop a bluff overlooking the wide river. Here Father Bannon earned a reputation under the Reverend Patrick J. Ryan for hard work and dedication.[19] "A man of no ordinary gifts [and] a personality of massive character, with a keen intellect" and compassion, Bannon might have helped defend his Cathedral against a nativist mob during August 1854.[20]

Not long thereafter, Bannon became pastor of the Church of the Immaculate Conception on Eighth and Chesnut,[21] where he now attempted to convert a rambunctious immigrant citizenry into good Christians. The problem was serious. As one St. Louisan complained, "the Irish specialize in drinking, fighting, politics, and religion."[22] The levee area near the Cathedral was especially bad, where rows of "drinking saloons and low groggeries," gambling and prostitution houses flourished.[23] Many common laborers from Ireland worked at the levee, loading and unloading steamboats, and at day's end, large numbers spent much of their time and money in these iniquitous dens.

Violence from drunkenness caused the St. Louis police to plead with the Irish priests for assistance. A possible solution called for giving the levee laborers religion each morning before work. Additionally, Bannon and other priests formulated plans to resettle their people away from the

Father Bannon, in St. Louis
before the War (Missouri
Historical Society, St. Louis)

corrupting city and outside St. Louis. But "nothing could be done to
change their habits." The colonization scheme failed as a whole, although
a limited success came at Millwood in Lincoln County, Missouri.[24]

In late 1858 Bannon was assigned to St. John's Parish on the western
outskirts of St. Louis. These fashionable suburbs contained many middle-
and upper-class Celts, most of whom were pre-Potato Famine immigrants,
now second-generation Americans.[25] The two thousand parishioners of
St. John's Parish were "one of the most intelligent and refined Catholic
congregations in the city."[26]

The setting was ideal. St. John's Parish was in one of the city's most
picturesque sections. The area contained tree-lined avenues with rows of
two-story, brick homes and trimmed lawns. Bannon and assistant pastor
Myles Tobyn, another Irishman, arrived at St. John's Parish on 4 November 1858. Father Bannon's assignment was to erect a church suitable for the
setting and its people.[27]

But because of internal dissent among the congregation, Bannon "met
no kindly reception."[28] The former parish priest had been popular, and
the financial health of St. John's Parish was poor. The parish was so impov-

erished that Bannon was quickly more than $1,000 in debt in trying to make livable his small quarters next to the old church. But he forged ahead courageously, doing his best under difficult circumstances.[29]

Within days after his arrival at St. John's Parish, Father Bannon held meetings to solicit donations for his new church. He wanted to erect more than an ordinary house of worship. The young priest envisioned a church that would shine its light across the parish and stand as a bastion for Catholicism in St. Louis. Within a few weeks he had collected more than $5,000. At last, the dream of a new church began to take shape. Finally, in February 1859, Irish laborers started digging the church's foundations.[30] The site was well chosen. When completed, the new church would dominate a rise at the intersection of Chesnut and Sixteenth streets, several blocks north of Mill Creek.[31]

The Archbishop laid the church's cornerstone in a ceremony on 1 May 1859. Church and city officials spoke while members of the Roman Catholic Total Abstinence and Benevolent Society stood in formation. But, lamented Father Bannon, "owing to a sudden shower of rain which fell about 4:30 o'clock, the people were thrown into such confusion that the contemplated arrangements for collecting the subscriptions were frustrated, and in consequence only a trifle was received. The rain likewise detracted much from the solemnity of the ceremony as it prevented our using the rich vestments on hand for the occasion."[32]

Work on the structure, meanwhile, progressed. During its construction, Bannon conferred closely with the architect. He was involved in the building process with the same concern as a parent raising a child. But a crisis developed in October of 1859 when it was ascertained too late that the architect's Romanesque barrel vault ceiling was too heavy, creating more lateral stress and pressure than usual. The architect had miscalculated. Bannon complained in his diary, that the "Side walls [were] bulging."[33]

Both walls and foundation should have been thicker and more solid. With the building near completion, the whole structure now faced collapse. The architect, offering no solution, quit in embarrassment, but Bannon found an answer. He proposed to a new architect, John Mitchel, that seven vertical columns be built along each outside wall. This adjustment would give the extra width and weight necessary to support the roof and keep the walls from spreading. Sturdy limestone bases would anchor each column. The new architect accepted Bannon's architectural innovation to save the church.[34]

By this time, Bannon was a member of the St. Louis Catholic Literary Institute at the library of St. Louis University, an institution that had suffered during the Nativist riots because of its religious material. Membership here allowed Bannon to quench his thirst for knowledge and bolster his intellectualism.[35]

Plans for the erection of St. John the Apostle and Evangelist Church, meanwhile, ran into another snag. The "lack of cooperation on the part of the people and insufficient funds brought [Bannon's] ideas from celestial heights to the more modest things of earth."[36] Prospects for success dimmed. Other means were needed to transform the brick structure of a distinctive salmon color into a beautiful church. Father Bannon discovered means to secure funds.

On 15 August 1860, a Concordia Park benefit raised revenue during a "Grand Fête Champêtre" festival. Multitudes responded to the ceremonies across from the United States Arsenal. "Hundreds of light footed tripped to inspiring music, while in every portion of the immense grounds knots of individuals engaged in various amusements."[37]

Also turning out en masse for the Fête was the Catholic Total Abstinence and Benevolent Society. Bannon had been the society's president since 1858. And wherever the Catholic Total Abstinence and Benevolent Society went, so marched the finest militia company of St. Louis, known as the Washington Blues. The two organizations blended Irish nationalism, militarism, and religion, and many Irishmen held membership in both the religious and military group, the best example being Capt. Joseph Kelly—the Washington Blues' leader and a high-ranking official in Bannon's temperance society. Members of both organizations were for the most part Irish and "an exceptionally fine body of men; intelligent, educated, spirited young fellows, every one of whom held an excellent business position in the city."[38]

A drill performance by the Washington Blues ensured the day's success by drawing a large crowd. Citizens responded with donations for Bannon's church on the hill with more than $1,000, which guaranteed the structure's completion. In a journalist's words, "Thus a worthy object has been benefited, multitudes delighted, and 'Lady Day' of August 15th, 1860, celebrated in a brilliant style."[39]

Bannon held another function in antebellum St. Louis. He served as the chaplain for Kelly's company and the whole St. Louis militia. The militia included men from St. John's Parish, but Chaplain Bannon's closest relationship was with the Celtic troops of the Washington Blues. Other

Irish companies—the Emmet, Washington, and Montgomery guards—were in the Missouri Volunteer Militia Brigade of St. Louisans under Brig. Gen. Daniel Morgan Frost.

Father Bannon mixed religious, civilian, and military roles. He had organized a "military temperance company [Kelley's militia] composed of the flower of young Catholic manhood." The Washington Blues and the temperance society were almost synonymous. This para-military organization met on the last Sunday of each month at St. Louis University.[40]

With the church near completion, Bannon had another idea to secure more funds for building expenses. He wrote in his diary on 15 October, "Church opened to public-occasion, a great bazaar." Among trees splendid with autumnal colors, Bannon's financial goal was finally realized in early October 1860, but the official dedication did not occur until 4 November 1860.[41]

The stately church was primarily of Renaissance architecture and commanded the rise dominating St. John's Parish. "It's interior decorations [were] beautiful and artistic." A painted fresco of the Apocalypse lined the inside of the circular roof above the altar. Outside and fronting the church high above the main entry stood a statue of the patron for both Bannon and his parish, St. John, the Apostle and Evangelist. The dedication marked the second anniversary of Bannon's arrival at St. John's Parish. Largely because of one man's energy and vision, one of the most beautiful churches of St. Louis now stood at the top of a small hill. The Archbishop changed his residence from the Cathedral to Bannon's church, designating it as his pro-Cathedral.[42]

The city's finest architects and skilled workers completed a magnificent brick structure of a Romanesque order. Two twin towers, each more than a hundred feet high, fronted the church on each side. Today the church still stands as a monument to Father Bannon.[43]

The first Sunday in November was Bannon's proudest day, but he enjoyed his church for less than six months. With the election of Abraham Lincoln, the Civil War impended. The many differences between two distinct societies would be settled on the battlefield.

Sectional conflict pulled Father Bannon away from his church only days after the first service. Like other churches, St. John's bells atop each tower rang on the morning of 25 November. As tolling bells spread the alarm for the St. Louis militia to gather, the sounds echoed over St. John's Parish and "mingled with the ringing of ramrods and gun-locks and the church

St. John the Apostle and Evangelist Church, St. Louis, ca. 1870 (Missouri Historical Society, St. Louis)

going people had a vision of other than a spiritual army."[44] Bannon put aside his normal Sunday duties for military service. Churches stood empty throughout St. Louis, which was aroused to a threat on Missouri's western border, and the militia brigade formed to defend the state almost six months before the Civil War.[45]

Sectional tensions had torn deep divisions in Missouri since the Kansas-Nebraska Act of 1854, negating the Compromise of 1850, and paving the way for popular sovereignty and "Bloody Kansas." Hence, the Kansas Territory had been turned into a battleground as opposing factions, North and South, clashed to determine Kansas's destiny—free or slave. Missouri border residents, who had been clamoring since the mid-1850s for protection, had petitioned the governor to send state troops. Kansas residents also sought protection. Once again citizens on both sides were caught in an emotional and ideological conflict.[46]

Civil war raged for years in Kansas, just over 300 miles west of St. Louis. During the fall of 1860, the Kansas Jayhawkers again raided along Missouri's western border. Some pro-Southerners were shot and hanged during a raid common to both factions.[47] Gov. Robert M. Stewart, answering requests for assistance, ordered Frost's militiamen to the border.

To protect the state's citizens, the Irishmen of St. Louis flocked to their company armories to answer the call.[48] Father Bannon left St. John's Church to join Captain Kelly's Washington Blues at the Verandah Hall Armory on Fourth Street. On 25 November, militiamen strutted in their navy blue uniforms and prepared for active duty, Bannon also wearing a militia uniform.[49]

Wrote one correspondent, "Our city this morning looked like a military camp—drums beating, troops marching by companies from the different armories to the place of general rendezvous, flags flying and troopers galloping in squads."[50] Thirty-six hours after receiving the governor's directive to muster, the militia prepared to depart. On the morning of 25 November, more than six hundred soldiers marched past a cheering populace and along snowy cobblestone avenues toward the Seventh Street Depot where they piled aboard cars of the Missouri Pacific Railroad.[51] Another priest held the last Sunday Mass in November at St. John the Apostle and Evangelist Church. Bannon climbed onto the train with his Irish boys. Some St. Louisans wore "States-rights badges" in support of the South, which now threatened to leave the Union.[52]

Under overcast skies the train churned westward from the depot with St. Louisans waving and shouting as the Southwest Expedition was launched. The soldiers were "in fine spirits, and only anxious to advance to the frontier, so as to have a chance of thrashing the enemy."[53] Militiamen dreamed of their own invasion into the Kansas sanctuaries of the raiders. "Ho, for Kansas" was the battle-cry.[54] The next day at noon, the expeditioners disembarked at Smithton, in west central Missouri within striking distance of the border. The command established camp near town and the western terminus of the railroad. During the next few days, Frost's troops prepared to march southwestward.[55] For the most part Bannon remained with the Washington Blues and other Irish units. In the tented city, he attended to religious needs.

When the brigade journeyed across the prairies on 28 November, Bannon remained behind at Smithton.[56] The "Kansas War" abruptly ended for the priest, who stayed to attend the sick. A major, thereafter, acted as the brigade's chaplain. One of the ill soldiers was Captain Kelly whose health, already precarious, had grown worse on the trip west. In St. Louis, he had been in a sickbed for six weeks when word came for border duty. Kelly had leaped to his feet to lead his company. The British army veteran initially remained in camp at Smithton, but despite being seriously ill, he soon rejoined the Southwest Expedition on the march, commanding the Washington Blues from a carriage until forced to return to Smithton as his condition worsened.

Other sick volunteers remained at Smithton with the brigade surgeon, who himself fell victim to typhoid fever. A chaplain's duty necessarily called for attending to the injured or sick. Bannon shortly returned to St. Louis and St. John's Church, apparently bringing back some diseased militiamen.[57]

Conditions soon returned to normal in St. Louis, and Bannon said Mass at St. John's Church on the first Sunday of December.[58] He held Mass each morning at 6:00, 7:00, 8:00, and 10:30 and then at 1:30 in the afternoon.[59] When the Kansas raiders slipped back into their territory and vanished, the Southwest Expedition, except for one battalion under Col. John Stevens Bowen, reappeared in St. Louis. The campaign had lasted almost three weeks. Sunday, 16 December, saw low attendance during Father Bannon's service at St. John's Church. In a journalist's words, "Yesterday [16 December] was another military Sunday—The churches were nearly vacant, because the church-goers, except those of the strictest orthodoxy, were out to witness the animated spectacle of 'The Soldiers' Return'."[60]

The Southwest Expedition was a harbinger of the Civil War. Missouri militiamen trekking far from home to stop an expected invasion from a neighboring territory and contemplating a strike within Kansas's boundaries signaled a polarization. Before the South's secession and Fort Sumter, civil war continued on the prairies of western Missouri. Missourians were placed on a war-footing, although North and South were only threatening and posturing. This expedition also, demonstrating the strength of state sovereignty, loosened further ties with the national government. When people of this western slave state protected themselves without the help of the United States government a stronger sense of States Rights was created among many Missourians. Bannon and his Irish soldiers were among those who embraced the new nationalism of the South. The Southwest

Expedition marked the end of the antebellum period and of the lull before the great national tragedy.

The brief winter campaign also signified the passing of an age of innocence. With the coming of the Civil War in less than six months, there would be no more bloodless military campaigns. Pro-Northern and Pro-Southern militiamen of St. Louis, who marched together on the Southwest Expedition, shortly would kill each other during four years of madness.[61]

As an uneasy peace settled over the border and the entire nation, Bannon now led an "active and full life of a parochial missionary in St. Louis with a zeal and energy which are not yet forgotten."[62] Archbishop Kenrick, most of his clergy, and most of the people were pro-Southern. As the pastor of St. John's Parish, Bannon impressed many individuals of influence. Few citizens forgot the "most energetic priest," who as a pulpit orator was "among the foremost in Saint Louis."[63]

With an eerie calm in St. Louis and the Western frontier, in the East events progressed rapidly toward open conflict. In late 1860 and early 1861, independence-minded Southern states left the Union. Southern nationalism severed ties with the North, and the United States of America ceased to exist. A new experiment took its place. The Confederacy was born.

Most Missourians, meanwhile, dreamed of a neutrality that had no place in the upcoming crisis.[64] The destinies of St. Louisans were manipulated by developments hundreds of miles eastward. Already St. Louis University students were leaving school and going home to Louisiana, Mississippi, and Virginia to join the military.[65]

St. Louis had been a divided city even before its North-South cleavage. Besides political divisions, the community's social foundations were ripped to shreds. With almost 60 percent of its citizens from outside the country's borders, St. Louis was the largest refuge for foreign-born people of any city in the United States by 1860. Thousands of Irish and Germans had poured into the community during the past decade. By 1860 Missouri contained the second-highest Irish population and the largest German population in the South. Many Irish fell into line with the beliefs of the Democratic Party, while the majority of the Germans were supporters of the Republican Party. A clash was inevitable between the culturally diverse peoples who were historic enemies.

For many Irish and Father Bannon, the conflict not only was about political, economic, and social issues, but also took on religious aspects. Irish Catholics felt that a religious way of life was under threat. For Bannon and other Celts, according to one Missourian, the "'infidel, Sabbath-breaking, beer-drinking Dutch who had invaded St. Louis' were of the same breed as those who harried Ireland and inflicted innumerable persecutions in 1689." The religious hostility and perceived immoral qualities of the Germans further blended the Irish mixture of religion and nationalism.

Many factors contributed to Bannon's pro-Southernism and decentralized view of government. Self-determination for the South was linked to Irish nationalism. Having felt the stirrings of nationalism in Ireland during the "young Ireland" rebellion, Bannon was familiar with revolutionary doctrine. He thought that the Southern people and the Irish people both had the natural right to choose their own leaders, systems of government, and destinies.

In addition, social factors combined with historical forces in the combustible environment of St. Louis to promote a militant pro-Southernism for Bannon and others. Many of the thousands of Germans who had flooded into St. Louis during the 1850s were Lutherans and refugees of the Revolution of 1848. They had unsuccessfully tried to oppose their Austrian rulers and unify Germany, and during their struggle, they identified Catholicism with the Austrians. The ex-revolutionaries of 1848, consequently, were strongly anti-Catholic. Hatred of Catholicism had been carried from Germany to St. Louis where it targeted the Irish Catholics.

This hostility from the German populace promoted a pro-Southern, anti-German, and anti-Union sentiment among many St. Louis Irish, who viewed themselves as threatened from all sides. They feared, besides native American hostility, the newly arrived Germans who might take away the economic, political, and social gains St. Louis had granted them. By 1861, many saw antagonists in both groups. In addition, the national government, the abolitionists, the newly elected Republican Party, and the populace of Kansas were viewed as threats. Indeed, the Irish saw a correlation between abolition and anti-Catholicism. Because the Germans were pro-Union, many Irish volunteers eventually destined for Confederate service were motivated by this antagonism alone.

But the majority of the St. Louis Irish in 1861 overlooked the historic antagonisms, the analogy of the plight of Ireland with the South, the social divisions, the Know-Nothing riots, the discrimination, and their life as second-class citizens. Most would side with the Union in large part because the Northern army provided an avenue by which they could obtain instant equality. Some, unable to ignore such considerations so easily, would soon wear Confederate gray, largely because of cultural, socio-economic, and historical conditions that existed long before the firing on Fort Sumter.

With the common man on both sides during the Civil War, the issue of slavery was not paramount in explaining motivations. Like most other pro-Southern St. Louisans, these Irishmen were neither slaveowners nor pro-slavery advocates. Bannon and the pro-Southern men of such units as the Washington Blues represented an atypical element among the Irish community. Despite their being a minority in the Irish community, Bannon and his comrades were among the most active, militant and pro-revolutionary in St. Louis. These Irishmen, ironically, were the radical types most needed back on the Green Isle for a successful nationalist movement against the British.[66]

TWO War in the West

NOT EVEN THE FIRING ON FORT SUMTER in April 1861 convinced Missourians to go to war. Gov. Claiborne Fox Jackson felt Missouri's future lay with the South, and thus he refused to comply with Lincoln's call for troops to suppress the rebellion. Jackson now prepared for the conflict. Father Bannon, also supporting refusal, found his stance made easier by the arrival of Capt. Nathaniel Lyon, new Union commander in St. Louis. Lyon was known for his uncompromising nature, pro-Kansas sentiment, and anti-Catholicism.[1]

To shift the state to a revolutionary course, General Frost had Governor Jackson order the state militia into its annual encampment at Lindell Grove during early May. This grove was located in the city's western outskirts, twenty blocks directly west of St. John's Church.[2] On 6 May the militiamen paraded westward through St. John's Parish and down Olive Street.[3] Under the pretense of a legal muster, General Frost eyed the United States arsenal to St. Louis's south. Whichever side gained control of the vast munitions depot would probably win the state. Once Frost received cannon from the Jefferson Davis government, pro-Southerners could lay siege to the arsenal.[4]

Besides being a principal religious leader of his community and a militia chaplain, Bannon might have played another key role. During the archbishop's absence, a member of the Catholic Church hierarchy had worked out an arrangement the previous winter with General Frost, a Catholic. The plan was calculated to arouse the city's militia for a strike on the arsenal. A peal of ringing bells of St. John's and other Catholic churches, with five-minute, interruptions, was to unite the militia. This signal, wrote one Unionist, would unleash "the enthusiastic, reckless Irishmen [who] were to take the initiative" and capture the arsenal. Father Bannon was probably involved in the plan, perhaps even formulating the strategy.

Unfortunately for him, Unionists discovered the scheme, and pressure forced Archbishop Kenrick to deter the attack. Captain Lyon, expecting a strike there, made defensive preparations, and the secessionists lost their chance. Kenrick was only "moderately sympathetic" to the South; Bannon was a zealot.[5] No doubt Lyon's anti-Catholicism increased after learning of the plot that centered around the Catholic churches. Governor Jackson had missed a good opportunity to capture the arsenal. Unlike other Federal arsenals throughout the South, the St. Louis munitions depot would remain controlled by the North.

As he had done during the early stages of the Southwest Expedition, Bannon stayed close to Captain Kelly's Irishmen at Camp Jackson. He probably tented in the company's bivouac. Named for the governor, Camp Jackson resembled a carnival more than a military encampment during the first week of May. Every day hundreds of citizens descended upon Lindell Grove to visit. One St. Louisan described the bivouac, where "daintily attired ladies and children were to be seen mingling with gaily uniformed soldiers, while the bands played, and nature, serene in her spring dress, seemed to smile on the beauty of the scene."[6] Frost, a Mexican War veteran, was lulled into complacency. No defensive preparations were erected around the encampment.[7]

But Captain Lyon, West Point Class of 1841 like Frost, held no such illusions. After moving much of the arsenal's arms and munitions across the river to Illinois, Lyon realized he must strike first, but he needed an excuse. He thought he had one in demanding the return of the four cannon lent to the state troops by the United States Army. These guns had only recently returned from the border with Colonel Bowen's Southwest Battalion. Frost refused to relinquish the artillery pieces, now belonging to Capt. Henry Guibor's Battery. Lyon responded in anger, threatening "that if he had to go and take them that he would take them, his men and munitions, in fact everything."[8]

Frost was not intimidated. But Lyon would not advance upon the encampment until he was certain of its Southern sentiment. A personal reconnaissance by Lyon revealed camp avenues named for Rebel leaders. Also in Camp Jackson was Confederate artillery captured from the United States arsenal at Baton Rouge, Louisiana, guns which had been sent to

Frost by President Davis. Lyon reacted quickly. More than six thousand United States regulars and Home Guards swung through the streets of St. Louis on the morning of 10 May. One column of bluecoats tramped through St. John's parish and passed near Bannon's church. Along the route, Colonel Bowen had earlier brought a letter of professed innocence from Frost to Lyon, but Lyon refused to accept it. It was now too late for diplomacy or compromise in the contest for Missouri.[9]

Frost's militiamen, meanwhile, sat before tents, played pranks, or strolled through Lindell Grove. Many soldiers left the encampment to visit friends and families. No one expected an attack on the afternoon of 10 May.[10] Father Bannon attended to his various duties. The dual role of religious community leader and military chaplain was not unusual. After all, colonial men of God were the foremost supporters of rebellion during the American Revolution.[11] As the morning grew warmer, Camp Jackson resembled more of a festive Fourth of July gathering than a military bivouac. Soldiers left their muskets stacked in the cantonment filling a wooded hollow. Suddenly, wrote one militiaman, "a battery of artillery [was] planted on the hill west of us, then another north and another south of our Camp, while regiment after regiment of infantry volunteers . . . gradually closed in on the ridges around our Camp."[12]

After thousands of Federals had surrounded Camp Jackson, Lyon demanded Frost's unconditional surrender. Union cannons and rifles prepared to fire from the high ground if Frost refused. Lyon had "so many men with him as to make any resistance ridiculous." Encircled by about ten-to-one odds and trapped in a meadow, more than six hundred militiamen capitulated.[13] Some of the men cried, broke sabers, and cursed, while the captors cheered their success.[14] Captain Guibor, commanding the controversial battery, and his cannoneers were ready for action,[15] but the order to fire never came. In one stroke, Lyon eliminated the most militant and active pro-Southern force in Missouri.

Corralling the prisoners took an hour or two during a chaotic surrender.[16] One militia captive rounded up was Father Bannon. Like most other militiamen, Bannon refused to take an oath of allegiance,[17] but instead, wearing his militia uniform, he joined the column of captives, sandwiched between two lines of Federals.[18] The victors erred in wasting much time and deciding to escort the prisoners through St. Louis. A mob of civilians, including many St. John's parishioners, gathered, and hovered on Camp Jackson's outskirts, and some who were armed rallied to assist the camp's defenders.

The column finally moved out in the late afternoon. With Federal drums pounding and flags waving, the prisoners trudged along the road leading out of the grove. When an unexpected delay occurred at a fence-line, the halt allowed the crowd to get closer. Militia officers who had been allowed to keep sidearms, defiantly broke their sabers against the rail fence with the mob applauding.

The trek to the arsenal resumed, but the column again stopped. Now the rear of the column was at the grove's entrance and the head stood within the city's confines. The throng approached closer. Citizens shouted for Jeff Davis, hurled stones and curses upon the Federals. Someone fired a shot in the confusion. The Unionists raked the crowd with a volley, and musketry crashed along the blue lines. Around one hundred civilians were hit. In one St. Louisan's words, "It was simply a massacre."[19] Father Bannon watched in helpless rage while his people were shot down.

Indignation rose across the state with the St. Louis killings. The Missourians' dream of neutrality was erased with the volleys unleashed in St. Louis. Lyon's rash capture of Camp Jackson transformed thousands of neutralists into Confederates, and war was forced on Missouri.[20]

After the shootings, the prisoners were escorted for the arsenal, prodded at bayonet point eastward down Olive Street and through St. John's Parish. The sight of Bannon as a captive must have incensed his parishioners, lining the streets along the route. Crowds were hostile throughout the parish. Perhaps Father Bannon's being surrounded by verbally abusive German soldiers might have helped incite the crowd at the "Camp Jackson Massacre," for St. John's was the nearest parish to Camp Jackson and the shootings occurred near the western boundary of the parish.

The rage among St. John's people was shown at "the windows of [houses where] women expressed their bitter scorn by spitting at" the Union troops. Militiamen and Bannon walked into the arsenal, some captives singing "Yankee Doodle." Near the arsenal's gate was Ulysses S. Grant in civilian attire. Frost's enlisted men were herded into a limestone building, where "we were crowded so closely that it was impossible to lie down." Bannon endured the night without food, while crammed into the building with more than six hundred other prisoners.[21]

Paroles were issued on 11 May. Frost's men complied except for one officer. Bannon stood in line on the arsenal's grounds with Frost's command when the parole process began late in the afternoon. A Union officer gave the order, "Attention! Hold up your right hands!" The captives swore aloud not to take up arms against the United States government.[22] Bannon took the parole oath no doubt with some reluctance: "We, the undersigned, do pledge our words as gentlemen that we will not take up arms nor serve in any military capacity against the United States, during the present civil war. This parole to be returned upon our surrendering ourselves, at any time, as prisoners of war. While we make this pledge with the full intention of observing it, we hereby protest against the justice of its exaction."[23]

After nightfall, the militiamen embarked upon a steamboat at the arsenal's wharf, because they feared that they might be attacked by the German populace. From the landing, the vessel churned north and upriver against the current. Far in the night, the parolees disembarked at the city's upper levee at Chesnut Street and near the Cathedral. Frost's First Regiment of the Missouri Volunteer Militia, Bannon's unit, marched up Chesnut to onlookers' cheers. At Fourth Street, "the ranks were then broken, each man going his own way."[24] Bannon walked west along Chesnut and toward his church, after learning much about war.

With Camp Jackson, Missouri was hurled faster toward civil war. The state legislature passed a military bill, arming the state in self-defense against Federal encroachments, and the Missouri State Guard was born. Despite last-minute attempts of pro-Southerners to maintain a thin veil of neutrality with the Harney-Price Treaty, in late May open warfare was inevitable. With the signing of the treaty in St. Louis, Governor Jackson had bought precious time to prepare for the confrontation with Lyon. But Lyon retained the initiative and shortly launched a campaign westward into the state's interior. Here he encountered little resistance, and he captured the state capital at Jefferson City in June 1861 and dispersed a Rebel force at Boonville.[25] Many of Bannon's parishioners rallied to Price's Missouri State Guard. Among these volunteers were Captain Kelly's Washington Blues, who had missed the Camp Jackson fiasco because of escort duty to the state capital. The army of pro-Southern volunteers was little more than a mob,[26] but as skirmishes spread across the state, the Guard won a respectable success at the Battle of Carthage in early July.[27]

Father Bannon, meanwhile, remained at St. John's Church while the nation self-destructed. Now absent from his Sunday church services were the many Irishmen of his temperance society and the Irish militia companies of St. Louis. These men now fought with General Price. The

Catholic Total Abstinence and Benevolent Society had members on both sides.[28] While his ex-parishioners were fighting, Bannon now faced a congregation that mostly was either neutral or pro-Union.[29]

Some priests in St. Louis, including Father Bannon, espoused pro-Southern views to their parishioners. One St. Louis Unionist complained that the Catholic clergymen were "urging prayers to the patron saint of Ireland to grant them greater aid than had been the case at Camp Jackson, and also to protect them during the impending uprising against the Germans."[30]

During the summer of 1861, Bannon lost more of his desire to continue in his passive role at St. John's Parish, while great events unfolded elsewhere. Nothing now affected Bannon more than reading the letters of former church members battling with General Price, the leader of "the Missouri sons of liberty." Soldiers' words scribbled by campfire and candlelight told of the engagements and needs of the Catholic Rebels. Such themes appealed more to Bannon than the daily concerns of his congregation. To his delight, no United States flag waved from St. John Church's twin towers. Pro-Southern Archbishop Kenrick refused the government's orders to fly "Old Glory" from the churches of St. Louis.[31]

The contest for Missouri intensified in early August. The Blue and Gray armies clashed along a stream called Wilson's Creek, near Springfield, to determine the state's destiny. After launching a surprise attack, Lyon's forces achieved initial success, but the Rebels eventually won the bloody contest in southwestern Missouri, killing Lyon and mauling the Federal army. A Southern victory at Wilson's Creek and the defeat of the state's primary Union force swung the balance of power in the Rebels' favor. Crowed one journalist, "a few more such victories and Missouri will be free."[32]

To exploit his success, General Price was determined to win the home state. In early September, Price's army swung north toward the Missouri River. The invaders envisioned capturing St. Louis. Success came at Lexington, where Price's Missouri Rebels bagged thirty-five-hundred Unionists with the use of mobile hemp bales. By September's conclusion, "Old Pap," an ex-Mexican War officer, seemed ready to reclaim the state. But much of the Rebel army dissolved with the approach of winter. "Summer" soldiers returned home by the thousands.

To arouse the state's people, Price implored them in a November appeal: "Awake, my countrymen, to a sense of what constitutes the dignity and true greatness of a free people . . . and we only now ask our fellow citizens, our brethren, to come to us and help to secure what we have gained and to win our glorious inheritance from the cruel hand of the spoiler and the oppressor. . . . Now is the crisis of your fate; now the golden opportunity to save the State. . . ." But a conservative people failed to respond to the call. Liberation on the Western border was a myth.[33]

Bannon was influenced by Price's "Proclamation to the People of Central and North Missouri," calling for widespread support from all Missourians. Or Father Bannon may have heard how Joseph Kelly, now a colonel leading one of Price's infantry regiments, and his men had their first contact with a Catholic clergyman in late September of 1861, when the Irish soldiers in butternut had heard Mass and taken Communion from a Union chaplain captured at Lexington. Clearly an urgent need for a Rebel priest existed in Price's army.[34]

More letters from Price's army stressing the desire for a Catholic priest came to St. John's Parish. Bannon felt that he could no longer preach in St. Louis with a free conscience. Another incentive to depart came in September with the capture of Lexington's garrison and the official exchange of Camp Jackson's prisoners. Federal authorities, moreover, now sought an excuse to arrest Bannon, who spoke his mind freely in the pulpit. During one encounter with Unionists in St. Louis, Bannon came close to losing his life. By December, consequently, he had many reasons to prepare secretly for the long trek southwestward through the Union lines to join Price's Missouri State Guard.[35]

Despite "being so deeply attached to [St. John the Apostle and Evangelist Church], as a priest will be to a church for which he has begged and for which he has fought, loving it tenderly, and loving with that great heart of his sacrificed all, and without hesitation [Bannon now made ready to leave] everything; because he heard that there were Catholic young men of this city in the Confederate army without a chaplain to minister to them who might fall in battle at any moment."[36] In addition, Bannon was targeted for arrest by December. His views, expressed from the pulpit, were common knowledge and stirred the wrath of Union authorities. But he continued his duties until the final minute. He said his last Mass at St. John's on 15 December. Bannon would never again see his church after that day.[37]

Before his departure, he paid one final visit to a family living on Walnut Street. After saying goodbye on the night of 15 December, he eased out the back door in a disguise and false beard, while a Federal officer simultaneously came in the front door.[38] This would be the first of many close calls for Bannon during his long journey to join Price. His mission, if ascertained, would have landed him in prison.[39]

He joined Judge Robert Armytage Bakewell and P. Bauduy Garesche. Law partners, they were both from distinguished St. Louis Catholic families. Garesche, of French heritage, had two brothers captured at Camp Jackson. An uncle would die wearing a Federal uniform. One of these Garesche brothers, a St. Louis University faculty member, had been General Frost's orderly at Camp Jackson. Like Bannon, both Garesche and Bakewell had refused to sign an oath of allegiance.[40] Much of Bannon's persecution had stemmed from his refusal to sign a loyalty oath from St. Louis authorities.[41] Other St. Louisans, such as Henry Guibor, also fled the city in the night for similar reasons.[42] These refugees all went to General Price's yeoman army in the field.

During the ride through the militarized city, Bannon, Garesche, and Bakewell escaped detection. The gallop southward continued all night.[43] Before embarking, Bannon left a farewell letter with the archbishop's secretary. He realized that any official request and permission to leave his parish might implicate Kenrick, already under suspicion of disloyalty. When Archbishop Kenrick later came to his office, a secretary offered, "Father Bannon has gone South, your grace." The archbishop responded, "I have heard so." Then the secretary said, "He left this letter to be delivered to you." Angry at losing the best priest of his Archdiocese, Kenrick snapped, "Keep it!" According to legend, Bannon's letter to his superior was never opened.[44]

Rumor said Union authorities applied a penalty upon the archbishop for Bannon's departure. A St. Louis woman, for instance, wrote in a letter, "Father Bannon has gone down to Price, and the report is that the Catholic archbishop has been assessed $7000 [in consequence]."[45] No doubt Federal military commanders regretted that one of St. Louis' most influential religious leaders and foremost Rebels had slipped through their hands. Bannon left behind much more than a beautiful church and a large congregation. He forfeited the dream of what many expected him to achieve one day—the episcopacy, a bishop's rank, of the American West.[46]

For five weeks, Bannon, Garesche, and Bakewell dodged Union patrols. The trek took them through winter rains and snows, across streams and over a hilly wilderness. They were often lost. The risky journey toward southwestern Missouri meant living off the land, hiding in thickets by day and riding at night. After the more than two-hundred-mile ordeal, the party reached Springfield on 22 January 1862.[47] Bannon now became a member of "the Patriot Army of Missouri." Price's Missouri State Guard was encamped around Springfield, the largest city in southwest Missouri.[48]

The following day Bannon met the commander about whom he had heard so much—"Old Pap" Price, the homespun Missouri general and former tobacco farmer.[49] Bannon, who had not shaved since leaving St. Louis, presented a rugged appearance. The Missouri Rebels felt their cause gain more credence with the addition of the well-known priest. Bannon "had been in charge of one of the most important churches in St. Louis and this appointment he gave up to join the Confederate troops."[50]

He was introduced to the army's top leaders on 23 January. For the first time in more than five weeks, he washed up. He got a change of clothes the following day. Since no regulation existed for a chaplain's dress, Bannon put on a soldier's uniform. Like other Missouri Confederates, he probably soon wore an undyed wool uniform, whitish in color. The new clothes were of a jean material. These uniforms were tough and durable, the common wear of slaves, and ideally suited for the combat requirements of Colonel Little's Rebels.[51]

Father Bannon went to work immediately. On 25 January, he officially joined his St. Louis soldiers. According to Bannon, he "visited Genl Price & got introduced to members of Col [Captain] Guibor['s Battery and] visited [William] Wades Camp in the [evening]."[52] The reunions with former parishioners were memorable. He found two artillery units containing two of the heaviest concentrations of St. Louis Catholics. Capt. William Wade commanded one of these batteries. Wade, a former leader of the Irish militiamen of the Emmet Guards, had been captured along with his men at Camp Jackson. The unit, organized recently in Memphis, was drawn from the St. Louis exiles and Camp Jackson parolees.

The other primary artillery unit that contained Irish Catholics from St. Louis was the First Missouri Confederate Light Artillery, under the command of Captain Guibor, a St. Louis University graduate of French ancestry. The battery's composition resembled an international unit. Among the gunners were British, Italians, Germans, Frenchmen, and Scotsmen. Guibor had worshipped at the Cathedral, where he probably knew Father Bannon during his early days there. The captain combined Mexican War and Southwest Expedition experience to mold what would become one of the Confederacy's best artillery units. Guibor, age forty, had also learned much under Colonel Bowen's West Point-like tutelage.

This invaluable experience had been gained on the border with the Southwest Battalion during the winter of 1860–1861.[53]

Guibor, Wade, and Bannon formed close ties. Without taking any rest, Bannon immediately heard thirty confessions from Wade's artillerymen on his first Sunday, 26 January, with the army. Wade's cannoneers confessed sins for three hours.[54] Captain Guibor's and Wade's batteries now had their Catholic chaplain, and Father Bannon became part of the First Missouri Confederate Brigade, containing around two thousand hardened veterans. This unit consisted "of the youths of the first families of Central and Northern Missouri. The Brigade would become known throughout the South during the war as 'The Fighting Missouri Brigade.'" Col. Henry Little, likewise exiled and from the easternmost border state of Maryland, led them.[55]

But Bannon had not officially entered Confederate service, for artillery units contained no position for chaplain. Therefore, wrote Bannon, "my position here is as volunteer chaplain."[56] He was caught in a bureaucratic dilemma. The St. Louis Catholic troops, he wrote, were "so disposed through the regiments [that] it is impossible to concentrate the votes for a regimental chaplain. A brigade or division chaplain does not exist, or I might secure such a position. Less I would not accept, as a lower regimental chaplaincy would limit my sphere of action and make me dependent upon the authorities."[57] Thus he demonstrated both his independent nature and his desire to serve as many men as possible.

Such widespread responsibility guaranteed that he could administer to the needs of his old comrades: ex-soldiers of the Washington Blues and other pre-war St. Louis militia companies and former members of his temperance society. These St. Louisans were scattered in various units. Since no pay was forthcoming from a regular Confederate commission as chaplain, Bannon survived "on the voluntary gifts of the Catholics whom I serve."[58] Filling the needs of the majority of St. Louisans and other Irish in the army had not only cost Father Bannon his church and a bright future within the church, but also now deprived him of regular army pay.

Unofficially, he served in a chaplain's capacity for the Missouri Brigade.[59] Colonel Little would recommend that the priest be promoted to chaplain for his Brigade, but the response from the Richmond bureaucracy dismissed the appeal, responding that a "Brigade is not entitled to a chaplain."[60] Bannon, consequently, "had the general care of souls throughout the whole army."[61] With more responsibilities than a regular chaplain, he "had no idle time."[62]

General Henry Little (Missouri
Historical Society, St. Louis)

Upon invitation, he joined Colonel Little and his staff officers as an unofficial member of the general's staff. With this cadre of the Brigade's highest-ranking leaders, Bannon slept, messed, and dined like an officer on the colonel's staff.[63] The fact that Little's staff contained two former St. John's parishioners, Capt. Wright C. Schaumburg and Capt. Francis Von Phul, allowed Bannon's entry into the top echelon of the Brigade's officer corps. The priest maintained a close relationship with Schaumburg, the son of a wealthy St. Louis judge, and Von Phul, also from a well-to-do, first family of St. Louis.[64] From this vantage point, Bannon obtained a bird's-eye-view of the army's inner-workings. At the headquarters established in a farmer's house or a thicket after a hard day's march, he would be intimately involved within the Brigade's leadership hierarchy during active campaigning. Chaplain Bannon often held Mass at Colonel Little's headquarters.[65]

Colonel Little, a Mexican War hero and the son of a Maryland congressman, became Price's "right-arm" and best lieutenant. Like so many others caught in the Civil War's insanity, Little had cast his lot with the South after much personal anguish.[66] A Memphis journalist understood the significance of Price's appointment of Little as his adjutant. According to the newspaper account, "Old Pap" wisely "seeks always to bring to his aid all the talent or experience of others within his reach; one of his first acts as Major General, was to select for his Adjutant an experienced officer [Henry Little] who had resigned from the U.S. Army, and whom he had previously known only by reputation."[67]

General Price could not have picked a better candidate to forge the First Missouri Brigade into a superior fighting machine. Like Bannon, Colonel Little embraced the struggle like a crusader waging a holy war. But Little's intimate association with Father Bannon, whom he affectionately called "the Padre," would be brief. The bond between the two would last less than one year.[68]

By this time, Bannon looked the part of a warrior. He allowed a jet-black beard to grow after leaving St. Louis in mid-December.[69] Additionally he was "a handsome man, over six feet in height, with splendid form and intellectual face, courteous manners, and of great personal magnetism, conversing entertainingly and with originality and great wit, in a manner all his own."[70] A veteran recalled Bannon's widespread influence:

> There was another gentleman connected with headquarters who can never be forgotten. This was the Rev. Father John Bannon, who, to extend his field of usefulness, left a comfortable living and prosperous parish in this city for the privations and discomforts of an army life. . . . He became chaplain of Wade's and Guibor's batteries, and in fact served in that capacity for everyone in Gen. Price's army that was of his persuasion. . . . Yet it can be said his influence, in a religious sense, was felt by all who associated with him, and his presence wherever he went repressed the rude manners of the camp. Not that he objected to gaiety and mirthful pleasure, for he had the most affable manners and genial nature, but he always frowned upon the soldiers' unrestrained expressions and rude jests. He was physically large, handsome, dignified, refined and cultured. While his mission was one of peace, he became noted for his bravery in the field in attending the wounded and dying in very exposed places. He was both a pious and a practical man, and became a ministering angel wherever broken and bruised humanity needed help and consolation.[71]

Such attributes quickly won for Bannon the admiration of First Missouri Brigade members. His high spirits, Irish wit, and laughter radiated over Little's headquarters at the William Fulbright House near the Fulbright Spring, south of Springfield.[72] Not restricting his services to Catholics, Bannon made himself available to soliders of all denominations. Years after the war, a Rebel surgeon "of no definite religion," recalled Bannon's "cheerfulness and the good accomplished by him," within Price's Army.[73]

The calm of winter soon ended. A Union army pushed southwestward toward Springfield to drive Price out of Missouri.[74] On 12 February, Bannon heard Rebel "scouts fighting 8 miles from town." The foe had arrived in force. The chaplain wrote that "all [were] on the Road [southwest] at 7 o'clock" that night.[75] General Price evacuated Springfield on the night of 12 February and moved southwest toward Arkansas. The withdrawal in the darkness brought the Rebels to the Wilson's Creek battlefield on the following morning. During an hour's break, many Confederates viewed the field where the battle of "Oak Hill" had raged the previous August. One young officer captured the mood in his journal, recalling how "down yonder slope came the vaunting invader to the fray, and here in unbroken line, stood the unconquered sons of liberty and welcomed him to the slaughter."[76]

No one was more curious in exploring his first field of strife than Bannon. While most of the troops rested, the chaplain "went to visit the scene of Battle."[77] Col. Benjamin Allen Rives, an ex-physician commanding one of the Brigade's infantry regiments, gave Bannon a walking tour across the battlefield of Wilson's Creek. The chaplain strode over a field still littered with skeletons and the debris of battle. Colonel Rives had performed admirably in the contest of 10 August. For the Missouri Army, this spot in Greene County was hallowed ground, for "never was a greater victory crowned by the efforts of the friends of Liberty and Equal Rights." Bannon, as if anticipating great events, now kept a diary, making daily entries. Involved in his first military campaign against the United States, Bannon scribbled in his diary that night that he "slept well in the open air first time."[78] Hereafter, not sleeping in the outdoors merited mention in Bannon's diary. The southwestward march shortly resumed with the Brigade following the army, protecting the rear.[79]

The night of 13 February at Dug Springs was one of the last of fair weather. Bannon learned the reality of February campaigning on the afternoon of the next day, when temperatures dropped. His enthusiasm for martial life dimmed with a storm of "hail & wind."[80] Ice, snow, and rain pelted the withdrawing Rebel columns, twisting over wintry hills.

Springfield, meanwhile, was captured by the Unionists. Price's forces became the next target. Gen. Samuel R. Curtis planned to crush the Southern army before it escaped into Arkansas' mountains. Curtis, therefore, hurried his pursuers southwestward.[81] While covering the army's rear, Little's troops retired into the rough terrain of Crane Creek's wilds.[82] In Bannon's words, the Confederates "marched to crane creek—& camped."[83]

Father Bannon listened to crackling gunfire on 14 February. Skirmishes erupted amid the fallow fields and brown forests as Col. Elijah P. Gates's troopers of the Brigade's First Missouri Confederate Cavalry held the foe at bay. Bannon wrote that the Brigade's "forage train [parties gathering food were] turned back by Enemy . . . during the day firing heard in camp 2 miles north."[84] Confederate infantrymen grabbed muskets and strapped on gear, leaving supper cooking on campfires. If Bannon was offering Mass then, it abruptly concluded. The Brigade formed in a battle-line on the creek's north side in minutes. But no bluecoats appeared. Bannon suffered at the front during the freezing night like a common soldier, while the Brigade stood vigilant. He wrote later, in an understatement, that there was "no resting at Cassville last night." Satisfied pursuit had slowed and after the army's wagons had pulled away, Colonel Little ordered his troops further southwest around midnight to rejoin Price's command.[85]

Half-asleep foot-soldiers hurried through the blackness, trying to catch up with the main body. The rear-guard Missourians finally halted around four o'clock in the morning. Father Bannon and his Confederate comrades spent the night in a wind-swept cornfield bordering Flat Creek. Little's men were tired, cold, and hungry. During this sullen withdrawal, a Missouri private wrote, the enemy "gave us no chance to sleep and but little time to eat."

The next day, 15 February, offered no respite. The sound of musketry erupted northward, and Federal horsemen and Gates's troopers again clashed. But this time the bluecoats pressed southwest more aggressively. To parry the threat, Colonel Little assembled his regiments across the Telegraph Road. These veterans protected the main artery leading from Springfield to northwestern Arkansas.[86]

Once again, Colonel Little's troops waited for the army's supply wagons to move out toward Arkansas on the morning of 15 February. But, according to Bannon's diary, "on the starting of trains the enemy drove in our pickets—Col Little took up position with [Col. Elijah Gates's] cavalry [and] artillery."[87] Light sparring continued with the Federals hunting for a weakness in Price's rear guard. Bannon and Little's infantrymen watched as hundreds of Unionists aligned before them.

Sunlight reflected off gun barrels and colorful battleflags along a hilltop covered with blue formations. Colonel Little ordered Captain Wade to fire a shell into the enemy's midst. The projectile landed in the line's center, scattering Union troopers and horses. Wade's shot forced the lines to retire, and no further engagement developed. Bannon wrote that Little's veterans "held them in check until evening [but the] enemy refused battle." The Missourians then fell back, following the army's trail southwestward. Later, wrote Bannon, Southern columns halted for a brief rest "& [then] moved at night to Keatsville [Keetsville]."[88]

The dawn of 16 February illuminated once more Curtis's advance elements and Price's rear guard under Colonel Little. Bannon and his comrades passed out of their home state and into Arkansas. The priest would never return to Missouri. In the most rearward ranks of the withdrawal as usual, the Irish chaplain jotted down in his diary: "In the morning [the] enemy drove in our pickets but refused battle." After the Missourians turned and withdrew down into Big Sugar Creek's valley, Cross Timber Hollow, the bluecoats again probed for an opening. The Brigade, wrote Bannon, now "twice offered battle to the enemy's" legions, but the pursuers backed down. Captains Wade's and Clark's batteries and Colonel Gates's dismounted horsemen kept holding the Federals at a distance.[89]

No doubt Bannon found encouragement during the withdrawal in Capt. Samuel Churchill Clark, a teenage St. Louisan, who commanded one of the Brigade's artillery units. The grandson of famed explorer William Clark, he had recently won renown at Lexington for shooting down a Union flag. A Catholic and a St. Louis University graduate, he hailed from one of St. Louis's influential families. A Brigade member described "Churchy" thus: "His appearance is boyish, he cannot be over seventeen or eighteen, rather small and delicately formed. He wore a dark overcoat, reaching below the knees to his boots; his hat was looped up on the side and surmounted by a black, waving plume. The free and easy intercourse between him and his men exhibits a kind and cordial feeling. He has left West Point to assist in upholding a cause that he loved, and is considered one of the finest artillery officers in the West."[90]

Clark was "the best artillerist in Price's army." Much like Father Bannon, Captain Clark saw the conflict as a grand adventure. He swore in a letter, "My motto is Conquer or die, and die I will before they shall take me." He would get his wish in less than a month.[91]

The bluecoat cavalry continued hunting for a chance to smash through Price's rear guard. Opportunities for the Yankees existed because the Rebel army was burdened by an immense wagon train. Springfield had been emptied of supplies, which were loaded into hundreds of wagons. The slow-moving vehicles caused General Price to complain: "Is there no end to the train?" One three-hundred-man State Guard Division, for instance, had 236 wagons! In addition, the wagons were continually breaking down.[92] The logistical nightmare repeatedly placed Colonel Little's guardian angels in precarious situations.

The most serious threat came on 16 February at Potts' Hill, just across the Missouri line in Arkansas. With evening, it appeared the Federals would not attack. The day remained relatively quiet—a sure indication of trouble brewing. Then suddenly Gates's rearmost company was caught by surprise when columns of blue horsemen unexpectedly charged.[93] Bannon described the onslaught. "[We were] leaving the valley [when] they made a fast charge on our rear."[94] Colonel Gates's homespun troopers had no time to react before the howling Federals were upon them. A hand-to-hand struggle ensued along the road. One northwest Missouri preacher of Gates's command was slashed on the head with a saber, but the preacher promptly "gave [the Unionist] both barrels, twelve buck-shot in each, and knocked him off his horse dead as a wedge."[95]

In an intermingled mass, cavalrymen of both sides poured down the road, cutting with swords, firing revolvers, and cursing in the crisp winter cold. Because of a turn in the road, Captain Clark and his cannoneers failed to see the sudden attack. The guns were still hooked to limbers when the struggling horsesoldiers engulfed the battery.

Artillerymen fought beside their guns, swinging sponge-staffs and blasting adversaries from their saddles with pistol shots. Some battery members were sabered by the Federal troopers, but Captain Clark and his artillerymen refused to run, despite their battery being enveloped by the blue onslaught. Fortunately Colonel Rives's regiment stood nearby, and Rives led his cheering Missouri infantrymen forward, charging the cavalrymen and driving them off. Losses were light during this first engagement between North and South in Arkansas. Always near the rear during the withdrawal, Bannon viewed his first hand-to-hand contest. The skirmish at Potts' Hill almost on the Missouri line was an inconsequential, albeit nasty, affair,[96] but it hastened the Missourians deeper into Arkansas. With the Unionists staying close behind, Price's hard-pressed command finally linked with elements of Gen. Ben McCulloch's forces. Many of these Arkansas troops had fought beside the Missouri Rebels at Wilson's Creek. Bannon felt elation with the reinforcement, writing that they "met the force [only] a few miles inside the Arkansas border [of] 2600 [men] under Col. [Dandridge] McRae & Cabel [William L. Cabell]." McRae led the Twenty-first Arkansas Infantry and Cabell would later command an Arkansas brigade.[97]

The arrival of McCulloch's troops, however, failed to end the enemy's design to smash through Price's rear guard. Skirmishing continued during the withdrawal. Since leaving Springfield, Colonel Little performed brilliantly in protecting the army. He demonstrated much ability in choosing defensive terrain and meeting each Union thrust.[98]

And no unit within the Brigade proved more invaluable than Colonel Gates's First Missouri Cavalry. Gates, a natural leader and citizen-soldier without formal military training, masterfully utilized his soldiers as dismounted cavalry. Throughout the withdrawal, he employed partisan-like tactics, a type of strategy especially effective at close range during the retrograde movement. The Missouri troopers' use of double-barrel shotguns and their hit-and-run and ambush tactics in the rough countryside of northwest Arkansas were effective guerrilla-like strategies that slowed the enemy's pursuit.[99]

The next day, 17 February, Colonel Little's rear guard expected another strike. According to Bannon, still in the rearmost lines during the withdrawal, "All the [wagon] train had left s[ugar] creek & the troops were leaving the valley of [Little] Sugar Creek [when] the enemy attacked our rear in force with a battery of howitzers—our rear under Col. Little 1st Brigade Confederate forces twice repelled the assault when the enemy fell back & troubled us no more."[100]

With the Southerners ready, the Union cavalry now ran into "a hornet's nest," where the Telegraph Road crossed Little Sugar Creek. Once more Gates's shotgun volleys and Captain Clark's cannon deterred them. In early 1862, the war's horrors had not yet corrupted the men. Rough-hewn frontiersmen of Gates's First Missouri Cavalry, C.S.A., held their fire when a major of the First Missouri Volunteer Cavalry, U.S.A., charged through their line, and the Rebels allowed the Federal officer to escape unmolested. The 17 February skirmish was the last engagement between Curtis's lead elements and Price's rear guard.[101]

Father Bannon learned the following day of the bluecoats' sudden lack of aggressiveness. Once more, Clark's artillery and elements of the Brigade prepared for action. Bannon wrote, "We expected the enemy all day with batteries in position." But no attack developed on 18 February. After being chased out of their own state, the Missourians were embittered. Many had wanted to fight to the death on the border rather than flee into Arkansas. Bannon heard the curses and complaints, writing that the "men [were] tired & angry." But, he continued, spirits were lifted "during the day [when they learned] that the Enemy had fallen back."

This intelligence caused an impromptu conference between Price, Little, McCulloch, and other officers. Bannon, an unofficial member of Little's staff, was present. He recorded the discussion "at a council of war." To reclaim Missouri, Price advocated making a stand and fighting. But McCulloch, keeping Arkansas' and the Confederacy's interests paramount as dictated by President Davis's defensive policy, refused. "Old Pap" offered McCulloch overall command of the joint force as an inducement for his compliance. But the general again declined.

For the first time, Bannon expressed frustration in his diary. The common sentiment among the Missouri soldiery was that had McCulloch's forces joined them earlier at Springfield, then the home state would never have been lost. Bannon reasoned that because of McCulloch's decision it "thereby left us of Mo. no choice except [further] retreat—we therefore started about 11 miles towards Fayetteville Arkansas." Thereafter the withdrawal to the south must continue into the Boston Mountains of northwestern Arkansas.[102]

The Federals' aggressiveness additionally diminished when Price's forces linked with the bulk of McCulloch's command at Cove Creek, Arkansas, on 21 February.[103] In spite of their common cause, the Missouri and mostly Arkansas armies shared an antagonism toward each other. Missourians felt that McCulloch's refusal to join the State Guard during its invasion in the fall of 1861 had doomed that effort to failure. Bannon shared in the anger about the lack of cooperation between Missouri and Arkansas troops.[104]

To pacify the hard feelings between the frontier allies and to take joint command of Price's and McCulloch's armies, Gen. Earl Van Dorn came from the East on 2 March with grand plans. St. Louis was targeted for capture by Van Dorn, "the pride of Mississippi and the terror of the Lincolnites." The merger of the two forces created the Army of the West. Bannon now met a fellow priest-chaplain of the Third Louisiana Infantry, a hard-fighting unit at Wilson's Creek. On Sunday, 2 March, the priest wrote of the day's activities, "Said Mass in Genl [Daniel] Frosts tent— Genl Van Dorn arrived at 4 o clock." Perhaps a turning point for Confederate fortunes in the Trans-Mississippi had arrived as well.[105]

At last the withdrawal ceased, for the Union pursuit ended. A quiet settled over northwestern Arkansas. During this tranquil period at Cove Creek, Father Bannon made special efforts to reach men's souls. He routinely said Mass within various units of the Brigade, hearing confessions and uplifting spirits with words of faith. On one occasion, Bannon lectured to the infantrymen of Col. John Quincy Burbridge's regiment of the Brigade about their Christian duties.[106] "Jack" Burbridge, a St. Louis University graduate also developed close bonds with Bannon. The colonel once had a young private from northeast Missouri in his ranks with a twisted sense of humor and not much promise as a die-hard Rebel, Samuel Clemens, subsequently known as Mark Twain.[107]

Perhaps Bannon's most important psychological and spiritual duty during this period involved giving Communion services. These prepared a soldier for meeting his God before an impending battle. Communion could only be given to Catholics and, as a spiritual strengthening, placed the individual in God's good graces. The timing could not have been more opportune. The Rebel troops would soon be thrust into the largest battle of their lives to date, the bloody "Gettysburg of the West."[108]

THREE A Tavern Called Elkhorn

GRANDIOSE PLANS UNFOLDED in the rugged Boston Mountains for the reconquest of Missouri. Before the thousand-mile Confederate defense line in the West was punctured by General Grant's capture of Forts Henry and Donelson in northern Tennessee in mid-February, an offensive in the Trans-Mississippi was planned. Confederate leaders understood the urgency of a push through northwestern Arkansas to smash Curtis. Such an offensive would relieve pressure on the line's center, stretched thinly across the mid-South. If the Rebels struck first and beat Curtis, then they could capture St. Louis and take the war into Illinois.

This Southern thrust might sabotage Grant's offensive. Price had penned a February letter to Van Dorn describing how the Union forces "can be met, they can be whipped. I can do it [if I had Gen. James] McIntosh and [Col. Louis] Hebert [both of McCulloch's force] with me, victory would be easy [and] my Army would be encouraged [and] Missouri redeemed & safe. . . . I confess myself infatuated, if I do not see [that Rebel reinforcements probably] will not come, unshod horses, a snow storm, presents, General, all these things combined, are nothing to the freedom of a State. . . . Your [presence will be] better here [with the Missouri army], will be more than welcome. Come and come at the earliest moment. An inch of time, may save a Kingdom." For the Missourians, the goal of reclaiming the home state was the top priority. With Curtis's forces scattered over miles of forested, hilly terrain, an opportunity was now presented to deliver the Federals a crippling blow during

the late winter of 1862. Van Dorn, therefore, planned to attack immediately.[1]

Word to prepare for a winter northern offensive came at last. The news
was relayed while the Rebels were aligned for an evening dress parade.
Afterward, the encampments exploded in celebration. The Missourians
"had been hoping and praying that ere long we would be able to redeem
the state and drive from her borders the hated invader." Father Bannon
wrote on 3 March: "Genl orders for march at sunrise tomorrow without
baggage—& with 3 days rations—Cavalry in advance.[2]

Before daylight on the morning of 4 March, the Brigade led the army's
advance north. Price's best troopers, under Colonel Gates, pushed forward
before the Army of the West. In the army's van and with Colonel Little
and staff, Bannon rode up the Elm Springs Road, his black mare trotting.
The invasion to reverse the Confederacy's fortunes had begun.[3] But,
according to one officer, "The column . . . was not in force sufficient to
accomplish the work expected of it."[4]

As if in another ill omen, a storm blew up from the northwest, bringing
cold winds, sleet and snow to sweep the files of men while the column
moved across the winter-hued landscape. The road shortly turned to mud
because the snow melted on the warm ground. The Rebels struggled
onward with visions of Confederate battleflags waving over St. Louis. No
doubt Bannon dreamed of the reception upon a triumphant return to St.
Louis and St. John's Church. But first, to "save a Kingdom," ten thousand
Federals must be defeated in the Arkansas wilderness.[5]

On the night of 5 March, the Southerners made bivouac near an old
mill at Elm Springs, south of Bentonville, Arkansas. Snow flurries cas-
caded down from black skies. Bannon wrote on a water-stained page of his
diary how the troops "camped in the woods without tents—snowed all
night."[6] Any supposed glamour of military campaigning had ended for
Bannon. While he and his comrades shivered in the icy gales, Curtis
learned of Van Dorn's approach and concentrated his Federals along Little
Sugar Creek, twelve miles north of Elm Springs. He had chosen excellent
defensive terrain. Federal troops deployed astride Telegraph Road and
along the wooded bluffs bordering the creek. Bluecoats cut down trees,
dug trenches, and fashioned abatis along the high ground on the north side
of the creek.[7]

Thousands of Rebels, meanwhile, continued north before the dawn of 6
March. Hardened First Missouri Cavalrymen again dashed forward, leading the army. A skirmish resulted when Southern horsemen smashed into

some of Gen. Franz Sigel's forces at Bentonville before they could rejoin Curtis. Colonel Gates's men were among the first to strike the foe. Bannon described one encounter in the running fight northeastward along "4 miles on the springfield road [when] Col. Gates overtook Sigel's & [Gen. Alexander S.] Asboth's men—captured one cannon & one ammunition wagon [and] took several prisoners." As could be expected in winter, the ill-shod Rebels took the shoes and boots off Federal dead and wounded.[8]

But Confederate success at Bentonville only allowed Curtis more time to concentrate his troops. Failing to catch the Unionists by surprise, Van Dorn's scheme of crushing the enemy's isolated units failed. The common soldiers of the Army of the West, who had raced north over fifty miles during the past three days, were in poor condition, cold, hungry, and tired, for a major action to decide Missouri's fate.[9] At 6:00 p.m. according to Bannon's watch, the Missouri Confederates bivouacked in the icy darkness of 6 March. Too frigid to write, Bannon penned no thoughts in his leather-bound diary that night.[10]

Van Dorn and his chief lieutenants, meanwhile, discussed an alternative strategy. General Van Dorn refused to throw away his men's lives against the breastworks above Little Sugar Creek. The wisdom of the decision was soon apparent when grayclad scouts discovered a little-known path, the Bentonville Detour, that curved around the Federal army. Van Dorn thereupon formulated a bold plan based upon this road, slicing through rough terrain. But no Confederate troopers were dispatched up the detour to ascertain if it was open. This negligence was a fatal blunder.[11] No time existed for such safeguards. Desperation resulted in a gamble with Missouri the pot at stake.

While trying to stay warm, Bannon and his comrades-in-arms could not have comprehended the importance of the Bentonville Detour. This ribbon of dirt near the vicinity of Camp Stephens was farther west and beyond Curtis's right flank. After running straight north from Camp Stephens and emerging from Little Sugar Creek's bottoms, the Bentonville Detour curved northeast. Then it swung east, past empty fields and through forests to rejoin the Telegraph Road several miles in Curtis's rear. The defenses along Little Sugar Creek could be outflanked by a successful march along the detour.[12]

An overcast night and Pea Ridge would mask the eight-mile trek around the mountain and a sleeping Federal Army. If the plan succeeded, the Union army would be facing south, while thousands of Van Dorn's Confederates swarmed into position north and behind the fortifications on

Little Sugar Creek. Victory seemed certain with a Rebel army across Curtis's line of retreat by the sunrise of 7 March.[13]

The proposed march was even more audacious than the trek of Gen. Thomas "Stonewall" Jackson's Corps of the Army of Northern Virginia at Chancellorsville in May of 1863. But unlike Chancellorsville, a Rebel army now attempted not only to gain an enemy's right flank, but sought to gain a Union army's rear during darkness and winter conditions.

To conceal the movement, Southern pickets were noisy in the bottoms on the south side of Little Sugar Creek. Butternuts peppered the defenses, keeping the Unionists focused to the front. The Federals, meanwhile, waited for the expected assault that never came. Rebels among the contingent of a thousand men remaining in front of Curtis threw more logs on bonfires. These actions, giving the illusion that the night's encampment was established, deceived the enemy.

Bannon and his comrades had stopped to rest around sunset, after double-quick marching forward much of the afternoon. After the three-day sprint from Cove Creek, the exhausted Confederates suffered severely in the cold.[14] Preparing to lead the march, Colonel Little's troops hustled into line when "ordered to move at 8 toward Little Sugar Creek," wrote Bannon.[15]

Rebel officers finally passed the word to advance. Meanwhile across "the northern sky a glow like that of the Aurora Borealis" shimmered from Union campfires. These distant fires glowed on the horizon as far as the eye could see.[16] Not far behind Gates's cavalrymen, Burbridge's Missourians were the army's foremost infantry unit leading the advance. At the column's head rode Price, Little, and staff. Bannon probably galloped forward in this group. The mounted party trotted west along Little Sugar Creek and away from Curtis's position, before turning north.[17]

Southern foot-soldiers waded the watercourse, swollen by melting snow, with muskets held high and with "our haversacks [now] entirely empty." Twinkling Union campfires and the routine sounds of a hostile encampment cut through the air, reminding the Rebels to keep quiet.[18]

The ill-clad Missourians, some shoeless, shifted to the north near the confluence of Little Sugar and Brush creeks, and entered the woodland's blackness by way of the Bentonville Detour. Hundreds of Rebels struggled onward through a narrow valley, pushing roughly parallel to Telegraph Road farther to the east. Dead leaves blanketing the roadbed and "orders to make no noise" ensured a silent march through Benton County. After leaving the valley, the troops encountered fairly level terrain because the land rose higher in the march north.

The pace was good over the country north of Little Sugar Creek. Despite no sleep and no food, morale remained high. Thoughts of winning Missouri kept soldiers optimistic. The pale light of a full moon occasionally drenched the fields, belts of forest, and the lengthy column. The trek continued, with Rebels easing past Round Mountain just south of Pea Ridge. Luckily no bluecoats picketed the Bentonville Detour.

Near-freezing temperatures made the hours pass slowly during the ordeal. After the column swung by Twelve Corners Baptist Church and spring, the detour straightened out in an easterly direction near the western edge of Pea Ridge. Many Southerners realized that they had "got within the lines of [the Federals] during the night." But the march slowed upon encountering rougher terrain and heavier forest.[19]

During this night, Father Bannon was "a noble man on the march. He always had an encouraging word and [stood] ready to help those who became exhausted &c I have seen him walking, while some tired fellow was riding his horse."[20] Some of Little's Rebels limped along the frozen ground on crippled feet, but even these injured soldiers attempted to keep up with their units.[21] Behind the Missouri Confederates came the State Guard.[22] As the night passed, temperatures fell lower in the black woodlands.

In the Brigade's van, Bannon reasoned that God traveled with the troops. To Bannon, these defenders of the South were crusaders in a holy war. He wrote that the "Southern men, ragged and starving, were fighting for the protection of their homes."[23] Dog-tired, Confederates pushed onward through the night, with empty stomachs and in thin uniforms, but they carried full cartridge-boxes and had high hopes. For four hours, all progressed according to plan. A few more hours' march and success seemed guaranteed.

Behind, or north, of Pea Ridge, Little's files at last descended into the rough, wooded terrain drained by Big Sugar Creek. According to one Brigade member, the Rebel infantrymen tramped "so silently that little was heard but the tread of the soldiers' feet." The cold, weariness, and hunger caused some Confederates to draw analogies with the deprivations suffered by their colonial forefathers during the American Revolution.[24]

But not long after filing past the Twelve Corners Church and several miles west of the Telegraph Road intersection, their good fortune ended.

Around midnight, Confederate ranks suddenly halted in the forests behind the western edge of Pea Ridge.[25] With the time element crucial for
victory, something had gone awry. The column piled up for miles. Southerners wondered what was wrong in the thickets surrounding Pea Ridge.
The delay threatened to upset the plan's timetable, for dawn was set as the
signal to launch the attack in Curtis's rear.

Some Federals had anticipated Van Dorn's march, felling trees across
the Bentonville Detour.[26] Bannon wrote nothing in his diary during the
traffic-jam along the narrow trail,[27] where roadblocks of felled trees and
brush clogged the way. Colonel Little instantly ordered axe-men forward
to clear the tangled barricades.[28] Brigade members, meanwhile, stood in a
stacked-up line. Uniform pants froze harder since getting wet during the
fording of the icy waters of Little Sugar Creek.[29]

Volunteers from Burbridge's unit slashed at the obstacles to dismantle
the barricade. With the sounds of chopping axes echoing over Pea Ridge in
the stillness, Rebels heaved aside logs, tree trunks, and brush. The column
again inched on into the night, but only after much precious time vanished. Finally the detour was reopened.[30]

In a futile bid to regain the lost time, Confederates hurried along the
roadway. Officers implored their troops to quicken the pace, trying to get
to Telegraph Road before sunrise. Rebels stumbled along in an exhausted
state. The "headquarters in the saddle" of Little, Price, Burbridge, Bannon, and others continued east, leading the infantrymen through the
woodlands. After passing almost half of the two-mile rear of towering Pea
Ridge, the race against the dawn appeared won. Curtis failed to ascertain
that more than fourteen thousand Rebels—eight thousand under Mc-
Culloch and over six thousand under Price—had disappeared from his
front to gain his army's rear.[31]

With success still in their grasp, Price's forces now ran up against yet
another roadblock, barring the avenue to Telegraph Road. According to
Bannon's pocket watch, this second, and largest, roadblock was encountered at 2:00 a.m. The new obstacle was fatal to the delicate timetable.
Bannon recorded of the delay that sabotaged the Confederate strategy:
"Found the ravine entering [Big Sugar] Creek blocked by fallen timber."
Work details from the Missouri regiment of Colonel "Burbridge advanced
[to] clear [the] blockade." Again the men started removing the piles of
hardwood timber.[32]

The dream, meanwhile, of reclaiming Missouri slipped further away,
along with the mists over the cold forests during the early morning hours

of 7 March. Large gaps needed to be cut in the barriers for Captains Wade's and Clark's cannoneers to push their field pieces, limbers, and caissons through the entanglements. As before, the entire column mired in the woodlands.[33] The forest's gloom seemed to swallow them up whole, choking off Confederate fortunes in the Trans-Mississippi for all time.

Fatigue-dazed infantrymen rested on muskets that felt like icicles, while a northwest wind moaned through the oaks and hickories. No fires could be lit for warmth lest they betray the movement. So cold was the night that some trekkers who laid down to sleep with only a blanket froze to death along the detour.[34] Butternut workmen labored far into the night, removing the barricades which cheated the Southerners out of success. It looked as if it might take all night to break through the entanglements.[35]

Then the most discouraging sign suddenly appeared straight ahead on the eastern horizon—a faint lighting of the sky. Rays of sunlight began filtering through the treetops, signaling a failed strategy. Bannon described how for the second time, in the pale sunrise, the hike was "stopped till 7 o'clock—Genl [Colonel] R[ives] & Burbridge Regiments'] then advance[d and we] entered the valley of little [Big] Sugar Creek proper," north of the eastern end of Pea Ridge.[36] Finally, the march had resumed. But this had been a costly traffic jam in the Confederacy's lifetime—a five-hour delay that carried the price tag of victory.

With noisy jaybirds and crows making the woods come alive around it, the Missouri column relentlessly pushed through a valley of Big Sugar Creek after moving in a northeasterly direction. Burbridge's trailblazers, still leading the Brigade and army, swung to the right and south as the detour met Telegraph Road. Around 8 o'clock, the Rebels finally gained their objective in the Unionists' rear several miles north of Elkhorn Tavern, a two-story hotel at the intersection of the Telegraph and Huntsville roads. Almost twelve hours had elapsed on the Bentonville Detour. Now the Confederates fanned out in battle lines. Formations soon lurched forward, ascending southward into gorge-like Cross Hollow Timber. In the Missourians' foremost ranks was Father Bannon.[37]

As Price encouraged his troops southwest, he did so without McCulloch's forces. The Arkansas, Texas, and Louisiana veterans never completed the encircling march along the Bentonville Detour. McCulloch's division spent much of the night in crossing flooded Little Sugar Creek on footbridges. McCulloch, therefore, now prepared to launch his assault to Pea Ridge's west, while the Missourians struck from the east side of the mountain.

Van Dorn mounted a two-pronged attack from the north with his forces divided and separated by several miles. This strategy was in clear defiance of sound military logic. Only hours before a likely victory, wrote one Rebel, was "in our own hands; but never was a well-conceived plan more completely defeated in its execution than ours was by the remarkable mischances which [had befallen] us."

General Van Dorn probably should have canceled the attack up Telegraph Road. A combined strike with the entire Rebel army to the west of Pea Ridge would have been wiser. But nothing would go right for Confederate fortunes during this campaign. "Old Pap" learned the bad news when he asked Van Dorn, "How long will it be before Gen. McCulloch will be up?" Now knowing the diminished chance for success, Price replied, "Gen. Van Dorn, I am exceedingly sorry to hear it, sir! I am exceedingly sorry to hear it, sir."[38]

After light skirmishing, Price deployed his State Guard to the left. Little, meanwhile, orchestrated the right's alignment in the forests one-fourth mile north of Jesse Cox's tavern. Incredibly, "the Missouri army, by an all-night march, had passed completely around the Federal right flank, marching" directly in Curtis's rear.[39] Unlike the typical Confederate chaplain who stayed behind as prescribed, Bannon remained in the front lines. While the majority of chaplains stayed to the rear with the surgeons for hospital duty, Bannon went forward in the Brigade's ranks. One of his motives was to enter the climactic battle beside the troops to ensure their admiration. In Bannon's words, the men of God who faced bullets and hardships "were much respected by all the men, whether Catholics or not; for they saw that [I] did not shrink from danger or labour to assist them."[40]

Bannon's unorthodox policy exposed the common chaplain's failings. Such men, explained Father Bannon, "were frequently objects of derision, always disappearing on the eve of an action, when they would stay behind in some farm house till all was quiet."[41] Unarmed except for a Bible and crucifix, Bannon took his chances with his troops. Few Rebel chaplains of the Catholic faith wore Confederate uniforms, but he wore a butternut-colored uniform and a slouch hat, with a red cloth cross on his left shoulder. Additionally, a black beard and an athletic physique belied his role as chaplain.[42]

While the infantry prepared for the fray, Wade's and Clark's artillerymen hauled their guns up through the timber. The cannon unlimbered on a commanding position atop the southern rim of Williams Hollow.

From the heights, the Rebels overlooked a wide plateau and the Federal position north of Elkhorn Tavern at the eastern edge of Pea Ridge. Curtis had recovered from the surprise of Rebels in his rear and about-faced his troops. The Unionists formed a defense on the high ground above the ravines drained by Big Sugar Creek and Cross Timber Hollow.

Bannon wrote of the intensifying conflict, "At 10 o'clock [when] the Feds fired the first [cannon] ball into Price['s] lines—voley [*sic*] answered," by Southern batteries.[43] Captain Clark returned the first cannon shot from Price's Army.[44]

An artillery duel ensued with Rebel guns attempting to blast the Union artillery off the plateau. Price needed to capture this strategic high ground to achieve success. Van Dorn ordered the Missouri gunners to silence the Federal battery. Wade's cannoneers gained the advantage. Suddenly "a loud explosion was heard and column of blue smoke arose in the Iowa battery." A St. John's parishioner of Wade's Battery, Captain Von Phul's brother, Benjamin, apparently hit the caisson. The artillerymen cheered their success, and Bannon, proud of his St. Louis gunners, wrote of them: "Wade's battery blew up a caison [*sic*] of the enemy [the First Iowa Battery] with shell (sperical) [*sic*]." Only ten minutes thereafter, the Missouri cannoneers hit and exploded another Hawkeye ammunition limber of the Dubuque artillery unit.

The second direct hit caused "a tremendous concussion, and amid the cloud of smoke . . . we saw the bodies of horses and men dropping down from the air." The explosion erupted from a chain reaction of half a dozen ignited ammunition chests. In addition, other Missouri batteries, such as Captain Guibor's unit, unlimbered along the ridgetop beside the blazing cannon. Wade's and Clark's St. Louis cannoneers concentrated their fire on the surviving Iowa guns, now positioned several hundred yards north of the Elkhorn Tavern. During the duel, some Missouri artillerymen grew faint-hearted. One soldier "never stopped [running] until he reached St. Louis."[45]

As both sides exchanged barrages, Little's foot soldiers in the wooded hollow braced for the encounter. At this time, wrote one Rebel, "the sickening screach [*sic*] of the shell could be heard as it plowed through our [the Missourians'] ranks, or went tearing through the boughs of the timber over us & scattering them in every direction." Passing down the formations as shells exploded nearby, Father Bannon blessed standing or kneeling soldiers and bestowed the last anointing on the dying, applying holy oil or ointment on their heads. Now "the roar of artillery was deafning. . . . For an hour the bursting of shells, the crashing of solid shot, and the hissing of grape was fearful, . . . the hills echoed and reechoed . . . untill it seemed that the whole of nature[']s field had become the theater of one vast volcanic eruption."[46]

Price's artillery virtually destroyed the Union battery from Dubuque, Iowa. Bannon watched the duel between Captains Clark's and Wade's St. Louis gunners and the Iowa cannoneers. Blasting away from higher ground and raking the plateau, the Rebel cannon gained the upper hand. The priest recorded the success, writing that the graycoat artillerymen "disabled 2 of their guns [of the First Iowa] which they abandoned." The Federal battery was silenced, but another enemy battery quickly replaced the decimated unit. The artillery duels continued, thundering over Pea Ridge like a summer storm.[47]

By this time McCulloch's forces were engaged. Bannon knew another battle raged to the southwest of Pea Ridge, for he heard the roar of "heavy musketry."[48] Colonel Little, meanwhile, prepared to hurl his troops to the south out of the depths of Cross Timber Hollow to capture the plateau and Elkhorn Tavern. According to Bannon's watch, a twenty-minute lull settled over the field.[49]

After the brief respite, Rebel waves poured uphill toward the high ground. Blue and butternut infantry clashed in the forests choking the rugged terrain. Now "the enemy shot well, for our wounded fell on everyside." Both sides stood face to face, trading volleys in the woodlands. Young men killed as fast as possible, demonstrating the mettle of America's citizen soldiery of both sides.[50]

With Bannon at the front line, a comrade noticed his bravery. The chaplain was "everywhere in the midst of the battle when the fire was heaviest and the bullets thickest."[51] On Pea Ridge's field, he raced over to the Brigade's initial casualties "armed with the viaticum, the tourniquet, and with a bottle of whiskey."[52] During the fierce fighting, he saw human beings killed and maimed on the battlefield. Nevertheless, he waded into the blood bath to help his men. Amid the piles of fallen soldiers, Bannon applied tourniquets and offered his whiskey flask, while minié balls zipped around him.[53]

During this fighting along Cross Timber Hollow, Bannon's performance caused Price to declare: "The greatest soldier I ever saw was Father Bannon. In the midst of the fray he would step in and take up a fallen soldier. If he were a Catholic, he would give him the rites of the Church; if a Protestant, and if he desired, he would baptize him."[54] Bannon's presence on the front lines increased the resolve of the troops.

The savage contest, meanwhile, swirled back and forth. Casualties mounted each minute. Twice the Brigade threw back enemy thrusts, but Colonel Little's advances were blunted as well. Ascertaining the foe's strategy and giving the Federals a compliment, Bannon recorded how "the enemy fight hard to force the [Telegraph] road." All such Union attempts were unsuccessful, however. Yet another lull fell over the field. It seemed as if each side needed to catch its breath for the next death grapple.[55]

Confederate ambulances ambled forward to collect the wounded. The cessation of firing allowed Bannon the chance to roam over the body-littered thickets and ravines like a shepherd attending his flock. At this phase of the action, exploding Union shells and fragments of half-burned paper cartridges set the woods on fire. Rebels now fought both Yankees and rings of fire on the bloody morning of 7 March. The wounded had to be carried or dragged away from the flames. Fire and smoke skirted across the slopes of Cross Timber Hollow. One Confederate recalled how "whenever there was a wounded or dying man, Father Bannon was at his side supporting his head" and administering aid.[56]

The quiet faded after thirty minutes. Colonel Little spied a Union build-up on the right. He, consequently, rushed the Sixth Division of the State Guard to the west to fill the gap between two of his regiments. Double-quicking behind the Brigade's lines, Col. Joseph Kelly and his foot soldiers swung across Telegraph Road to bolster the right. Bannon recorded the movement in his diary: "Col Little & Genl [Mosby M.] Parsons [the Sixth Division's commander] crossed [the] ravine [Cross Timber Hollow]." This timely reinforcement was made to "save the Road" from being enfiladed by encroaching Federals and to reinforce Colonel Burbridge's regiment on the right.[57]

With pocket watch in hand, Father Bannon noted how the stillness lasted "from ¼ to 2 till 5 past 3." Bannon wrote that "for 1 hour, no fighting" occurred in the immediate front. But the battle had only begun. Price, ignoring an arm wound, marshaled his forces to yet capture the high ground at the head of Cross Timber Hollow. Rows of Union cannon suddenly bellowed. Fortunately, according to Bannon, the artillery "fired shell [over] our heads to [*sic*] high."[58]

Just after 3:00, wrote Bannon, Colonel Little's regiments lurched up Cross Timber Hollow for the final time. Shouts of "Charge!" rang down the line. Hundreds of Rebels surged forward, attacking to the south through the forest. At last, the bluecoats were pushed out of the hollow. Cheering butternuts spilled out of the cavern-like gorge, overrunning the mouth of the hollow. The attackers finally gained a toehold on the commanding terrain. The battered forces of Col. William Vandever's brigade retreated to take up defensive positions around Elkhorn Tavern.[59]

Along the timber at the hollow's head, the Confederates halted to reload. Here, Missouri veterans caught their breath and realigned for the final push. Before them stood Elkhorn Tavern, nestled in the brown fields of the Cox farm. The tempo again slowed. Both sides rested and prepared for heavier fighting. Analyzing the tactical situation, Bannon observed: "Price's left silent—his right answering occasionaly [with] artillery until 3¼—no firing."[60] But the most disturbing portent was the lack of musketry southwest of Little's position, the silence indicating McCulloch's inactivity due to either a quick victory or a defeat.

Van Dorn's right wing under McCulloch had initially won success. The Rebel assault south of Pea Ridge had driven all resistance before it. But Union firepower, poor Confederate discipline, and a timely enemy counterattack had routed the Southerners after the death of McCulloch and his top lieutenant. Van Dorn's right wing, nearly two-thirds of his army, was no more.[61]

Suspicious of the silence, Bannon recorded in his diary that there was nothing "heard [from] McCullogh['s] line. . . . " Bannon, emphasizing his worst fears, wondered at the implications of having only "heard [heavy firing from] McCullogh . . . for ½ an hour [after] we first heard his [attacking] army."[62] Unknown to Price's followers, the fiasco on the right wing ensured an eventual defeat for Price's troops on the east side of Pea Ridge.[63]

The Third Iowa Battery, meanwhile, boomed from around the tavern stronghold. Reinforcing blue formations gave new confidence to the stubborn defenders. A heavy shellfire crashed into the woods, knocking down Confederates and tearing apart trees. Explosions uplifted the ground, spraying dirt in every direction.[64] At some point, Bannon encountered the commanding general. Van Dorn curtly ordered a vulnerable Bannon to leave the battle lines and go to the rear. But Bannon refused to obey the order. The hot-tempered major general again ordered him to the rear to attend the field hospitals. Bannon explained in his Irish brogue: "I can attend there later. I must attend now to those who are not able to be removed from the field." The commanding officer then threatened to arrest him and, again, Bannon refused to leave. General Van Dorn soon gave up, riding away in frustration.[65]

Father Bannon, summarizing his attitude at Pea Ridge, wrote, "I am doing God's work, and He has no use for cowards or skulkers. A Catholic priest must do his duty and never consider the time or place. If I am killed, I am not afraid to meet my fate. I am in God's keeping. His holy will be done."[66] Throughout the engagement, Bannon stayed in the foremost ranks. He continued to serve under fire, ignoring Van Dorn's threat to "arrest [him] because he did not keep within the proper lines when someone had fallen among the rushing balls in the midst of the greatest danger."[67]

The sun finally dipped lower in a smoky 4:00 p.m. sky. Confederates prepared for the day's last bid to crush the Unionists. Colonel Little held the center with Price on the left and Colonel Burbridge's regiment and another State Guard Division on the right. The plan was simple. Price's Guardsmen would launch the strike to the east, while Colonel Little led the assault south on the Federals' left. Here, around the Elkhorn Tavern, the regiments of Col. Eugene Carr's division were poised. Little prepared to hurl his troops forward in the late afternoon.[68]

Rebel artillery exploded to the left in rolling waves. Price attacked once again. One final push before dusk might achieve complete victory. Bannon wrote that "at 4½ heavy cannonading from our [far] left" proclaimed that the drive to carry the field was to begin.[69]

Blaring bugles, beating drums, and Rebel Yells echoed over the fields around Elkhorn Tavern. Little's troops poured forward with Grizzly Bear State flags of blue flapping above the ranks and the cry of "Forward Missourians!" Wrote one of Rives's officers, "They began their fire, and poured volley after volley of grape [canister shot] onto us, but the regiment, never swerving with loud cheering moved on to the [Third Iowa] battery, driving both infantry and artillery before us."

Colonel Gates's troopers charged on foot with the infantry. Butternut horsemen destroyed Federals with blasts from their double-barrel shotguns at close range. After hand-to-hand combat the hard-fighting blueclad defenders were cut down, for "the shotgun thus used is a terrific weapon." In the fading light, Little's Confederates overran the position. The Rebels captured two Iowa cannon, prisoners, and battleflags in the day's last charge. But before departing, an Iowa cannoneer lit a blanket and threw the fiery cloth over a caisson full of ammunition. Not until a mass of Gates's and Rives's cheering men had crowded close to the captured guns, limbers, and caissons did the ammunition explode. Some of Little's Confederates were literally blown apart. But during the struggle, the Missouri attackers had also smashed into and thrown back the bluecoats of a Missouri Union regiment.

At last Elkhorn Tavern fell. Chasing the fleeing Yankees, the Missourians were "wildly enthusiastic." The howling Rebel tide continued charging past the tavern without halts to regroup. Despite enraged officers, the momentum carried the assault onward. The attack roared south down Telegraph Road and over the fields with a will of its own. Price's troops also advanced all along the line, chewing up blue units and gaining ground.[70]

Bannon joined the day's final charge. Quickly jotting down the facts in his diary, he recorded the highlight of 7 March: "the bayonet [charge] by the [First] Brigade on the right—the enemy fell back & the Brigade occupied his camp" around Elkhorn Tavern. For a half-mile southward, the Missourians' drive continued. Only darkness, exhaustion, and disorganization finally stopped them. Bannon wrote of the gains: "Col Little['s] first brigade [has] possesion of the road beyond the Elk horn Tavern at Sigels [probably Carr's Fourth Division] headquarters when firing ceased at 6½ o'clk." The success was almost complete. Colonel Little's troops hurled the Federals back more than a mile.

The price was high, however. As one soldier wrote shortly after the charge, the ground was covered with many a "martyr for his country, and her rights . . . there quiet in death, and stained with gore, lay gallant young men, whose voices had been forever hushed by the fatal 'minnie'." The cost of the roadblock delays was now apparent. With only another hour of daylight, Price's troops would have swept everything before them. A few more minutes of sunlight might have allowed for a decisive victory at the "Gettysburg of the West" and the eventual winning of Missouri.[71]

Little's victors, wrote Bannon, "bivouacked on the field for the night after 7½ hours fighting." It seemed as if the destruction of Curtis's army would be inevitable the next morning. Bannon left the front and walked north back to Elkhorn Tavern after blackness settled over the field. The tavern, decorated with elk antlers, was turned into Van Dorn's headquarters and a hospital. In Bannon's words, I "visited Genl Frost & Col Little & the wounded at Elk horn" Tavern during the night. Working for long hours beside surgeons, the chaplain assisted the wounded. The Cox family, hiding in the tavern's cellar, experienced "pools of dripping blood [running] through the floor." Bannon probably never knew that Elkhorn

Hunt P. Wilson painting of the Battle of Elkhorn Tavern. Father Bannon is the kneeling figure at the left. The painting shows Bannon's Confederate uniform and the cross emblem on his left shoulder. (The Museum of the Confederacy, Richmond, Virginia, Photograph by Katherine Wetzel)

Tavern once served as a Baptist Church.[72] Nighttime at Pea Ridge was as hellish as the daylight hours.

Around midnight, Bannon returned to the front. Almost within a stone's throw of the Federals, Little's Rebels lay on arms in the cold. Fires were not lit to ward off the low temperatures. Indeed "it was a gloomy night on that battle field, a cold March wind swept across the ridge and struck a chill like a death damp to the hearts of the men." Famished Confederates feasted on captured supplies, their first food in more than thirty-six hours. Bannon again noted a detail having important implications: "At 1^{am} o clock heard the enemy in motion."[73] Creaking wagon and artillery wheels, braying mules, and shouted orders from the Union lines drifted over the field.

Either Curtis was withdrawing or moving forward reinforcements. Since no news of McCulloch's debacle had reached Price's wing, it seemed reasonable to assume that Curtis was beaten. Apparently the Federals, confused and seeking to escape destruction before dawn, accidentally drove a caisson into the Brigade's position. Colonel Rives and a few followers rode forward to capture prisoners and the caisson. In this exposed sector, Father Bannon remained with Little's troops. He wrote in the bright moonlight of taking the prize: "Captured a caison & horses sent by Genl Sigel to Genl [Jefferson C.] Davis—which by accident strayed into our lines."[74]

Evidently, with only a thin blanket to shield him from the cold, he now caught a few hours sleep. Few realized that the half-beaten opponents before them were being heavily reinforced. Thousands of Federals bolstered the Union right after defeating McCulloch. Curtis's entire left moved eastward to amass before Price. But even worse, Van Dorn's ammunition wagons failed to accompany the army along the Bentonville Detour. Ammunition supplies were left at Camp Stephens some twelve miles to the southwest, so that the Federal army now stood between the wagons and Price. Little's infantrymen, consequently, carried only a few rounds in cartridge-boxes with which they would face thousands of Union soldiers at sunrise.[75]

The dawn of 8 March revealed the worst possible scenario. Before the Confederates stretched seemingly endless blue formations, clusters of batteries, and heavy reserves. In an engagement of the first modern war, the side with the most efficient logistical support system, command structure, and superior resources would win the battle.

It became clear that fortune favored the most modernized and best supplied army. An artillery duel unleashed its fury upon the Brigade's position along a wood-line. Bannon recorded: "The fight has resumed by the artillery on both sides & continued with varied intensity until 10 o'clock."[76] While St. John's Church services began back in St. Louis as usual, the chaplain kept his head down low as shells burst nearby and whizzed overhead.

With only dwindling ammunition, the Rebel guns could not win that day. Wade's Battery retired, after losing gunners and expending its last round. Amid the barrage, Captain Clark and his cannoneers immediately took Wade's place. Leap-frogging Union batteries advanced ever closer. These advancing guns poured a merciless cannonade into the Southern ranks, which now included some of McCulloch's units.

Rebel infantry volleys only sputtered as cartridge-boxes were emptied. With Confederate fire slackening, Union artillerymen became bolder. Their artillery crews inched their cannon closer to hammer away with ammunition reserves that seemed limitless. The largest number of Southern artillery—almost sixty guns—ever to be concentrated in the Trans-Mississippi, ironically, could not be employed because of the ammunition shortages. As if realizing the end was near, Bannon wrote, "10 o clock . . . the small arms came into play & continues in one voley for 20 [of] the enemy." Even worse, the diminishing musketry allowed the Federals to build up their strength to the west, overlapping the Southern right. Little's formations would soon be hit with an enfilade fire and a crushing flank attack. Much of the Confederates' fire had ceased before 10:00 for want of ammunition.[77]

Van Dorn ordered a withdrawal. The Rebels started heading to the rear across the plateau, taking more losses while retiring toward the tavern. Price's Grenadier Guard, Little's Missouri troops, covered the rear as usual. The cornered Confederates, according to one Unionist, "fought like tigers." Under the punishment, Father Bannon remained with the Brigade, assigned the position of honor.

. As First Brigade members died, Van Dorn's army retired east down the Huntsville Road, just east of the tavern. Out of rounds and luck, Colonel Little's regiments faced destruction. Van Dorn ordered Colonel Rives and his regiment "to hold [his exposed position] at all odds!" To throw the blue legions off balance, Rives screamed, "Forward Missourians!" The fierce counterattack, "to [allow a] retreat down the Huntsville road," blunted the

Union's momentum. Trying to steady his wavering ranks as his infantrymen were "being slaughtered like hogs," Colonel Rives galloped down the lines. A bullet soon tore into his stomach, but the mortally wounded colonel straightened up in the saddle.

Near Bannon just before the Elkhorn Tavern and close to Guibor's Battery astride the road, Colonel Rives made a dying wish to his nephew: "Help me to keep my seat until I ride down the line to encourage my men. They will break if they see me fall." Colonel Rives remained upright to make sure the Brigade's ranks held firm under the pounding and to gain time for the Army of the West's survival. But heroics were not enough.[78]

More of Little's exiles dropped each minute, after retiring to the north near the tavern. Rebel rifle-fire had virtually ceased when Bannon first earned his reputation as "the Fighting Chaplain." Near this St. Louis battery, he entered the struggle to join one of Captain Guibor's artillery crews and help man a bronze field piece near Telegraph Road. Beside the Irish gunners he knew so well, Bannon helped the gun crew maintain a continuous rate of fire at this critical juncture of the battle.

Bannon's volunteer duty was not based upon unnecessary bravado. The chaplain's contribution could not have been more timely. Enough cannoneers had been shot down that replacements were urgently needed. In addition, the Army of the West remained in danger. The situation of those Missourians remaining on the field was even more precarious, for much of the Brigade had departed the field and those left had expended their ammunition. It was now crucial that the artillery maintain its fire to ensure the Brigade's survival.

After his duty with the battery, Bannon noted the Brigade's final spurt of defiance at Pea Ridge, when the outnumbered and nearly surrounded Missourians unleashed a last "voley of small arms . . . in the side of the federals," who were attempting to outflank the Brigade's position. Colonel Little's survivors, the "regulars" of Price's army, now made a final stand around Elkhorn Tavern. Father Bannon stayed in the fray's midst, close to the St. Louis artillerymen. Holding the enemy at bay, Missouri guns belched flame beside Elkhorn Tavern and astride Telegraph Road.[79]

Cheering Unionists charged forward by the thousands so that the fields seemed alive with bluecoats, spilling onward in an unstoppable tidal wave. Captain Clark held the Federals back not far from Rives's unit, while the Brigade's last regiments withdrew. Captain Clark, the Army of the West's John Pelham, was decapitated by a shell, while withdrawing his last cannon. But his battery helped save the Brigade and permitted Van Dorn's army to leave the field. The end was near when Father Bannon viewed the Rebel army's "batteries retir[ing] by the Bentonville [Huntsville] road."[80]

All was confusion during the hectic withdrawal. Federal artillery continued punishing the retiring Southern formations as cheering bluecoats closed in for the kill. Some Rebel units lost contact, fragmenting into the woodlands drenched in smoke with Union cavalry leading the chase through Benton County. Many Confederates who stayed around Elkhorn Tavern until the last moment were captured or separated. Bannon was among those last defenders who were cut off. Luckily he found his mare and galloped through the woodlands to escape, while Union victory cheers echoed through the valley. Bannon was taking a risk, because blue cavalrymen pursued and he wore a Confederate uniform. He wrote that he "took the bluff East with the intention of joining Genls Price and Van Dorn & Col Little who with our left wing had retired by the Van Winkle [Huntsville] road." This road led to Van Winkle's Mill on the White River, southeast of Pea Ridge.[81]

Despite the confusion, Father Bannon shortly found the rear guard of Colonel Rives's regiment under Capt. Thomas Jefferson Patton. These Company B infantrymen might have been among the rear guard stand made by some of Burbridge's companies, including one under Capt. Pembroke S. Senteny. Isolated from the Brigade, this contingent played a role in ensuring a successful withdrawal by repulsing a cavalry attack. Once he was with Company B, the chaplain was relatively safe from capture. According to Bannon, this cutoff party escaped by a "march northward on the supposition that our boys held the passes of little [Big] sugar creek sth [south] of Keatsville [Keetsville]," northeast of Pea Ridge.[82]

With Captain Patton's band, Bannon kept moving to link with Van Dorn's army. When it appeared safe, the forlorn group of Rebels rested at a farmhouse. Here at Moore's Hill, northwest of Gateway, Arkansas, and near the Missouri border, Bannon found some wounded Rebels. Among the injured was Brig. Gen. William Yarnell Slack, who had been mortally wounded on the first day of battle while leading the Second Missouri Confederate Brigade. Bannon baptized Slack before he died. After assisting the wounded soldiers and giving another hasty baptismal to an injured Rebel, Father Bannon left with his band to continue their journey. That night they stopped at another isolated cabin "where we had supper & slept in the woods near [the] house." But local residents could not enlighten the party about the location of Price's command.[83]

On the morning of 9 March, Bannon and comrades "proceeded northward toward Keatsville—stopped at a house [then] sent a man to town for news of the enemy." Captain Patton's squad and Bannon, meanwhile, parted company. Evidently differences of opinion existed as to the proper course of action. The group was moving in the wrong direction, north, while most of Van Dorn's army, initially pushing north toward Cassville, Missouri, had about-faced, circled around the Unionists, and moved farther south into Arkansas. Danger remained high, for Federal cavalry and "old Sigal [Sigel were] still after old Price."[84]

Bannon and a few others now reversed course and galloped southeast toward the White River on a hunch that proved correct. The guess gained credence when the horsemen encountered two Southern batteries also separated from the army. As yet no Unionists were met. Curtis erred much as Bannon had initially. The enemy continued north in pursuit up Telegraph Road toward Missouri, while most of the Army of the West now fled deeper into Arkansas.[85] After getting into Curtis's rear to cut off his retreat on 7 March, Van Dorn had risked the consequences of a defeat which would almost eliminate a withdrawal south.

Rains and swollen creeks made the journey arduous. For days the band of Rebels rode southeast through the cold downpours. But on 12 March, the party finally reached safe territory, and Bannon wrote that they "took up the divide between the Arkansas and White Rivers," directly south of Pea Ridge.

The days slowly passed in traversing a flooded landscape north of the Arkansas River and to the White River's south. Making good time, the mounted party entered Frog Bayou County, east of Van Buren, Arkansas, late that day. Fear of capture kept them moving south, but they rode too far south toward the Arkansas River. The following day, 13 March, Bannon "learned that the [Rebel] army was back north of us 15 miles." Indeed Van Dorn's battered command had turned southwest for Van Buren after passing through Huntsville.[86]

Near the eastern edge of the Indian Territory in present-day Oklahoma, the chaplain at last gained the Army of the West on 14 March. The sight of Father Bannon in the Brigade's encampment along the Arkansas River lifted spirits of a demoralized soldiery. Never had the Confederates needed more to hear the words of faith than now. Little's troops, hundreds of miles from home and families, now realized that their state was lost. Many Rebels felt anger for General Van Dorn, who had "deemed it expedient to withdraw his forces from the field [at Pea Ridge on 8 March]. Tis said that Gen Price objected to it . . . and stated that he could whip the enemy with his Mo. Troops, but Van Dorn, it seems thought it expedient to retire."[87]

Much discontent lingered. This rainy period during the last days of winter was one of the Brigade's most trying, for the abandonment of Missouri and heavy losses at Pea Ridge had hurt morale. As subsequent events proved, the Battle of Pea Ridge was another reversal leading to the Confederacy's defeat. Not only was Missouri lost forever, but Grant's offensive farther east and into the midsection of the South continued as planned. Forts Henry and Donelson, ironically, fell even before Van Dorn reached Cove Creek. Victory at Pea Ridge allowed the North to gain the advantage and momentum needed eventually to win the war in the West and secure possession of the Mississippi River.

Curtis's victory in northwest Arkansas and the Army of the West's transfer meant that the Trans-Mississippi would never again witness a Rebel offensive on the scale seen during March of 1862. Hereafter, Confederate forces would scatter and not again concentrate for a united effort to reclaim the Trans-Mississippi. No large-scale Rebel offensives in the future meant Missouri would stay under Union control until the war's end. From the conflict's beginning, the Richmond strategists had considered Missouri expendable because of the defensive strategy. The roadblocks on the Bentonville Detour were formidable barriers for the fortunes of the South.[88]

Bannon rejoined Colonel Little and his staff at the camp in the Ozark Mountains. He very nearly lost some close friends on 7 and 8 March. Little had been under fire almost throughout the two-day battle at Pea Ridge. Captains Schaumburg and Von Phul had both played prominent roles as well. Von Phul had delivered Little's orders to various units during the contest, before taking an arm wound. During the risky withdrawal from Pea Ridge, Schaumburg had helped keep the Brigade's lines in order. Then came even more danger for Schaumburg when he had led a burial detail back to the battleground to secure Captain Clark's body. The Unionists, fearing a Southern cavalry attack, had opened fire, despite a white flag among the graycoats. Schaumburg survived and returned safely to the army with the remains of "Churchy."[89] The reunion between Colonel Little and staff members and the "lost" chaplain from St. Louis uplifted spirits at headquarters.

The only positive gain from bloody Pea Ridge was the enhanced reputation of the Missouri Brigade. Indeed, the Brigade's fame as the elite force not only of Price's Army, but of Van Dorn's entire command grew further. General Van Dorn, for instance, summarized their importance at Pea Ridge by reporting to the Richmond government: "During the whole of this engagement, I was with the Missourians under Price, and I have never seen better fighters than these Missouri troops, or more gallant leaders than General Price and his officers. From the first to the last shot, they continually rushed on, and never yielded orders to fall back, they retired steadily and with cheers." Other high-ranking officers compared Colonel Little's Missourians to "Napoleon's Old Guard."[90] Battling for the home state had fueled a ferocity in action. Father Bannon also basked in the fame his men earned.

The Missourians' camp shifted further west on 22 March to the environs of Frog Bayou. On the following day, Bannon was in a foul mood. In anger, he "rested in camp as my vestments [religious robes for Mass ceremonies] were 10 miles behind with Wade['s] battery. I couldn't celebrate Mass." Since first joining Price's Army, Bannon had kept his religious regalia in Captain Wade's care.

Eulogies were held in the camps for the many Pea Ridge dead and Father Bannon participated in these regimental ceremonies, important psychologically. During this period, also, Bannon "preached [lectured] for Dr. [William N.] Dodson," a regimental chaplain in the Brigade. Days grew longer and milder with the approach of spring but rains increased to drench the land.[91]

The Army of the West recuperated on Frog Bayou only briefly. Confederate strategists conceded the loss of Missouri, continuing to believe in early 1862 that the South's heartland was more important than the Trans-Mississippi. Van Dorn, consequently, received instructions from Gen. Albert Sidney Johnston to bring the Army of the West across the Mississippi River to reinforce Johnston's command. General Johnston, a West Pointer in overall command in the West, assembled an army in northeastern Mississippi to confront the North's great hope in the West—General Grant and his invading army.[92]

Colonel Little, soon to be appointed brigadier general for his Pea Ridge performance, ordered his troops to prepare to move out. The Confederates trekked east across central Arkansas. Nature now became the enemy. Rains, overflowing streams, cold weather, and mud slowed the march. After staying wet for days, Bannon finally got an opportunity to change soaked and mud-stained clothes on 28 March. Just east of Clarksville, in east central Arkansas, he took a quick "swim in the [Illinois] creek," flowing south into the Arkansas River.[93]

His dip into the icy waters was unwise. The next day, Sunday, 30 March, he was ill with chills and fever. He nevertheless continued his duties and "said Mass & preached" to the troops as if he were well. Near Springfield, Arkansas, the following day, the ailing priest discovered an oasis of comfort in the wilds of central Arkansas. Bannon and Captain Schaumburg halted to rest "at a farm house under the bluffs [of Caldron Creek], got some warm milk for myself & Schaumburg—Baptised Sick baby—better before I left house." In a frontier cabin along Caldron Creek, a miracle had seemingly occurred: an esteemed priest from faraway St. Louis suddenly came out of the wilderness to save an infant, while he recovered from a serious illness.[94]

Father Bannon and some others left the Brigade early on the morning of 3 April for Little Rock. Surprisingly he had gained enough strength for the trip. At the city on the Arkansas River, Bannon received a warm reception, for his fame evidently preceded him. He dined at the state arsenal, said Mass at a Catholic church, and obtained supplies for future campaigning. But, for the first time, he considered leaving the army. Little Rock's religious community had offered him a position to head one of the community's churches. Having already sacrificed such status in St. Louis to go to war, he again declined an appointment many a religious man coveted.[95]

After a two-day visit, Bannon took a Memphis & Little Rock Railroad train for a short journey east to De Valls Bluff, on the White River. Here, he waited for the Army of the West to be transported down the river. Confederate soldiers had came close to losing Bannon to the lures of Little Rock.[96]

On 7 April the Missourians finally reached Des Arc, Arkansas. Soldiers were worn after the more than two-hundred-mile eastward march. After a parade through town, the exiles from the frontier slave state, now under Federal control, heard stirring news: a big battle had been fought on 6 April along the Tennessee River in the Volunteer State. The information boasted of a Southern victory around Shiloh Church, a Methodist house of worship. To celebrate the success at Pittsburg Landing, Captain Wade's gunners fired salutes and Confederate infantrymen also celebrated the victory. But the first day's gains at Shiloh were reversed on the next day, for Grant's forces had rallied with the arrival of reinforcements to defeat Johnston.

Because the rains, flooded countryside, and swamps had hampered the march east and because of the lateness of Johnston's orders, Van Dorn's army failed to unite with Johnston's Army of the Mississippi for Shiloh. It is possible that the addition of the Army of the West's veterans to Johnston's command would have resulted in the most impressive Southern triumph to date. But as at Pea Ridge, Confederate success had slipped away because of poor timing, lack of coordination, and the narrowest of margins.[97]

Van Dorn's troops filed aboard steamboats on the White River at Des Arc on 8 April. In a massive logistical effort for the Confederacy, around fifteen thousand Army of the West Rebels embarked for Memphis. Cavalry units, such as Colonel Gates's First Missouri Cavalry, now became infantry because the army's horses were left west of the Mississippi. Cheering citizens gave the army a festive sendoff, ironically, because Confederate troops heading east only increased Arkansas' vulnerability. One Brigade infantryman wrote in his journal "As the boats glided down stream, cheer after cheer went up from the multitude on shore, for the success of the veteran soldiers of Missouri, and their aged and honored leader," General Price. On the night of 8 April, Bannon rejoined the army and dined with General Price and Colonel Little, before boarding a steamboat.

The spirited mood belied a cruel reality. Most of Little's troops were seeing the Trans-Mississippi for the final time. A high percentage of these Missouri Confederates would be killed east of the Mississippi. Father Bannon would never again set foot on Missouri soil.[98]

The paddle-wheelers churned southeast under overcast skies, riding the currents of White River for the following two days. After a leisurely trip through a flooded terrain, the boatloads of soldiers reached the Mississippi about one hundred miles below Memphis. Bannon, on the same steamboat as Colonel Little and staff, took notes in his diary. He wrote on 9 April how it "rained all day. Entered the misspi [Mississippi] at 8½ o clk [p.m.]. High water very—moon light," which made the night voyage memorable. Bannon was enchanted with the moon's sheen, which cast a romantic spell over the wide river. The last full moon night had occurred under less agreeable circumstances—during the night march along the Bentonville Detour and around the enemy army at Pea Ridge. After swinging north against the Mississippi's current, the steamboat armada carried the Army of the West toward Memphis, and a rendezvous with disaster east of the Mississippi.[99]

FOUR # Hard Fighting in Mississippi

ON 11 APRIL, TRANSPORT STEAMERS docked at the Memphis wharf, where thousands of citizens welcomed the Missourians. As the Brigade's band played "Dixie," Little's troops disembarked to cheers. After meeting the top religious and civic leaders of Memphis, Bannon assisted at one of the city's hospitals. From Memphis, the Missourians traveled to northeast Mississippi, Father Bannon writing that they took cattle "cars for Corinth at 7 p.m." on 12 April.[1]

Early next morning, the Memphis & Charleston Railroad train churned into strategic Corinth. Because the small community was the all-important railroad intersection linking all corners of the Confederacy, the rail terminus became a bone of contention for the opposing armies. After replacing the slain General Johnston in Shiloh's aftermath, Gen. Pierre Gustave Toutant Beauregard concentrated the largest number of Rebels in the West at Corinth to defend the key railroad junction.[2]

Bannon now met the Sisters of Charity. These volunteer nuns served the infirmaries and occasionally served on the battlefields. After the war, Bannon reflected: "Twice only did I come into relations with the Sisters' hospitals. The first time was at Corinth, Miss., after my arrival with the Missouri troops from Arkansas. There I found the Sisters of Charity (bonnet blanc), from Mobile, Ala., in possession of an hospital, located in a large brick building situated on a hill overlooking a railroad crossing—for the town of Corinth was little more at that time."[3]

Shortly after the Missourians disembarked at the Corinth depot, orders came to proceed ten miles down the Mobile & Ohio Railroad to Rienzi.

While the Brigade went by rail, Bannon galloped southward across country in company with Little's staff. Rains, muddy roads, and washed-out bridges made the journey longer than expected. Bannon, in his own words, during "crossing the creek—went under—horse fell," an incident which caused much amusement. In poking fun, Colonel Little wrote: "The Padre having tried a swim at Corinth had to stop & dry."[4]

The ducking caused Bannon to be perhaps the last Brigade member to reach Rienzi. He finally arrived at 10 o'clock on the night of 13 April. Once in the railroad town, he lodged in a private house, Little's headquarters, and on the following day, he made repairs from the "swim" and "mended my boot." In a fruitless exercise (to be repeated numerous times during the upcoming months), the Brigade hurried north on the next day and beyond Corinth to meet a threat that never materialized. Cautious Gen. Henry Halleck postured and bluffed, but seldom struck. The greatest danger in northeast Mississippi was disease. Various illnesses would steal more lives than Yankee bullets this spring and summer.[5]

Since it appeared the camp might be permanent, Bannon talked a Mr. Bennett into providing a vacant warehouse for his personal use. With the same zeal that built his house of worship in St. Louis, Bannon transformed the Rienzi storehouse into a church and had notices printed that announced the church's opening. A Rienzi printer may have assisted Bannon, or help might have come from the press of "The Missouri Army Argus," the newspaper of Price's Army. The church's opening proved a failure, however. It stood empty on 17 April, Holy Thursday.

Bannon could not fathom the reason, unless it was due to a rainstorm. But he later learned that "my circulars not having been [distributed] to the command I had no congregation." Employing leverage, Bannon convinced Colonel Little to pen a notice of the church's opening for distribution throughout the Brigade. The second opening was an ensured success when, wrote Bannon, "Col. L[ittle] wrote circular for my congregation for this evening on account of storm."

The idea of a soldiers' church was timely. At no point during the struggle had spirituality among the common soldiery in the West ebbed so low. For many Rebels, the war represented adventure and excitement. Away from social restraints for the first time, the boys expected to have their fun. As much as possible, large numbers of soldiers engaged in whoring, fighting, cursing, drinking, and gambling. Many chaplains, therefore, quit the Confederate army out of futility. But Bannon never lost faith. No doubt he beamed at the thought of divine intervention with

Little's assistance. With the evening, Rebels flocked to the "new" St. John's the Apostle and Evangelist Church in Rienzi. Bannon was elated when "30 or 40 of them arrived," after braving a thunderstorm.[6]

A typical day in northeast Mississippi, like 19 April, could be deadly. Diseases were rampant among the unacclimated Missourians from the western prairies, woodlands, and agricultural lands. Deluges of rain bred conditions for the spread of illness. Bannon described one dreary Saturday: "Rain all day & every night . . . mud-mud-mud—confessions at 8 o'clock heard 5 Mass & Sermon at 10½ oclk . . . wet all day [and] preached at night." With hospitals overflowing, constant burials in Alcorn County, and a demoralized soldiery, Bannon's work continued from sunup to after sundown.

General Beauregard's Army was decimated by sickness. Before the end of spring, eighteen thousand Confederates filled the infirmaries and private houses. Father Bannon, consequently, spent much time at the regimental hospitals. He also serviced in the Sisters of Mercy Infirmary at Corinth. For instance, wrote Bannon: "During the temporary illness of Father [Patrick F.] Coyle [of the Mobile Diocese], who was chaplain of the nuns, I visited the [Sisters of Mercy] hospital for him a few times. On one occasion a Sister indicated to me a cot in a distant corner of the ward, whereon lay a large, burly man, heavily bearded and of uncompromising aspect. He had been questioning the Sister about her religion and desired further explanations; so I was asked to go see him and give him satisfaction." Father Bannon made the soldier feel more comfortable by asking "a few questions about his home and family, and wounds and personal comfort."[7]

The remainder of spring saw little activity between the armies of Beauregard and Halleck, but frequent alarms occurred. Little's troops rushed to Corinth several times to repulse imaginary attacks. Bannon, preoccupied with his infant church and the sick, stayed in Rienzi. To his disgust, Bannon's dream of a church in Mississippi ended on 22 April. He complained that "Mr. Bennett occupied his store with cotton bales & closed my church sermons." The priest hunted for a new residence from which to preach but met with frustration. He wrote that he "could not get any house for church purposes."[8]

Without a church, Bannon now relied more on the assistance of such men as Capt. Patrick Canniff. The former St. John's Parish member probably had been one individual responsible for Bannon leaving his parish. Canniff became the Brigade's most noted Catholic and Irish fighter. The captain's battlefield exploits reached legendary proportions before the conflict's end.[9] In the military field, Canniff's and Bannon's association went back at least to the Southwest Expedition. Then, the captain served in the militia's Emmet Guards.[10]

Canniff, a devout Catholic, was soon Bannon's right-hand man. On 1 May, scribbled Bannon, "Coniff [sic] went to [Wade's] Battery to arrange for Mass next day." Mass was regularly conducted at Canniff's tent. As with so many Brigade Irishmen, Captain Canniff would die in battle. Father Bannon devoted much time to Canniff's unit. This elite command consisted "of Irishmen from St. Louis—all Irish from the captain down. They were recruited [mostly] from the wharves of St. Louis."[11]

But, ironically, Captain Canniff's Celtic soldiers caused the chaplain the most headaches. Some officers already had given up attempts to control the St. Louisans' turbulent spirits. These Irishmen were the army's best fighters and the most troublesome soldiers in camp, for the Irish Confederates loved alcohol. On some occasions within the encampment, every member of Canniff's company was found drunk. Liquor abuse often led to fist-fights, broken arms and noses, and black eyes.[12] So bad were some altercations that Father Bannon, of a robust physique at six foot four inches, gained a reputation for the "settling of drunken rows occuring [sic] among the Irish of his flock."[13] He quelled fights by force whenever necessary.

Despite their vices, these feisty Irishmen were the Missouri Brigade's crack troops. The unit was known throughout the army as the "Fighting Irish Company." Clearly, these infantrymen were "the pride of the Missouri division."[14] As one soldier stated about the Irish Missourians' contributions during the conflict and the historical analogy, "Whoever tells the truth as to our war will [also speak of] Ireland in her struggle for self-government for Irish blood asserted itself in our war."[15] Father Bannon and his Irishmen equated Ireland's struggle with the South's bid for nationhood. A legacy of oppression and the desire to combat it were factors causing the Irish Confederates to be "the best fighters . . . in the army."[16]

Bannon viewed the struggle in basic terms of good versus evil, the forces of lightness against darkness. Marching into battle under the flag bearing the symbolic St. Andrew's cross became a religious duty in this holy war. Since the war's beginning, religion served as the basic building block for Confederate nationalism, and Southern churches were the moral and spiritual foundations for the Confederacy's cultural nationalism. One Rebel, who perceived the interwoven relationship between religion and

nationalism, wrote that "there is no patriotism without Virtue and Religion; and we can not expect to find the practice of self denial and patient
endurance of privation for one's country among those who never give one
thought to the Deity."

The themes of the cause's righteousness and a divinely sanctioned nation were emphasized by the chaplain in his sermons. Southerners were
God's chosen people, while the Unionists were the Egyptians or Phi-
listines. According to him, the conflict was one between "the cross and the
crescent for which last the Yankee substitutes the dollar; a war between
materialism and infidelity of the North, and the remnant of Christian
civilization yet dominant in the South." This was the ideology embraced
by the average Confederate, inspiring him to march for miles without
food, rest, or water and charge impossible odds.

Bannon also understood how two distinct civilizations—one agrarian
and the other industrial—were clashing on battlegrounds to decide which
political, social, and economic system survived in America. To Bannon,
the conflict had been caused by one region of the country trying to domi-
nate the other economically and politically. In his words, the North's
attempt to coerce the Southern states back into the Union by force was an
"UNHOLY AND CRUEL WAR." In this view, the North's *moral* objective was to
turn the South into a dependent colony to exploit a populace and raw
materials.

The South's fate, according to Bannon, would become that of Ireland.
In his opinion, the North "proclaimed such high-sounding and attractive
sentiments as 'the old flag' 'the Constitution,' and 'the union,' when the
only object of the war is to enrich the nation of Yankee manufacturers by
the plunder of the farmers and planters of the South."

He viewed the South as the last bastion of true Christian values in
America. In part, he now served in the Confederate army because the Irish
historical experience long ago fused nationalism and religion. The two
philosophies merged to become inseparable. God had given all peoples—
including Irish and Southern—the natural right to revolt to preserve
a national identity. He equated states rights with "Home Rule." This
struggle for self-determination also generated a peoples' war. An entire
society had mobilized to repel invading armies. Explained a Southern
journalist of this modern type of warfare that galvanized a whole society:
"Government usually make the wars, and the people who fight have really
no animosity for those against whom they are contending. But in this war,

every Southern man is animated with feeling of hatred and revenge. It is the People's War. . . . Not only all the blood, but all the wealth of the South, is freely offered in such a holy cause."[17]

During the rainy weather Little's lingering malaria and dysentery worsened, and his fever and chills increased. Knowing negligence might cost the Confederacy a fine leader, Bannon took immediate action and became forceful. Technically a "volunteer chaplain" he could step beyond the normal bounds of military protocol. He therefore convinced Little to take more interest in his failing health. The colonel now could leave camp only in an ambulance and under Bannon's care.

The illness was potentially more harmful because the Marylander had sunk into severe depression. Colonel Little not only sorely missed his family but perhaps regretted his decision to fight against his former country. He also had learned that some Missouri senators in Richmond opposed his pending promotion to general. Proud, sensitive, and pessimistic by nature, Little sulked at the insult, but the advancement to general would be forthcoming. Such distress caused Price's top lieutenant to request "Old Pap" to relieve him from command. But General Price knew better, denying the request.

On 6 May, Little described in his diary Bannon's efforts: "Still sick had severe chills [and] Father Bannon proposes to take [me] to Hospital—Consented to go—rode over very weak thought my head would split." Bannon's mission of getting Little immediately into a Corinth infirmary probably saved his life.[18]

By this time, the special relationship between "the Padre" and General Little had grown even closer. Each held respect for the other—an unusual example of a high-ranking military officer forming such a close bond with a chaplain. But Bannon had proved his ability on the battleground of Pea Ridge where he earned fame as a soldier-chaplain.

General Little's admiration for Bannon's heroics knew few bounds. The general wrote to the Richmond government in a recommendation for the chaplain's promotion: "Rev[d] John Bannon of the Roman Catholic Church (late of St. Louis Missouri) for the appointment of Chaplain in the P[rice's]. A[rmy]. He also has been with the Brigade since its organization and in the Battle of 'Elk Horn' he was on the Battle field in the Midst of the action administering the last consolations of his religion, to the wounded and dying."[19]

Bannon, thereafter, often visited Little. But the officer's condition worsened. General Little had been admitted to the hospital just in time. His illness was so severe that on 8 May, Little wrote that he could "sit up [only] a little while [and had a] long talk with Father Bannon." Another of Bannon's functions at this time included baptism. He baptized Col. James Avery Pritchard, the Third Missouri's commander. A promising leader, Pritchard had replaced Colonel Rives. Destined to suffer the fate of his predecessor, Colonel Pritchard would fall mortally wounded in action before the year's conclusion.[20]

Bannon's routine broke when the stalemate threatened to heat up. The eyes of two nations remained focused on the chess game for Corinth. Halleck's army of more than one hundred twenty thousand bluecoats continued to advance south toward Corinth, reconnoitering the Rebels' strength and dispositions. Ironically, the huge Federal build-up occurred because Van Dorn's army had left the Trans-Mississippi, releasing thousands of Unionists for duty east of the Mississippi. Beauregard had less than half as many troops to stop the North's largest offensive in the West. In closing a ring around Corinth, Halleck probed forward on 9 May, but the thrust was blunted by Southern attacks. Once again, the Brigade had raced north from Rienzi to help repel the threat.

During this offensive, Bannon accompanied the Missouri regiments to bolster Corinth's fortifications. The Brigade's attack northeast in the sharp skirmish at Farmington, to Corinth's east, was described by Bannon in his diary: "At 10½ oclock over 40,000 of the Enemy [were engaged and the Southern forces] captured 300 of his men & quantities of arms & supplies—only 3 companies of the first Brigade engaged as skirmishers— captured blankets our forces retired to their camps & to town—bad head ache." Farmington was the most consequential meeting around Corinth that summer between blue and gray. Wrote one soldier, but "for unaccountable [Confederate] delays and mistakes of guides, it is probable that 'Farmington' would appear in the list of the great battles of the war."[21]

After the skirmish, the Missourians returned to the Rienzi area. Colonel Little's troops now established Camp Churchill Clark, an encampment named for Bannon's teen-age friend killed at Pea Ridge. Bannon basked in the observance of 16 May. This Friday was one of nine days set aside by the government for "Fasting, Humiliation and Prayer" to secure battlefield success, give thanks for victory, or ask penance. Such days represent the Confederacy's dual combining of religion and politics to boost nationalism. In Bannon's words, it was a "day of Prayer & devotion [set] by [President Jefferson] Davis—had Mass at Battery Wade at 7 o'clock [at Rienzi] came in to Corinth in the afternoon" to visit Colonel Little. The fighting spirit yet burned strong in the general. He had regretted having to "lay here & listen to the fight [Battle of Farmington] for liberty." Opium, administered under the surgeon's direction, perhaps only made Little's condition more precarious. The general never fully recovered. [22]

With days like 16 May, President Davis strengthened bonds between nationalism and religion to legitimize the struggle. Bannon understood the strength of such ties. The day of official observance served as an invoking of God's favor to repel the invading armies. Bannon had helped blend a lingering Irish nationalism, religion, and militarism in pre-war St. Louis with his temperance society and the Washington Blues. But for the Missourians, that date would have ironic implications as a day of thanks. More of the Missouri troops would become casualties on 16 May 1863 during a brutal Saturday in Mississippi than on any other day. [23]

Having worn out his Confederate uniform, Bannon needed new clothes. He, therefore, gave Captain Von Phul two hundred dollars to buy him another uniform of Confederate gray. [24] It was fitting that a man who acted on the field of strife like the common soldier should wear battle dress.

Halleck's Army, meanwhile, maneuvered closer to Corinth, so that by mid-May the Union juggernaut had pushed to within four miles of the railroad intersection. In preparation to batter down Corinth with siege guns, the Federals completed a fortified line about five miles in length before the city. It now appeared that, during the summer of 1862, the most decisive contest of the war would be at Corinth. The Brigade again hurried forward to blunt an expected attack on 18 May. Instead of remaining at camp, Bannon joined his troops on the battle-line. As usual, he endured the front's dangers alongside his comrades. [25]

With General Little still as sick as hundreds of his men, Colonel Gates retained Brigade command. Later in the day, Bannon returned briefly to camp. On his own, Bannon then galloped back to the front and "went to the field at 6 o'clk—men under arms [and] visited the skirmishers [under] Col Gates—Enemy entrenching at Farmington—firing last night by [Col. John F.] Hill[']s regt [the Sixteenth Arkansas Infantry, now assigned to the Missouri Brigade] at some hogs. Picket firing on Gate[s's] left—returned to the lines." Bannon had refused to remain at the safety of the main line. He had suddenly left the defenses and ventured forward to give services to the Brigade's advanced skirmishers. A chaplain on the skirmish line, the army's foremost troops, was a rarity, but it won the soldiers' respect. The troops' main criticism of chaplains on both sides was that they talked much of reaching heaven, but seemed fearful of reaching it themselves. Bannon shattered the stereotype, increasing his prestige within not only the Brigade, but the army as well.[26]

Two days later, the Missouri regiments rushed southeast of Farmington to again parry another probe, and Bannon accompanied the marching Rebel column. On the firing line during an artillery duel, Bannon recorded how Captain Wade's cannoneers were "shelling a log house occupied by Feds." Such fire kept the enemy at a distance during the siege of Corinth. The action subsided at nightfall.[27]

After Mass on Sunday, 25 May, Bannon helped a relapsed General Little from a Corinth hospital. The infirmary became overcrowded and understaffed as the weather grew hotter and disease spread. Bannon realized that Little's best hope was for constant attention in a clean, open-air, and sanitary environment. Consequently, he took the initiative, removing the general from Corinth. A healthier environment on higher ground away from the sweltering lowlands and having decent care might make the difference between life and death. To Corinth's south in Monroe County Bannon assisted General Little off the train at Aberdeen with the aid of Captains Von Phul and Schaumburg. In the Tombigbee River country of rich cotton lands, a critically ill General Little was taken to a physician's home.[28]

The move was timely. The day after Little was rescued from the hospital, he improved, and he continued to gain health. After again ensuring the general's survival and visiting him almost daily, Bannon boarded a train for Mobile. While on leave, he visited the South's most beautiful, most sinful city. Mobile had the reputation of being "the Paris of the Confederacy."

He now looked more like a highwayman than a priest. Sunburned from active campaigning, with a rough appearance and acting more like a soldier than a chaplain, Bannon "arrived bearded like a Pard, with a long black beard hanging over his chest." He kept this rugged look throughout the conflict.[29]

On the journey southeast, Bannon viewed the Deep South and a tropical-like environment for the first time. This land for which he fought fascinated him. It was a world apart from his native Ireland on the North Atlantic. He looked with keen interest upon the sloughs, forests of magnolia and cypress. He took special note of a cup-shaped flower, the chalice, and sketched the flower in detail in his diary. The chaplain found significance in the flower's name, since the chalice is the gold or silver cup that holds the wine for Holy Communion.[30]

Bannon as he appeared during
the Civil War (Missouri
Historical Society, St. Louis)

At the Gulf of Mexico port, Bannon secured goods that were run
through the Union blockade. He bought new sabers for General Little and
others and a luggage box, even communicating with Little by personal
letter from Mobile. After completing his mission for the general, Bannon
entrained for Corinth. The return trip was made just in time. Faced with
overwhelming odds, Beauregard decided to evacuate the strategic railroad
center without a fight.[31]

Bannon realized something was wrong upon reaching Corinth. Preparations were being made for leaving. More than one hundred twenty thousand Unionists were closing the vise on Corinth, threatening to crush the
Rebel army caught in the snare. The priest sought to locate the Missouri
Brigade. He "went out to camp—no camp then returned to town—heavy
artillery till the afternoon." On the following day, 29 May, he finally linked
with his comrades. After rejoining his unit, the chaplain "staid in [the]
field all the [time] & moved from the field at 11 at night" during the
evacuation of Corinth.[32]

On the night of 29 May, after supplies and the wounded were transported, Confederate troops flooded into railroad cars to depart Corinth. To

fool the enemy into thinking the increased railroad activity meant the arrival of Southern reinforcements, the Rebels cheered each arriving train. Then, they entrained. The ruse worked, fixing Halleck's army in place. Beauregard's whole command was shuffled south in the blackness. Again given the most risky assignment, the "1st [Missouri] Brigade [served as the] rear guard of the army," wrote Bannon of the risky withdrawal. He stated that the "town [was being] evacuated of everything belonging to the army—Hospitals empty, Artillery in the city at head of our column."

After the last Rebels had ridden the rails south and Corinth stood silent, the Missourians and Bannon boarded the final train out of Corinth. More than fifty thousand Confederates had slipped south to Tupelo, while Halleck's forces expected an attack. But daylight revealed the truth to Halleck. One Missouri officer bragged in his journal that "the enemy's advent into Corinth, will be welcomed only by deserted camps and that ominous silence pervading, the scenes of nature, when her children have forsaken her bowers." Corinth's evacuation, wrote another Confederate, represented another "great drama of this revolution."[33]

Bannon stopped at Aberdeen to visit General Little on 1 June. The general wrote with pleasure of having his confidant, good friend, and faithful nurse by his side once more. In his words, "Feel quite happy to have Father Bannon with me again—We drove out in buggy." Little's spirits were so rejuvenated that he attempted to walk the next day. Bannon also quartered at the physician's home to be near the general.[34]

After another brief trip to Mobile for more supplies, Bannon rejoined the Brigade encamped in the pine woodlands around Tupelo.[35] Here, around fifty miles south of Corinth, the Confederate Army took a new position. Affairs in this sector of the West settled down into a relative calm after Corinth's evacuation. Failing to destroy Beauregard, Halleck's army was dismantled to various theaters during the summer of 1862.

General Little's health, meanwhile, gradually improved, a turnaround in large part due to Bannon's assistance. Because of his accomplishments during the Arkansas withdrawal and at Pea Ridge, Little won command of Price's two-brigade division in mid-June. Other changes came as well. Van Dorn had stepped down from the Army of the West's command. Now Price led the Army of the West. Bannon continued as a chaplain for the whole Brigade, under Colonel Gates. Little's other brigade leader was an officer of equal quality, Col. Martin E. Green, an ex-State Guard general. Green had proved himself under Price in 1861. He had joined the army as a private and would earn a general's rank this summer.[36]

Throughout June, Bannon stayed busy with the Brigade. He continued saying Mass, hearing confessions, presiding at burials, and performing other duties. And he administered to General Little hour after hour, offering comfort, hope, and good cheer. The priest was even handy around Little's unofficial headquarters. General Little, for instance, wrote that "Father B[annon] built chicken coop." At his headquarters among the cotton plantations, Price, other leading officers, and Bannon often dined and conferred on military affairs.[37]

The quiet summer was a killer. Crude wooden headpieces and crosses popped up like spring flowers on the hillsides in increasing numbers. Seemingly stranded forever on the wrong side of the Mississippi, the Missourians saw morale sink further, and Father Bannon's role became more crucial. His influence was instrumental in keeping the exiles from deserting. Some parts of Missouri had been under Federal control for more than a year. Soldiers' families lived under the occupation rule of Union troops. For the Brigade's enlisted men, it made little sense to die of pneumonia, dysentery, and typhoid fever in the relatively quiet Magnolia State with Missouri held by the enemy.[38] Even General Price had traveled to Richmond to seek approval from President Davis to lead his Missouri troops back across the Mississippi.[39]

Bannon continued to stir religious feeling among the troops. For example, the priest's sermon on 15 June moved one young Confederate—a non-Catholic—to write in his diary: "I attended Church this morning. Father Bannon officiating we had a very good sermon."[40] Bannon's emphasis that God stood on the Confederacy's side and blessed the Southern nation served as a psychological force convincing the average graycoat that his cause was righteous. A Mississippi bishop implored in 1862: "Stir up thy strength, O Lord, and come and help us; for thou givest not always the battle to the strong, but canst save by many or by few. . . . Strengthen the hands and the hearts of our soldiers. Protect them from the violence of the enemy. Be thou their shield and defence in the day of battle. Give success to our arms." Such religious fervor increased motivation among Confederate soldiers.[41] Bannon's guidance affected large numbers, regardless of faith. Indeed "both Protestants and Catholics alike felt his influence and his memory is cherished by all survivors of whatever religion."[42]

A Protestant officer, for instance, long remembered the "good chaplain, whose name was Father Bannon, a young Catholic priest from St. Louis, who came down South with our command and served the Catholics as their chaplain. We had a number of good Irish Catholics in our army who had been gathered up around St. Louis; and, wonderful soldiers they made. We all loved Father Bannon. Everybody who knew him loved him, for he was so faithful, good and efficient in every way in all of his duties." A Rebel surgeon, who knew Bannon well, described the chaplain's importance by writing, "As strange as it may seem, the war improved the moral tone of many a soldier."[43]

In June, General Price officially commissioned a Confederate mail carrier, Absalom Grimes. An ex-Brigade member, Grimes had long been engaged in the dangerous undertaking of carrying mail. Grimes's duty consisted of supplying the Missouri troops with letters from home and delivering soldiers' correspondence to the home state. With Missouri occupied by the Federals, this was hazardous duty. Grimes's official appointment as mail carrier "was made at General Price's headquarters in the presence of the troops in camp, together with General Henry Little, Colonel Elijah Gates, Colonel Frank M. Cockrell, Colonel Burbrage [sic], Colonel Thomas Snead, Chaplain Father Bannon, and some other officers. General Price made a few appropriate remarks as to caution, keeping my own council, dangers, etc., and that I was to be ever mindful not to jeopardize the welfare of the Southern people at home in old Missouri. He shook hands with me and bade me 'God speed.'" Then the army's leaders and Bannon also shook the mail carrier's hand and gave encouragement.

Toward the end of June, Bannon briefly visited Columbus. He then went to Verona, with General Little and Captain Von Phul. The Fourth of July saw much celebration. Such festivities verified the Confederates' belief that their young country had inherited the political, moral, and philosophical legacies of the founding fathers. To Southern minds, the Confederate soldiers were defending the true principles of the American Revolution and the early republic. The United States was only an impostor. On this day also, news arrived of the repulse of Maj. Gen. George B. McClellan's drive on Richmond. Bannon wrote that the Rebel artillerymen "fired salute of 13 guns for repulse of enemy from Richmond & Chichominy [Chickahominy River]."[44]

Parades and drills dominated July. The Missourians spent much of the summer prefecting their skills so that the Brigade's reputation as the best drilled unit in the Confederacy might be established. General Little and staff, with Bannon alongside, often reviewed the troops on the drill field. But Little was so sick during one July parade that, wrote the general, "Father B[annon] had [to] button my bridle"—a gift from Captain

Schaumburg. Bannon probably had helped General Little into the saddle before adjusting the bridle over the head of the general's horse, "Trumps." Then General Little galloped down the formations in review.[45]

On 9 July, wrote Bannon, he was beside General Little during a "parade of 1st Brigade at 3 oclk [lasting] 3½ hours." But the exertion of reviewing the troops further sapped the strength of the commanding officer. The following day, therefore, Bannon took Little back to Aberdeen in an ambulance. Away from military duty and with the chaplain's care, General Little once more recovered, after two days.[46]

The date of 13 July saw hectic activity at the Brigade's encampment. A review began the day. As so often in this war, Bannon performed a sad duty. According to General Little, "Man to be shot—Father B[annon] over to see him." After the "parade at 5 o'clock Mass at 8 o clock [and] 12 communion" given, Father Bannon visited the condemned soldier from Tennessee. James Doyle of the Second Tennessee Infantry was evidently a deserter. Gen. Braxton Bragg, who had replaced General Beauregard as the commander of the principal Western army, imposed high standards on the Southern soldiers, who were some of the most individualistic in the world.[47]

After the execution of the Tennessean, Bannon met with one of Price's followers also fated to be shot. The death sentence was for taking corn from a Lee County farmer to supplement army rations. But "Old Pap" countermanded the order, further endearing himself to the troops who saw him as a father figure.[48]

Mail-runner Grimes had returned to the Missouri camps by mid-July, delivering and picking up letters. Bannon, therefore, penned a letter to a St. Louis friend on 16 July. He detailed some of the religious and social demographics of the Army of the West and his own situation:

> Some regiments have Catholic chaplains, the number of Catholics being so many as to give them the majority in the election. Other regiments are entirely Catholic—Louisiana, Hibernian, Irish and French in Price's army . . . about 1500 Catholics [in total] trusting as I do on the voluntary gifts of the Catholics whom I serve, I think I fare much better than as a commissioned chaplain. Since my arrival in Price's army I have messed with Col. Lytle [*sic*], for 22 years an officer in the Federal army and a relative of Col. Morrison of Carondelet. In the same mess are W. C. Schaumberg [*sic*] of St. Louis and Frank Von Phul of Gen. Lytle's staff. All articles procured for the mess are in the account and the amount divided between us when the bill comes in to be paid. Considering that we are represented to the world as

starving, we fare very well. . . . The only privation we have yet suffered is separation from our friends. We have never suffered for want of provisions [except when] at times we have been marching to the field or retreating. . . . We are very apprehensive that England or France will rob us of the honor of forcing a recognition from the North by interfering in our affairs. They have now a justifiable excuse for interfering to open the way home.[49]

But what Bannon, ironically, failed to understand was that French and British recognition was one of the Confederacy's best hopes for maintaining an independent nation. He, himself, would be a player in the game to obtain foreign recognition in the following year.

During July, the Brigade moved ten miles north up the railroad and encamped around Saltillo. Ever-developing strategies caused other changes. By the conclusion of July, General Bragg had shifted most of his troops north to Chattanooga to initiate his campaign to liberate Kentucky. North of Tupelo and just south of Corinth, meanwhile, the Army of the West waited for events to unfold. Price's forces remained around Tupelo, making sure the Federal army in Tennessee received no aid from Corinth to stop Bragg's northern offensive. For most of the summer, consequently, northeastern Mississippi stayed quiet.[50]

By early August, Bannon was writing more letters to St. Louis. A network of dedicated women, including Col. Joseph Kelly's daughter, operated a clandestine Rebel postal service in Federally occupied Missouri, a network that supplied the Confederate troops in Mississippi with an invaluable source of morale. These courageous women risked imprisonment. As Bannon noted, on 8 August, "letters from St. Louis [arrived] by [Absalom C.] Grimes." Grimes, the mastermind postal service organizer, had fought with Colonel Gates's First Missouri Cavalry at the Battle of Pea Ridge. The ex-steamboat pilot, age twenty-five, repeatedly risked his life in running cargos through the Union lines.

During this respite, Bannon demonstrated a talent for foraging. General Little recorded in his diary Bannon's success in supplying their mess with eatables. Despite Bannon's assistance, Little continued to be seriously ill. But the general was determined to fulfill his responsibilities, ignoring the sickness as much as possible whenever duty called.[51]

As the summer faded away, the South mustered everything she had to win the victories necessary for foreign recognition and independence. The great dual offensive of the Confederacy swept into two theaters of operation. Gen. Robert E. Lee's Army of Northern Virginia swung toward

Maryland, while the Army of Tennessee under Bragg marched for the Ohio River. Bragg's Confederates drove north to liberate Kentucky, expecting the populace to rise up.

Never had the South mustered so much muscle and never would it again. Foreign recognition would probably be ensured with autumn victories on Northern soil. The odds that the new Southern nation would survive were never better than by the late summer of 1862. Hence, the Army of the West's important mission in conjunction with these offensives was to keep thousands of Union troops occupied and away from the invasions.[52]

As if knowing as much, Bannon conveyed to General Little that he sensed an impending movement. According to the general's diary entry of 23 August, "Father B[annon] went to Tupelo [and] Thinks we will soon move."[53] Bannon was correct. To assist Bragg's Army of Tennessee in its offensive, Price made preparations to keep the Union forces at Corinth under Maj. Gen. William S. Rosecrans pinned down. Price's watch on Grant's troops in northeastern Mississippi meant that these bluecoats could not aid Union forces in Kentucky and Tennessee.[54]

With the final phase of the Confederacy's three-part northward thrust under Price imminent, Father Bannon "went to Guntown [Mississippi, and farther up the railroad from Saltillo] to find a house [headquarters] for Genl. L[ittle]."[55] While he made housing arrangements near the Mobile & Charleston Railroad, the Missouri Brigade underwent a reorganization. On 1 September, the Brigade gained a new addition with the Fifth Missouri Confederate Infantry. Among the new regiments was Captain Canniff's company [F] of Emerald Islanders. This crack company, containing some St. John's Parish members, held the reputation of being one of the army's finest skirmish companies. Bannon had serviced Canniff's Confederates since his arrival in the army.

Colonel Cockrell now led the Second Missouri; Colonel Pritchard headed the Third Missouri; Col. William D. Maupin commanded the First Missouri Cavalry (Dismounted); Col. James C. McCown led the Fifth Missouri; and Colonel Hill was in charge of the Sixteenth Arkansas. Colonel Gates retained command of the Brigade. In the upcoming contest for Corinth, every Missouri regimental commander would be hit, two of them fatally.[56]

After finding housing in Guntown, Bannon took General Little by ambulance to the new divisional headquarters.[57] Little's troops swung up the iron rails to Baldwyn, north of Guntown, on 6 September. Three days later, another move was ordered by Price, but in a different direction.[58] Fearing that the Unionists were heading for Kentucky to oppose Bragg, "Old Pap" planned to strike at once.

General Rosecrans and a small force held a vulnerable salient at Iuka. This Federal position jutted southward from the main defensive line, anchored on Corinth. The target southeast of Corinth and on the Memphis & Charleston was tempting.[59] Besides the Kentucky campaign, General Price had another reason to be aggressive this September. He desperately needed a victory that might release him and his Missouri troops from service on the east side of the Mississippi River. Reclaiming Missouri remained the top priority among Little's followers.

By 10 September Southern columns were pushing northeast through the hot pine forests to snatch Iuka and keep the Union forces in northeastern Mississippi from hastening northeast to oppose Bragg's invasion. Bannon, meanwhile, galloped ahead of the division "to search [for] a house for Genl [Little]." The general had not yet recovered from disease. Quinine and opium prescribed by the surgeons failed to help. Despite having a high fever and being hardly able to eat, General Little rode toward an engagement from which he would never return.[60] As never before, the Army of the West needed a victory.

The Southerners' march through the parched countryside was tough. Thousands of Rebels churned up clouds of dust while a scorching sun singed the column. Confederates were hobbled by blistered feet. At bivouac in the pine thickets beside the road, Bannon said Mass under shade trees. He distributed Communion and heard confessions after each day's march. Perhaps Bannon gave his sermons from atop a tree stump, a log, or an artillery caisson while speaking traditional prayers in Latin in the Mississippi forests. Fearing that a big battle was imminent, more Confederates came forward to receive Communion—a spiritual insurance policy to reach heaven if killed. Atheists, Protestants, and perhaps even Jewish Rebels came forward to seek spiritual comfort. An impending action and the fear of death erased denominational lines and made nonbelievers into believers. These were Father Bannon's long-time goals.[61]

The pace toward Iuka was rapid. Rebel columns pushed through the woodlands of Prentiss County, for Price envisioned crushing Rosecrans before he ascertained the movement. It was feared that "Old Rosey" might shortly rush into Tennessee to face Bragg's invasion. At all costs, Bragg's western phase of the high water mark of the Confederacy must be assisted by Price.[62] On the night of 13 September, according to Bannon, Price's army was within striking distance of Iuka. A quick attack now might catch the Federals unprepared. Bannon felt confident of success when Price's army maneuvered to within only "3 miles from Iuka [the] troops ordered out at 5 p.m." It now seemed possible that an all-night march might snatch the town and its garrison.[63]

But most of Rosecrans's forces were already withdrawn. General Grant had correctly ascertained that the Southerners were up to mischief. Only Union cavalry were left at one of Grant's largest depots. Rosecrans had fled northwest toward Corinth in such haste that supplies could not be destroyed, and tons of commissary stores were stacked in warehouses for the newcomers. After sweeping away the Federal rear guard, Price's troops enjoyed a feast.[64]

Bannon and Little's staff officers obtained "our share of the plunder." The chaplain may have also acquired wine for his mass services. General Little, his staff, and Bannon made headquarters at a Mr. Pride's house in Iuka.[65] This bloodless victory yielded a bonanza to the under-supplied Confederate soldiery.

With Rosecrans absent, Price became careless. Complacency settled over Iuka. The Southern army, meanwhile, lived off the enemy's commissary and its good fortune, and Grant now spied a chance to entrap the Army of the West. A modern warrior, Grant understood the wisdom of immediately striking "Old Pap" before he linked with Van Dorn. The Union commander would employ a masterful strategy suggested by Rosecrans. First, he would send sixty-five hundred bluecoats southeast from Corinth toward Iuka. This Union force was to be the bait that Price would surely pounce upon to win the success that might ensure his army's transfer to the Trans-Mississippi. Such a victory would boost Price's fame as "the grey-haired Hero of the West."

With Van Dorn held in place by a feint and Price distracted, Rosecrans and nearly nine thousand Northerners would slip around the Army of the West from the southwest. These Federals would slam into Price's Army from flank and rear below Iuka, in a strategy calculated to "capture the whole Army of Price" and perhaps destroy it.[66]

As Grant hoped, the old Mexican War general remained at Iuka for five days. This inactivity was a much longer period than sound military axioms recommended for a small force without support and deep in enemy territory. The lapse of vigilance at Iuka by Price now almost made "his annihilation . . . inevitable." Price's butternuts continued to live in grand style, while the snare began to close. The Army of the West's commander was kept looking in the wrong direction by probes from a force in its front under Gen. Edward Otho Cresap Ord. This was the decoy contingent sent from the northwest. General Price failed to ascertain the danger at a seemingly secure Iuka.

The Unionists' feints caused many Southern troops to race back and forth to meet probes at various points.[67] On 18 September, for instance, Bannon described one such bluff: "Troops out all night—rain at 4 o'clock. [The] Enemy [continues to] advance from Burnville [Ord advancing from Burnsville, to Iuka's northwest] at 7 o clk [p.m.] Troops ordered to the field." The Federals, meanwhile, maneuvered stealthily into positions from which to strike a killing blow.[68]

Ord's forces played their role to perfection. This Union force appeared ready to attack from the direction of Corinth. While Rebels stayed in a stupor, Grant plotted the destruction of the Army of the West for 18 September.[69] As their annihilation came closer with each passing hour, Missouri Confederates ate rations in the piney woods four miles north of Iuka. Little's troops were prepared for an attack by Ord from the northwest, expecting danger in the wrong direction.[70] But luckily Rosecrans's encircling columns encountered problems with guides, roads, and rough terrain. Grant, therefore, delayed the closing of the pincer movement until the morning of 19 September. Price remained ignorant of Grant's strategy, playing into the enemy's hands instead of withdrawing to the south.[71]

Dawn brought sunshine over the autumn-hued land of northeastern Mississippi. Rosecrans swung into position in Price's flank and rear. Thousands of Yankees eased closer to their prey, approaching from Iuka's southwest. Ord's sixty-five hundred bluecoats were to attack when they heard firing southward—the start of Rosecrans's assault. But a northwesternly wind howled toward Confederate forces and away from Ord. Muffled battle noises would keep Ord from striking. By this time, Price had received orders from Van Dorn to withdraw and link with his force. Price, consequently, had ordered a withdrawal, but it was too late. Fortunately Rosecrans's troops had trouble aligning in the rugged landscape and woodlands, allowing Price another respite.[72]

Ord now sent a summons for Price to surrender. General Little hardly believed the proposal "for the sake of humanity to lay down our arms." Price responded to the ultimatum with a taunt "to come and try the experiment of an attack." Despite the enemy's threats, few Rebels were concerned about their situation.

General Little now had a premonition of death. For the remainder of 19

September, therefore, Little was "melancholy and unusually reticent."
Uncharacteristically, the general severely chastised a Mississippi colonel
for a blasphemous oath. Then upon entering a log cabin on the Burnsville
Road, the Marylander instantly left upon seeing a blood-splattered floor.
After returning to his Iuka headquarters after breakfast, General Little
now contemplated an impending "return to Baldwin or Jacinto—dread
another night march." Little and most others anticipated no fighting that
day, since Price had been ordered to leave Iuka and join Van Dorn's army
for a combined strike on Corinth. The Southerners, consequently, leisurely loaded wagons for the Army of the West's departure.[73]

Crashing musketry to the southwest around 2:30 unraveled the riddle:
Rosecrans's forces swarmed up the Jacinto Road. This road was strategic as
the westernmost artery and one of the escape avenues out of Iuka. Rebel
pickets were posted along the road hewn through the forests. Price, waking from his trancelike state, responded quickly. He ordered Little's units
about face and to the south to counter the threat in his left rear and flank.[74]
In Bannon's words: "About 4 oclock Genl Little went to take command of
our left wing on the Jacinto road."[75]

With alacrity General Little recovered from the shock of an unexpected
attack from the flank and rear. The general mustered all available strength,
despite being so sick as to be unable to ride a horse for more than a short
time. In the late afternoon sunlight, General Little rode frantically
through Iuka and down the Jacinto Road to face a crisis threatening to
result in the Army of the West's annihilation.[76]

Little, half-ill and worn out from the early morning reconnaissance,
"arrived upon the field none too soon, and at a glance comprehended the
situation."[77] Federal regiments poured north up Jacinto Road like a blue
flood. Immediately, General Little hurled his Second Brigade down the
road to stop the attack about to spill into Iuka and to tear into Price's flank
and rear. Butternut-colored formations smashed into the enemy tide
head-on.

The fury of Little's counterattack at the decisive moment blunted the
Union attack. But more importantly, General Little saved the day by
striking Rosecrans so fiercely that "Old Rosey" failed to get astride the
Fulton Road. If Rosecrans had gained the easternmost road running south
from Iuka, the Army of the West's escape would have been impossible.[78]

Bannon, meanwhile, responded to the musketry by riding southwest,
after leaving the Iuka headquarters. In Bannon's words, he "went out to
the field with a canter of water to Genl L[ittle]." He galloped down the

Jacinto Road, clogged with artillery and troops rushing toward the raging storm. In this column moved the Missouri Brigade. Ignoring the danger, Bannon sought to reach General Little during the crisis.[79]

Into the heat of action, Little hurriedly threw his newly arriving regiments forward through the drifting smoke and exploding shells. The attacker now became the attacked, and Rosecrans was caught unprepared for the counterstroke. Little's blows smashed the momentum of the Union surge in the late afternoon. Further, General Little's assault accomplished more than just forestalling defeat. Howling Rebels drove the Unionists back hundreds of yards through the bloody fields and woodlands. The Southern counterattack overran an Ohio battery and threatened to rout Rosecrans's forces before nightfall.[80]

Price arrived on the field to survey the accomplishments of his top chieftain during Little's finest hour. General Little may well have saved the Army of the West during a crucial forty-five-minute period on the afternoon of 19 September. Here, two miles southwest of Iuka, Little pulled up to confer with Price and his staff. The "brave Marylander," covered in dust and sweat and probably wearing a blue United States cavalry coat, met his commander just before 5:00. Bullets whizzed around the officers. Beside the Jacinto Road, Generals Price, Little, Louis Hebert, and Col. John Whitfield discussed whether to press the assault in the fading light or wait until the next day.[81]

General Little had begun the conference when a minié ball whistled under Price's arm and struck Little in the forehead. Without a groan, Little raised his arms in the smoke and spun backward off "Trumps." He then fell into the arms of a soldier. The South lost a rising star in the West. General Little's death "was an irreparable loss to the army, to his State, and to the Confederacy."[82]

Father Bannon described for the general's family the details of Little's death in the last entry of Little's diary:

> He was shot whilst our line advanced. He was immediately behind our line conferring with Genl Price at the moment—Being struck with a minnie [sic] ball on the line of the scalp over the left eye and bullet passing thro his head & stopping only under the skin on the occuput—his Death was without pain & his passage was instantaneous—he never spoke nor moved after being struck.[83]
>
> Rev. Jno. Bannon
> St. Louis

The loss of the Army of the West's best leader came as a severe blow to Price. "Old Pap" dismounted and "wept over him as he would for a son."[84] Galloping down the Jacinto Road with his canter of water for General Little, Bannon never forgot the moment when he "met [Capt. John G.] Kelly [from Carondelet, one of Little's staff officers and Dublin-born] with the intelligence of Genl L[ittle]'s death by a minnie ball on the scalp over [the] left eye—met ambulance with body." Now he fittingly "took charge of the body & conveyed it to his head Quarters." During the heart-breaking journey northeast to Iuka, Bannon was once again by General Little's side as he had been so often in the past. This was the saddest journey of Father Bannon's life.[85]

The Confederate attack down the Jacinto Road, meanwhile, continued with greater ferocity. Rebels charged forward to avenge Little's death. While its first commander died, the First Missouri Brigade gained the field and joined in the surge at sunset. The Missourians pitched into the fray, pushing onward and unleashing volleys in the dimming light. A Federal later learned that his Missouri regiment had faced Missouri Rebels, who were some of the Confederacy's finest troops, "known as the 'Flower Brigade.'" By this time, the Missouri Brigade had the reputation of being the flower of the Southern Army.

Yelling Rebels poured onward toward the Yankee position along the high ground. But the blackness closed the door on further Southern gains. Had not General Little and night fallen, Rosecrans's forces might have been destroyed. If so, much credit for the victory would have gone to General Little. Confederate success was also easier by the exclusion of Ord's forces from the action. Price fought Rosecrans only on 19 September. Iuka, nevertheless, was a hard and bloody fight. The Unionists took nearly eight hundred casualties and the Confederates suffered losses of more than five hundred men.[86]

With the night, General Price "returned sorrowfully to town, for he had lost his most trusted lieutenant,—the very best division commander I have ever known,—Henry Little."[87] Price remained distraught, despite the battle's success. For example, Captain Von Phul could not get a coherent response upon asking the commander-in-chief: "General, what shall I do with General Little's body?" Price, "crazed with grief," could only choke out, "My Little, I've lost my Little, my only Little."[88]

General Price had ample reason for remorse. He described the soldiers' feelings about Little's loss: "No one could have fallen more dear to me or whose memory should be more fondly cherished by his countrymen.

Than him, no more skilled officer or more devoted patriot has drawn his sword in this war of independence. He died in the day of his greatest usefulness, lamented by his friends, by the brigade of his love, by the division which he so ably commanded, and by the Army of the West, of which he had from the beginning been one of the chief ornaments."[89]

Bannon had the body of the Confederate general "laid out [at the house of] Mr Convers of Iuka." Later at Little's headquarters [Convers's House known as "Twin Magnolias"] on Quitman Street, Price and his leading commanders met during a conference, while General Little's body was in an adjoining room. Initially General Price wanted to complete his success with the sunrise of 20 September, but he grew wiser about his predicament. He, therefore, ordered the evacuation of Iuka to proceed in the night. It was time to leave before Ord and Rosecrans further closed the trap. Orders were circulated to withdraw down the open Fulton Road—an escape route left open for the Army of the West by General Little. But the cost had been Little's life. With orders to depart Iuka, Price stressed to Father Bannon and Von Phul how, "General Little's body must be buried at once for we retreat before the dawn."[90]

Some Rebels, meanwhile, dug a grave in a small garden in the yard behind Convers's House. Here, at the "Common House" and across from the old Tishomingo County Courthouse, General Little at last found the peace which eluded him on earth. The ad hoc funeral started near the midnight hour while evacuation activity swirled around the headquarters. First, Bannon solemnly passed out his set of Mass candles for the ceremony. Nearby he had positioned Little's body for burial.[91] Captain Von Phul never forgot. "The saddest funeral train I ever witnessed in my life formed in line and moved to where the fresh earth had been rolled back." In the darkness and in the yard behind the old house

> each of us carried a lighted candle that flickered mournfully in the night air, and we gathered about the open grave as the rough coffin was lowered in the earth. Father Bannon, of St. Louis, the chaplain of the First Missouri brigade, stood at the head. Wright Schaumburg, came next. Then we were all grouped around the sacred spot, each man with a lighted candle. There were Colonel Thomas Snead, the adjutant to General Price; Lieutenant Peter Saugrain [from a leading St. Louis French Catholic family and captured at Camp Jackson] of the army; John Kelly, a civil engineer; Colonel John Reed [Reid], myself and General Little's orderly. There may have been some others whom I have forgotten.
>
> It was just midnight as the last spadeful of earth was placed upon the

grave and patted into shape. Our candles still flickered in the darkness, sending out weird shadows. A plain piece of pine board was set at the head marked: "General Henry Little."[92]

During the "weird, pathetic ceremony," Bannon gave his most brilliant eulogy. He spoke pained words for the man whom he loved as a brother. Unable to master his emotions, Bannon "made the oration and in a feeling manner spoke of the character and virtues of the dead General, not, as he said, in the capacity of a priest, for he was not of his church, but as a warm admirer and friend."[93] Von Phul recalled, "The way we laid General Little in the cold ground that night, cautiously and hastily, will cling to me until the last."[94]

One Brigade officer summarized the mood upon Little's death: "The whole army mourned him as a father lost, and we buried him at midnight in solemn silence and beneath the pitying stars, 'with his martial cloak [perhaps the United States cavalry coat], around him.' Many a heartfelt prayer went up for his wife and little one in a distant State, and we murmured, with bated breath, our requiescat in pace as we left him 'alone in his glory'."[95]

The Army of the West's wagon trains, loaded with captured supplies, and artillery ambled south through the night. Around 3:00 a.m., the Missouri Brigade departed the front and headed for Iuka.[96] Hundreds of Missouri Rebels quietly tramped past the Convers's House, not realizing that their commander lay buried behind the now vacant headquarters. But in a fitting gesture, the Brigade was paying the highest tribute to General Little by bringing up and protecting the Army of the West's rear.[97]

According to one Confederate general: "No more efficient soldier than Henry Little ever fought for a good cause. The magnificent Missouri Brigade, the finest body of troop I had ever then seen, or have ever seen since, was the creation of his untiring devotion to duty and his remarkable qualities as a commander. In camp he was diligent in instructing his officers in their duty and providing for the comfort and efficiency of his men, and on the battlefield he was as steady, cool and able a commander as I have ever seen. His eyes closed forever upon the happiest spectacle they could behold, and the last throbs of his heart were amidst the victorious shouts of his charging brigade."[98]

Under the yellowish moonlight bathing the column, Bannon and his comrades marched to safety along the Fulton Road that General Little had kept open. In one Brigade member's analysis: "The brave hearts that beat in the bosoms of the members of the First Brigade, pulsated with sadness and sorrow as they pursued this retrograde march. Their leader and first brigadier had fallen. . . . In Henry Little our brigade lost its main stay and support, and the army its best subordinate general. He did more, both while belonging to the Missouri State Guard and in Confederate service, towards organizing and disciplining the Missouri troops than any man connected with them. To him it owed its proficiency, steadiness in danger and excellency of drill, and to his labors it was greatly indebted for the high rank it achieved among the armies of the South."[99] More than anyone else, Henry Little had been instrumental in developing the superior quality of the Missouri Brigade.[100]

Besides the general's family, no one experienced greater pain with the death of General Little than Father Bannon. But Bannon would have many more such heartbreaks before the war's end. Henry Little, ironically, finally won an official promotion to major general, for the army's headquarters received Little's promotion orders only a few days after his death. Since the beginning of 1862 and throughout the summer, Bannon had been closer and more helpful to General Little during those nine months than anyone else. His encouragement and assistance ensured that General Little would be on the Jacinto Road at the most critical moment to save a Rebel army, which was a key player in a new nation's struggle for independence. On Iuka's battleground, Bannon received the greatest shock of his life when he lost General Little.[101] An officer of Henry Little's caliber would be sorely needed in less than a month during the next confrontation between blue and gray.

FIVE Autumn Fury

PRICE'S ARMY EASED OUT OF GRANT'S GRIP. Fortunately the Unionists sent no cavalry in pursuit after finding Iuka empty. The Rebel command moved south until halting for several days at Baldwyn, on the Mobile & Charleston Railroad north of Saltillo and south of Corinth. Then the Army of the West pushed northwest for Ripley, where Van Dorn and his forces awaited its arrival. The two armies finally linked on 28 September.[1]

The race to unite with Van Dorn caused Bannon to complain on the last Sunday of September that there was "no mass [because] we would march to day [for] Van Dorn."[2] The combining of the two Confederate forces massed twenty-two thousand Southerners into the newly styled Army of West Tennessee.[3]

Planning as he had before Pea Ridge, Van Dorn formulated an aggressive strategy. In Napoleonic fashion, the Westerners in gray would swing rapidly north toward Bolivar, Tennessee. This move was calculated to disguise the Confederates' main objective, Corinth. Then the Rebels would turn and push southeast to snatch the railroad center. After capturing Corinth, Van Dorn's victorious army would join the Confederacy's greatest offensive in the West for future successes in Kentucky, Tennessee, Ohio, and beyond. Such a northward drive would also keep the enemy from mounting an effort to capture Vicksburg.[4]

The campaign to help turn the tide began on 1 October. Butternut columns "marched before day," wrote Bannon, to beat the hot weather. Lengthy Rebel formations twisted like a snake over the countryside of northeastern Mississippi. The Confederates were eager to avenge Iuka and

Little's death. General Maury, a native Virginian, was in close contact with Bannon, who now served as a mess member and volunteer aide on the staff of either Colonel Gates or Gen. Louis Hebert, the new division commander in Little's stead.[5]

Maury was paid a tribute by a Mississippi journalist, who proclaimed that the general's attributes "justly entitled him to be classed . . . along with the officers and soldiers of Missouri. That is the highest praise we know how to bestow." After crossing into Tennessee during the northward feint to keep Federal garrisons from reinforcing Corinth, the Army of West Tennessee, wrote Bannon, "camped at Davis Bridge on [the] Hatchie River." Spirits among the Missouri troops lifted upon leaving the Magnolia State—a tragic land for the frontier exiles.[6]

Like other high-ranking officers, General Maury never forgot Bannon. According to the division commander: "The good and great Father Ohannon [sic], chaplain to Price's Missourians, was near me [and said] 'General, you are very tired; take a drop of the [whiskey] cratur'; 'twill do you good, and then you can get a nap till half-past one.' The good Father never drank a drop himself, but he was indefatigable in his care of his wounded and wearied people, and always carried into battle a quart canteen full of good whiskey."[7]

In the bivouac along the Hatchie, Bannon was busy with an imminent engagement. There was much less drinking, cursing, and card playing during the night, for just to the southeast and down the Memphis & Charleston Railroad were around fifteen thousand Federals. Beside the river, Bannon heard confessions from young men, who knew they might soon meet their Maker.[8]

Before the dawn of 2 October, wrote Bannon, the march through blistering weather continued "eastward across Hatchie at 10 o clk [then] crossed Tuscumbia [River] bottom—camped sth [south] of Chiwella [Chewalla]," only ten miles northwest of Corinth.[9] Rosecrans, commanding at Corinth, was not fooled by the Tennessee ruse. He had marshaled plenty of reinforcements from the surrounding area. In a strange duplication of Pea Ridge almost seven months before, Van Dorn had lost the element of surprise immediately before an important battle.[10]

The next day dawned clear and hot. Colonel Gates ordered the Brigade up before daylight to make final preparations for again engaging the Yankees.[11] From the movement's beginning, Bannon encountered difficulties for, he wrote, when we "marched at dawn—Horse lame & road blockaded—delayed" in an eerily familiar scenario reminiscent of the Bentonville Detour the previous March.[12] With his horse unserviceable, Bannon either secured another mount on the journey or continued forward on foot. Then he "heard artillery at 7½ [7:30 a.m. and] small arms at 20 [minutes to] 10."[13]

Skirmishing escalated briskly, when the Confederates encountered the Yankees in Corinth's outer fortifications north of town. Sweating Missourians double-quicked down the road with Bannon in the column as well. The troops halted and readied for action. Now, Bannon scribbled in his diary, "1st Div[ision] loaded small arms at 10 to 10."[14] The Battle of Corinth was about to begin.

The Army of West Tennessee prepared for its first action, aligning in neat battle formations. Price's units shifted to the left, or north, to deploy in the open fields for the killing to begin. The Missourians' ranks sprawled for hundreds of yards, while a blazing sun beat down. Throughout the deployment, blue skirmishers continued banging away. A sharpshooter killed one of Price's staff officers.[15]

Reminded of death, Capt. Clay Taylor, Price's aide-de-camp and Capt. Churchill Clark's cousin, rode up to Bannon, who, as usual, was at the front. By this time, Bannon was famed throughout the army as "the Catholic Priest who always went into battle." Captain Taylor, a St. Louisan, and veteran of the Mexican War and California gold rush, asked for a quick baptism on the field around noon. As cannon roared, Bannon performed the baptism at a nearby creek.[16]

Beside the Brigade's formations, the cannon of Wade's Battery were unlimbered. Soon Rebel guns hurled fire, raking the network of earthworks. A ferocious artillery duel commenced around noon, and again the Brigade's cannon demonstrated precision.[17] A mounted Lt. Samuel S. Farrington, a former St. Louis militiaman and Captain Wade's top lieutenant, directed accurate fire from his guns. As the growl of cannon echoed over the hills, the young officer was a conspicuous target in the rain of incoming projectiles. Lieutenant Farrington shortly fell from his horse after a cannon ball ripped through his neck and shoulder.[18]

Bannon immediately rushed over to assist the fatally wounded Farrington, "an intimate friend, and one of the noblest spirits of the war, beloved by all who knew him." Farrington had been a member of St. John the Apostle and Evangelist Church. Bannon offered Farrington the last rite if he still lived. Afterward, Farrington "was carried from the field by the ever vigilant and faithful Father Bannon who selected a spot for the temporary interment of his remains."

Clay Taylor, CSA
(Missouri Historical
Society, St. Louis)

The chaplain took the lifeless body of his ex-parishioner and "buried him at the . . . mound on which stands a cotton gin north of the Chewalla road." He selected a spot that could be found by Lieutenant Farrington's relatives, who later retrieved his body, bringing it back to St. Louis before the end of October. Near a clay knoll and an old cotton gin, Bannon performed yet another solemn burial that would be repeated many more times during the struggle.[19]

Not long after he lowered the officer's body into the soil of Alcorn County, the Army of West Tennessee rolled forward. Charging Rebels overran the fortifications all along the line. Corinth's outer defensive line quickly fell. Resistance was light, for Rosecrans fought only a delaying action. The bluecoats retired to their stronger, and last, line of earthworks ringing the town.[20] After the funeral on the battleground, Bannon returned to the front to follow the Brigade's attack. He wrote in his diary how Colonel Gates's Missourians "took the enemies first line of entrenchments on [the] N[orth] & W[est]" of Corinth.[21]

The Rebels' advance only stopped when the sun set over the smoke-wreathed forests. In the diminishing light Captain Canniff and his Irish company (Company F, Fifth Missouri) led the Brigade's surge toward Corinth as skirmishers. The Missourians ended their drive by taking cover behind the Mobile & Ohio Railroad's embankment northwest of Corinth and before Rosecrans's right-center.[22] Van Dorn's whole army swung into position before the fortifications. The stage was set for the showdown to determine the fate of Corinth the following day, 4 October.

Casualties were light, and Bannon's duty with the injured was brief. Before the charge, one attacker had written in his journal the common prayer: "God only knows what the [battle's] end will be, we are sure He will do right, may he grant us success."[23] Van Dorn, meanwhile, was jubilant. The general dreamed of a sunrise victory; he would telegraph Richmond and proclaim success. A Friday triumph seemed to promise greater gains on Saturday—the Pea Ridge formula.[24] And, ironically, a reinforced enemy would adjust to face a confident Van Dorn on the second day and with the same results as at Pea Ridge. Rosecrans's veterans, primarily from Ohio, Illinois, Indiana, Missouri, and Iowa, were among the North's best troops.[25] Once again, Price's soldiers would face battle-seasoned men.

Knowing all hell would break lose in the morning, Rebels, wrapped in thin blankets, lay down on arms and rested, the last night's respite for many. Soldiers were worn out from the day's march, the fighting, and the summer-like weather. As they had during the night at Pea Ridge, the Unionists stirred with activity. Now Rosecrans was either reinforcing or departing; no Southerners knew the answer. But throughout the night the Federals bolstered weak positions and threw up more fortifications. The best chance for Confederate success vanished with the setting sun of 3 October.[26]

One man not sleeping that night was Bannon. Since sundown he had engaged in hectic activity. Knowing it was his best opportunity to reach the hearts and souls of the soldiers, he went from one Missouri unit to another, seeking out Catholic Rebels. The men he visited were for the most part Irish, but included some men of German and French ancestry as well. First, Bannon left the railroad embankment's safety—the Brigade's position—to reach the army's most advanced posts on the skirmish line.

Lying in skirmish positions were the soldiers who would first face the Unionists on 4 October—Captain Canniff's Irishmen from St. Louis's streets and rural Missouri. These men of Company F were young men who loved Catholicism as much as they loved meeting the Federals. Canniff's Rebels were perhaps the army's best skirmish troops.[27]

They were scattered in the open woods before the enemy's defenses. Cool weather, no rations, no fires made the night miserable. Racing the sunrise, Bannon "would go up to a watch-fire, and waking one of the men, call him aside, hear his confession, and send him to summon others. The whole night would be spent thus in going from campfire to campfire. The men were always willing to come, generally too glad of the opportunity; some would even be watching for me." Reliable Irish soldiers, like Color Sgt. William Walsh of the Fifth Missouri, gave their last confessions forever in the dark woodlands. Walsh would never return to his St. John's Church in St. Louis.[28]

While hearing confessions and giving advice in the darkness, Father Bannon heard the rumbling noises to the south. The sounds of the bluecoats preparing for battle in only a few hours speeded up Bannon's pace on a night in which everyone must be reached. As the early morning hours grew cooler, he finally returned to the Brigade at the railroad. In the moonlight, he took advantage of the grace period. Many Rebels rose earlier than usual because sleeping had not been easy with the tension of approaching battle. Bannon administered his services to Colonel Gates's Brigade members further into the night.

After completing his religious duties with the infantrymen, Bannon hurried to the Brigade's rear to find Captain Wade's Missouri Light Artillery. The battery was unlimbered behind the Brigade in protective fashion. Now Bannon heard sins against God's laws and instilled faith in those from the largely St. Louis battery. Within the artillery units, he talked to such Ireland-born Celts as Lt. Richard C. Walsh, John Kearny, and James Barron, Sgt. William Brooks, Pvts. Maurice Daniels, James Kane, and others.[29]

His duties ended around 4:30 a.m. when the action erupted. Van Dorn's batteries opened the battle, throwing projectiles into the Union defenses. The optimistic belief of marching unopposed into Corinth vanished when Federal artillery replied with spirit. A sleepless Bannon recorded in his diary: "We [were] assailed with artillery at 4½ [half past 4:00] in the morning—24 [pounder shells] passed us for 2 hours."[30] Bannon could identify the caliber of the projectiles that landed around him.[31] The barrage of iron slammed through the trees, frightening horses, tearing off branches, and raising dust. Colonel Gates, meanwhile, formed the Brigade behind the protection of the railroad, while a red sun inched higher.[32]

Brigade members soon poured across the railroad embankment as gear clattered and buglers blared over the russet forests. After swarming through the open woods, the Missourians realigned before a high ridge crowned with artillery, blue formations, and earthworks. Before them, the ground was open for the three hundred yards to Battery Powell. This fort was the main defensive bastion anchoring Rosecrans's right center, and they were the most powerful fortifications Bannon and his comrades had ever seen. Clearly, many attackers would not live to see tomorrow because thousands of Rebels would shortly be ordered to overrun these formidable defenses.[33]

By mid-morning, the Army of West Tennessee was poised to strike. Price's troops were ordered to attack when firing opened to the left as one of Van Dorn's three divisions advanced. But orders and communications were bungled, and the assault, consequently, was delayed so that Van Dorn's plan self-destructed before the engagement began. General Price's infantrymen waited in attack formations for hours under a hot sun and the fire of blue skirmishers and artillery.[34]

Bannon could only pray for Captain Canniff's skirmishers as he watched them die before the Brigade. Skirmishing escalated all along the line, swelling to a nearly full-blown engagement.[35] Bannon wrote that the morning was filled with sporadic "firing [at] intervals until 9 [o'clock]—Artillery vollied [sic] for 2 hours—Small arms occasionally."[36]

But the long delay was like a God-send to Father Bannon, who was rejuvenated by the opportunity despite no sleep and perhaps no rations for some time. He went "along the line [to] hear the men as they stood in the ranks" and sprinkle holy oil on upturned faces. He administered the last anointing for a final blessing, before the Rebels charged headlong into the rows of cannon and rifles atop the high ground. The Irish Confederates would soon attack with an abandon bordering on madness, for "no men fight more bravely than Catholics who approach the sacraments before battle."[37]

While artillery boomed louder, Father Bannon went to each regiment. Passing down the formations, he talked to frontiersmen from southeast

Missouri's swamps, the southern forests, and the prairie lands bordering Kansas on the western border, and the grasslands flowing into Iowa on the state's north. He may have used, appropriately, the Biblical words from Verse 1, Deuteronomy 20: "When Thou goest out to battle against Thine enemies, . . . be not afraid of them; for the Lord Thy God is with thee . . . let not your heart faint; do not fear, or tremble, or be in dread of them; for the Lord your God is he that goeth with you, to fight for you against your enemies, to save you."

Holding the Fifth Missouri's flag, Sergeant Walsh found solace in Bannon's encouragement as he had at St. John's Church. Before the Third Missouri under Colonel Pritchard, Bannon moved relentlessly down the ranks with crucifix, Bible, and words of faith. He may have given the last anointing to such Third Missouri Irishmen as Pvts. Richard Burke and Lewis Quinan who would die in battle during 1864.[38]

Nearly five hundred Brigade members shortly would become casualties in Corinth's tempest.[39] Suddenly around 10:00, the signal came to attack.[40] The long lines of Rebel infantrymen snapped to attention. Fixed bayonets reflected the morning's sunlight, gleaming for hundreds of yards along the ranks. Battleflags flapped in the light breezes of October. Beardless drummer boys pounded drums and buglers blew horns.[41] The signal to charge uphill caused Father Bannon to speed up activities. "When the time came for advancing," he wrote, "I made a sign for them all to kneel, and gave them absolution [and] I then went to the second line, or the reserve, till it was their turn also to advance."[42] Confederates swung forward in double battle formations with the resolve of veterans and with red banners snapping overhead.

It is not known if Bannon stayed behind with the wounded and surgeons or joined the advance. He may have followed the Brigade, for soon after the engagement a former St. John's parishioner emphasized to his family, "Father Bannon is safe and well," after listing his company's losses (Company F, Fifth Missouri).[43] Such a performance was in keeping with Bannon's reputation.[44]

After tearing through an abatis, the Missourians charged ahead with high-pitched yelps. Dozens of attackers were cut down during the onslaught up the slope, but the charge continued through the din. The Brigade rolled forward like a well-oiled machine, churning onward to punch a hole in the Federal line. Gates's troops overran the ridge, routing hundreds of Unionists and capturing Battery Powell and Fort Richardson. In one of the war's most impressive gains, the Missourians took at least forty pieces of artillery. Bannon was proud when he saw the Brigade's colors waving from the ramparts of Battery Powell. But the victory was short-lived.[45]

The Brigade's charge ground to a halt after encountering massed reserves and artillery fire beyond Battery Powell and near Corinth. Stubbornly the Missourians fell back to the body-littered ridge and took cover. But heavy losses and a shortage of ammunition meant that their gains could not be held. More bluecoats rallied on counterattacking reserves. The Rebels were being pushed out of Battery Powell and Fort Richardson and off the high ground. If Van Dorn's assaults had been better coordinated and gray reinforcements had been hurried forward, then perhaps the day might have been won. Farther to the right, Green's brigade likewise ran into a wall of Federals after also breaking through the Union lines and achieving success.[46]

Mounted riders had galloped off the ridge to find grayclad reinforcements for salvaging the victory. Captain Von Phul's brother Benjamin, the St. John's Parishioner of Wade's Battery, dashed to the rear to hurry forward an Arkansas brigade. Knowing the Missourians were being wiped out in holding the captured defenses, Von Phul screamed to the Arkansas troops: "Colonel Gates has captured forty guns, but cannot hold them unless you reinforce him at once—follow me!"[47] But it was too late. Out of cartridges, luck, or support, the outnumbered Missouri defenders were driven from Battery Powell and Fort Richardson at bayonet point. Scores of Gates's dead lay sprawled along the slopes, the ridge-top, and beside the captured artillery. Elsewhere were the same tragic results. All of Van Dorn's attacks were repulsed. Instead of providing victory, Corinth brought only death on 4 October.[48]

In the rear after the repulse, Bannon most likely attended to duty at the hospitals, overcrowded with wounded. At the infirmaries, Bannon baptized and anointed the dying while physicians amputated limbs, stopped bleeding, and patched holes from lead balls. Bannon's hospital service concluded with orders to withdraw. The nightmare of bloody Corinth ended with more than twenty-five hundred Federal casualties. Almost twice as many Rebels were killed, wounded, and captured.[49]

Glancing at his pocket watch, Bannon wrote in his diary that the withdrawal began at noon.[50] Fortunately Rosecrans's forces failed to immediately pursue. In that event Van Dorn's beaten army might have been destroyed.[51] Determined not to be separated from the main army as he had been after Pea Ridge, Bannon kept close to the men. After retiring northwest the way they had come, the beaten Confederates encamped around Chewalla.[52] With the sunset of 5 October, Bannon joined a general's staff and continued farther west to the Tuscumbia River.[53]

On 5 October, the Army of West Tennessee was almost boxed in by two opposing forces—one from the west under Gen. Edward O. C. Ord and then Rosecrans's pursuers to the east. In addition, the crippled Southern army was sandwiched between the Hatchie and Tuscumbia rivers. With Ord on the Hatchie and Rosecrans on the Tuscumbia, there seemed no escape between the two Union forces and without any means to cross two rain-swollen rivers. In desperation, Van Dorn's army fought for its life during the Battle of the Hatchie. The Rebel command remained trapped after blunting initial Federal attacks. At the last moment, however, an escape route was discovered across the Hatchie six miles south at obscure Crum's Mill. It must have seemed to Bannon that the Red Sea had parted allowing escape from the Egyptians now in Yankee blue.[54]

Bannon wrote of the salvation for the Army of West Tennessee, when "the [munitions and supply] train [was] ordered to retreat by boneyard [Road]"—a dirt path that snaked through the forests to the Jonesboro Road. This road led to Crum's Mill on the Hatchie and freedom.[55] In the rainy blackness after sunset, Bannon joined the columns of weary men stumbling down Boneyard Road. With his Missouri troops, he toiled through the road-turned-morass, while "verry [sic] hungry and almost worn out."

He had to endure a dismal march and "traveled all night" in the rain and mud. Around 9 o'clock, the Missourians and their chaplain picked their way over the makeshift bridge along the mill dam. The Army of West Tennessee had escaped destruction.[56]

The retrograde movement continued south. But when lingering too long with either stragglers or wounded, Bannon was almost surrounded by Unionists. Capture for the chaplain in a Confederate uniform would have resulted in a stay in a Northern prison. While being hotly "chased by Fed cavalry last night at Rockford [Mississippi]," Bannon escaped because of his own horsemanship and because his mare was a fast one. Van Dorn's army, meanwhile, encamped in the Holly Springs area. Rosecrans had not followed. Father Bannon rejoined the Brigade on 18 October at Waterford Station, south of Holly Springs.[57]

After he had nearly run his mare to death in his flight from the Union cavalry, his horse needed medical attention. Captain Wade, consequently, gave him the horse of his battery's best lieutenant, Farrington. Here, in north-central Mississippi, Van Dorn's Army remained while the theater grew quiet after Corinth.[58]

The Corinth disaster was not the worst reversal to befall the Confederacy in the decisive autumn of 1862. Bragg's invasion north ended along with the dream of Kentucky's liberation. Most Kentuckians, like most Missourians, rejected revolution. The Corinth defeat guaranteed as well that the Army of West Tennessee would not assist in the Western offensive. Grant had not only whipped Van Dorn, but rushed forces northeast in time to help beat Bragg at Perryville, Kentucky. The dream of Southern columns marching across the Ohio River and into Ohio and Indiana slipped away.

Setbacks came in the East as well. The Army of Northern Virginia's drive into Maryland ended in a bloody clash on the banks of Antietam Creek, near a town called Sharpsburg. The high tide of the Confederacy ebbed simultaneously in both the East and West.[59] In addition, chances for foreign recognition faded further with the Northern victories at Antietam, Perryville, and Corinth. The Union ascendency led to Lincoln's Emancipation Proclamation.

Camp life resumed its normal routine after Corinth. Winter was near and both armies needed to prepare for harsh weather.[60] Bannon resumed his regular duties once more—saying Mass, attending to the sick and wounded, holding dedication services for Corinth's dead, and distributing Communion. In his 19 October diary entry, Bannon recorded an eventful Sunday: "6 commun [Communion]—went to town [Holly Springs]—a flag of truce with two Fed officers from Rosecrans army [probably to discuss the situation of thousands of Rebel wounded on their hands or an exchange of prisoners]—accident on RR [the Mississippi Central] Pemberton . . . on board."[61] Indeed a new commander took Van Dorn's place to defend the Mississippi, Lt. Gen. John C. Pemberton. He arrived with "the reputation of an accomplished and thorough soldier."[62]

Fair autumn days quickly passed, while the Brigade fine-tuned for future battles. Corinth had heightened the Missourians' reputation across the Confederacy. One Deep South journalist, for instance, stated how the top leaders of the Confederacy agreed "that no troops in the West, or in the East, in the provisional army, or in the old United States regular service, have ever exhibited more perfect and beautiful drill and military order than the Missouri troops. These veteran soldiers never falter in battle. They are never whipped! They do not seek sick furloughs. They do not straggle. When batteries are to be taken, they take them! When an enemy is [to] be routed, they charge him with a shout of defiance. They have met the foe on fifty battle-fields! They may be killed, but they cannot be conquered!"[63]

Besides spreading across the South, the fame of the Missouri Brigade infiltrated deeper into the enemy's ranks after Corinth. A Northern newspaperman declared: "It is high time to throw aside the idea that the Missouri rebels . . . are to be put down with mild or conciliatory measures. When men march barefooted miles after miles over rough and filthy roads their feet exuding blood, at every step; when their rations consist of a single ear of corn, and when their clothing hangs in rags about them, with its safety endangered by every gust of wind, it is time to know that these men believe in the cause they have espoused. When men thus shod, fed and clothed, fight with a desperation unparalleled in history, as instanced by that terrific charge on our batteries at Corinth, it is time for us to understand that only an active and vigorous war will end the rebellion with honor to the Federal cause. Well said for the Missourians." This is one of the rare existing compliments to the Missouri Brigade from the North.

In typical Mississippi winter fashion, cold rains pelted the encampment instead of snow. Fall turned into winter. One storm struck late on 24 October, a hard night for Bannon. He had his "tent blown away last night." On the next morning, Bannon said good-bye to an old friend and former St. John's parishioner, Captain Von Phul. The officer left for a new assignment in the Trans-Mississippi army.

Price would soon recross the Mississippi to continue the struggle for Missouri. In addition, he would lead a large contingent of Missouri troops to the Trans-Mississippi to regain the home state. But Price would take with him only State Guard units. Missourians in Confederate service, like Bannon and other Brigade members, remained in the Deep South.

With Vicksburg as his objective, Grant sought to strike a blow before the coldest winter weather. Strong blue columns pushed into northern Mississippi in early December. Pemberton's graycoats, therefore, retired deeper into the Magnolia State. The withdrawal would not stop entirely for the Missourians until they encamped on the Yalobusha River, southwest of Grenada, after Grant's drive stalled. Here, in central Mississippi, the Southern forces established permanent winter quarters,[64] and it was winter that became the chief enemy for the poorly clothed and underfed Confederates.

Bannon parted with Lieutenant Farrington's horse because he needed a durable animal for his duty, which consisted of constantly traveling to scattered regimental encampments within the entire division. To find a new mount, he went to the state capital, Jackson, "on a plank wagon." The trip south was wet and long. He was alone, except for "Bridle & Saddle" for a new horse. In Jackson, Bannon demonstrated horse-trader qualities by driving a hard bargain. After much haggling, he obtained a spirited mare for "$300 cash [in Confederate money] & not for $100 [in United States currency]." With the Confederacy's spiraling inflation, this was a good purchase during the winter of 1862.[65]

Three days later, Bannon galloped into the Brigade's encampment around Grenada. Much spiritual work was needed. Long winter nights bred mischief. One Missourian wrote, "Orders in camp forbidding all gambling, . . . Cock fighting has become a sorce [sic] of gambling." Perhaps Bannon helped initiate this directive from headquarters. Another constant worry for him was money. Since his first day with the army, Bannon subsisted on personal loans, largely from Irish soldiers like Captain Canniff. The chaplain noted in his diary each amount for repayment.

Despite having served as a Confederate chaplain for nearly a year, Bannon never received one cent in pay. Through bureaucratic omission and because his position as brigade chaplain did not exist officially, an appointment to chaplain of the First Missouri Confederate Brigade for Bannon was not forthcoming from the War Department.[66]

He finally decided to do something for himself after working so long for others. Consequently, he entrained for Mobile on 21 December to confer with the Reverend John Quinlan, Bishop of Mobile. A friendship had already been struck between the two men, for he and Bannon had met on the train to Corinth the preceding April.

Bannon arrived in the Gulf of Mexico port city two days later. No doubt he appreciated the local Creole and French culture—an old St. Louis atmosphere heavily laden with Catholicism and hospitality. He now sought to secure an official appointment to chaplain. A commission would guarantee regular pay and rations so that Bannon could continue service as long as the conflict lasted,[67] and by the winter of 1862, it was clear that the struggle would last much longer than anyone—North or South—had originally expected.

Bannon explained his impoverished situation to a receptive Bishop Quinlan. The bishop then sent the all-important letter on 7 January 1863. Quinlan wrote to the Confederate Secretary of the Navy, Stephen Russell Mallory—a West Indian-born Catholic of Florida:

There is a little matter I would urge on your consideration, affecting a large body of brave Catholics, and indirectly, as far as it goes, the welfare of the Confederacy itself: It is in reference to Rev. John Bannon of St. Louis. This Rev. gentleman was chaplain (state) to the Missouri State Guard . . . In May 1861, it was dispersed at Camp Jackson, by the Federal Government. Father Bannon's devotion to our cause was so well known at the time, in St. Louis, that it earned for him at the hands of the Lincoln officials much prosecution & in one instance nearly cost him his life. When Genl. Price was gathering his noble band of patriots, many young men (Catholics) from St. Louis left that city to join him: the separation from Family & home they murmured not, but fought on unflinchingly for the cause of the South. There was one thing, however, they could not do without—the ministration of a Catholic chaplain. They wrote to Father Bannon to St. Louis, for assistance: and he, with a noble sacrifice of all self interest, relinquished his comfortable position of Pastor of St. John's Church, in this city and, thro many dangers, succeeded in reaching Price's Army, which he has followed faithfully ever since January 1862. Ever since then, he has been the faithful Apostle to about 1,800 Catholic Missourians of Price's Army; has been in the trying conflicts of Elkhorn, Farmington and Corinth & is yet with the same army. During all this time, he has not received a cent of the public money. He started from St. Louis with 300 hundred dollars in gold & has been serving since without any remuneration, depending entirely upon the generosity of the officers. He is now without funds, 1000 dollars in debt & unable any longer, unless assisted, to continue his services w[ith] the army. I would most earnestly request, then, Hon. & dear Sir, that you would procure for him a chaplaincy, with orders to report to Major Genl Price, and, if possible, to have it antedated . . . to cover his services [from January] 1862 to the present. I know it does not belong to your department, but I am sure, for the Sake of our cause, and the spiritual interests of so many brave men you will do all you can to obtain the granting of this request.[68]

Bishop Quinlan's influence proved decisive. The Confederacy's Secretary of War, James A. Seddon, officially appointed Father Bannon a Confederate chaplain on 12 February 1863. As Bishop Quinlan suggested, the commission was antedated from 1 February 1862. This cutting of bureaucratic red-tape entitled Bannon to a past payment up to 30 January 1863—$960 and almost enough to cover a $1,000 debt to his men.[69] Despite wearing a soldier's gray uniform for a year and repeatedly risking his life on the battlefield, Bannon only then became an official member of the Army of the Confederate States of America.[70] Regular pay of $80 per month guaranteed that Chaplain Bannon's services would continue.[71]

After a year of active field service, Bannon found his Mobile furlough to be a much-needed respite. He visited pro-Southern families banished by Union authorities and exiled from St. Louis, among them Captain Schaumburg's relatives. He also found a quantity of prayer books, an ideal source of religious guidance for the enlisted men. Bannon's extended stay was highlighted by the arrival of Captain Wade, also on furlough. Eventually, on 7 January, Bannon embarked by rail for the Brigade's encampment around Grenada.[72]

Upon rejoining the army, Bannon "distributed [the] p. [prayer] books in camp." In addition, he sought out such faithful men as Captain Canniff and "settled bills" with a cash advancement based upon his antedated commission. The balancing of the ledger relieved the chaplain's conscience. Less than a week later, he took the train west to Vicksburg, a town that would become more important during upcoming months. Here, on the banks of the Mississippi River, Father Bannon preached at the house of worship atop the bluffs overlooking the river. St. Paul's Catholic Church reminded Bannon of his own church five hundred miles northward and upriver from Vicksburg. The Vicksburg cathedral was known throughout the South as "one of the finest and largest Catholic Churches on the Mississippi." At the conflict's beginning, a Catholic priest here had blessed the battleflags of Confederate troops before they marched northward to meet the Yankees.[73]

Bannon soon returned to his Brigade, continuing his duties as eagerly as ever. Not long after his arrival in camp, General Little's ex-servant took Bannon's horse. With some indignation, Bannon wrote in his diary, "My Mare [was] stolen last night by Bob." This African American had been "brought in" the army during the summer of 1862.[74]

By January 1863, the Missouri Brigade had gained a new commander, Gen. John Stevens Bowen. He was from Carondelet, south of St. Louis, and native of the coastal lands southeast of Savannah. He had been wounded at Shiloh while leading a brigade to victory on the first day against some of the Camp Jackson captors. Bowen commanded Little's old division during the upcoming campaign for Vicksburg.[75]

Mary Lucretia Preston Kennerly-Bowen had joined her general-husband and stayed in the army's encampment. Of French ancestry on her mother's side, the Catholic woman became close to Father Bannon. The two St. Louisans had much in common. She had been captured at Camp Jackson with her brothers (now in the First Missouri Confederate Infantry Regiment) and her husband, who had been Frost's best lieutenant and a regimental commander. But unlike Bannon, Mary had slipped through the Union lines at Camp Jackson on 10 May 1861, carrying with her the Second Regiment's colors out of Lindell Grove. Then upon joining her husband in Mississippi, the young woman had presented the flag to Bowen's First Missouri, now part of the Brigade. Mrs. Bowen had again smuggled the regimental banner past the enemy. Mary now found a means of worship with Father Bannon in her absence from St. Boniface Catholic Church of Carondelet.[76]

SIX   Battleflags Amid the Magnolias

AT THE END OF JANUARY, the Missourians piled aboard the cattle cars of the Mississippi Central Railroad on a train moving south for Jackson. With the Unionists threatening Vicksburg from the Mississippi River, Pemberton shifted his reserves closer to the citadel.[1] Not long thereafter, in Bannon's words, he watched a "review of Bowen's Div[ision] at Jackson—Mo troops uniformed" in new gray jackets with blue trim and pants. After fighting a year and a half in undyed wool and butternut, Brigade members finally obtained regular Confederate uniforms.[2]

By the beginning of February, Father Bannon was occasionally preaching at the Catholic Church in Jackson. He reached a receptive audience. These parishioners had donated the church's bells to be melted down and recast into cannon.[3] Bannon also visited the Sisters of Mercy infirmary. He described the hospital at Jackson: "The hospital was located in a large hotel, downtown. As I entered the door I found the hallway occupied for its length by two rows of sick soldiers stretched on the floor, each wrapped in his old worn blanket with his small bundle for a pillow. A tall, gaunt, poor fellow had just come in and was spreading his blanket, preparing to lie down."[4]

The Brigade, meanwhile, swung farther to the west and close to Vicksburg, still threatened by Grant. By mid-February, the Missourians had taken position along the Big Black River, halfway between Jackson and Vicksburg.[5] Bannon stayed busy in the capital, continuing to visit the church near the city's center and its large immigrant congregation to conduct Mass.[6] Meanwhile General Grant continued attempts to win control of the Mississippi. One Southern newspaperman commented that the war would be won in the West. "It grows more and more apparent every day that the great contest for freedom in which the Confederate States are now engaged is to be decided in the valley of the Mississippi."

Mississippians foresaw dire consequences if Union forces gained control of the Mississippi River. "The loss of Mississippi, and the unqualified surrender of the Great Father of Waters to the use and control of the enemy will be a calamity which, if it does not deprive us of our liberties, will strip us of our possessions, and consign our wives and daughters to brutal insults, and turn our children bare footed upon a devastated and ruined country." But Vicksburg, the South's "Gibraltar," stood squarely in the Union's path to victory.[7]

North of the city, Bannon understood Vicksburg's strategic value when he spied "13 Yankee boats on [the Yazoo] river this afternoon [6 February] from above."[8] The Northern fleet had swung south down the Yazoo Delta and toward Vicksburg during the Yazoo expedition. But this attempt to find a suitable route through the delta jungle for an offensive from the city's north was futile.[9]

For much of March, Bannon continued making the religious circuit between the Brigade's encampment, Mobile, Jackson, and Vicksburg. A Catholic priest in the Deep South was a much sought after individual. With the warmer and longer days of an early spring, the Missouri Confederates felt frisky. Wrote one officer, the "soldiers are fiddling and dancing." Expecting trouble, Bannon stayed closer to the Brigade's bivouac after the unit was transferred to Grand Gulf in early March. The Brigade, and later the entire division, was ordered to hold Vicksburg's southern flank at Grand Gulf.

On the Mississippi and near the mouth of Big Black River, General Bowen took command of the strategic position. He planned to transform the heights of Grand Gulf into a fortress. The first glimpse of impending trouble came on 19 March when Wade's gunners exchanged fire with two Federal warships ascending the Mississippi after passing Port Hudson, Louisiana.[10]

The outbreak of fairer weather burst upon the land, diminishing thoughts of the war's horrors and lifting spirits. Grand Gulf's bluffs turned green and lush by mid-March. A Sixth Missouri officer destined to experience only one other spring in his lifetime wrote, "This is beautiful weather, and the birds seem to praise God for it." Some Rebels drifted away from Bannon's influence. At night these Missourians found merri-

Brigadier General
John Stevens Bowen
(Collection of Dr.
Thomas P. Sweeney,
Republic, Missouri)

ment at a local plantation's slave quarters. The Confederates drank, played music, and danced with the blacks in an intermingling of cultures reminiscent of the Missouri frontier. In this atmosphere, sexual unions with African American women were not uncommon. Only a nighttime raid by Captain Canniff's company ended the carousing. No doubt Bannon felt satisfaction in that his Irish Catholics had stamped out this interracial sin in Claiborne County.[11]

He also obtained comfort in working closely with the Brigade's other chaplains. The clergymen included the following: Lt. Archibald D. Manning, Presbyterian, an acting chaplain-soldier of the Fifth Missouri destined to be killed in battle; Charles H. Atwood of the Fifth Missouri; Joseph S. Howard of the Second Missouri; Edward M. Bounds of the Third Missouri; and William M. Patterson of the Sixth Missouri.[12] A Missouri officer summarized the role of the Brigade's chaplains: "With our

Missouri troops, no harder working men were found than the regimental chaplains. In battle, up with the fighting lines, or serving as hospital stewards; in camp, ministering at a divinely simple altar, beneath the stately forest trees."[13]

The building of Grand Gulf's defenses by both Rebels and impressed slaves progressed under the supervision of General Bowen, a West Point trained engineer and civilian architect. He had been one of the United States Military Academy's most gifted students in the Class of 1854.[14] Wade's and Guibor's cannoneers took position at the fortification's southernmost, or lower, point. On a shelf of the bluff before the river and above the ruins of Grand Gulf was Fort Wade. One of the two most formidable bastions on the Southern line, this fortification was named for Col. William Wade.[15]

Grand Gulf provided Bannon, he thought, with additional proof of the foe's ungodliness. Union forces had destroyed the community during the summer of 1862 "in retaliation for an attack with which the town had nothing more to do than had the city of St. Louis."[16] Grant decided that Fort Wade and Fort Cobun, the upper defensive bastion, must be knocked out for his Mississippi invasion to begin.[17] Much of Vicksburg's future depended upon Colonel Wade, now commanding the artillery of Bowen's Division, and his cannoneers. In addition, a Louisiana battery also bolstered Fort Cobun. Captains Wade's and Guibor's men garrisoned Fort Wade, a Missouri fort on Mississippi soil. Nearby, the Brigade's infantry encampment sprawled across the fields of an old cotton plantation.[18]

A special occasion for Bannon was on 27 March. "This is a day that was appointed by our President as a day of humiliation and prayer," wrote one soldier. "It was observed by our Brigade, in suspending all Military operations [sic] that drill as well be suspended, and attending Church in the evening, under arms the five Regiments, under the command of Gen. Bowen, assembled on the same ground, drew up as near the stand as, was convenient and remained standing while the services were conducted."[19] Unlike in 1861 and 1862, religion had grown stronger among the Confederate troops. As the war lengthened and grew bloodier the Rebels became more committed to God.[20] One Brigade member remembered the unique intermingling of militarism, religion, and nationalism in the Confederate Army:

> The camp fire often lighted the pages of "The Best Book," while the soldier
> read orders of the Captain of his salvation. And often did the songs of Zion

ring loud and clear on the cold night air, while the muskets rattled and the guns boomed in the distance, each intensifying the significance of the other, testing the sincerity of the Christian while trying the courage of the soldier.

Stripped of all sensual allurements and offering only self-denial, patience and endurance, the Gospel took hold of the deepest and purest motives of the soldiers, won them thoroughly, and made the army as famous for its forbearance, temperance, respect for women and children, sobriety, honesty and morality, as it was for energy and invincible courage.[21]

The earthworks of Grand Gulf were completed just in time. Prowling Union warships prepared to slip down the Mississippi and past Vicksburg to test seriously the strength of the newly erected fortifications. Throughout western Mississippi, trees were budding along the hillsides. No longer cotton country, the land lay ready for the spring planting of crops eventually to feed Rebel armies, and recent rains and warmer temperatures brought new life. Majestically, the swollen Mississippi turned below Big Black River, cutting close to the bluff's edge and the Rebel trenches.

Veteran Confederate troops understood the importance of Grand Gulf. A Mississippi newspaper praised the Missouri exiles. The Brigade's "sons sleep on the bloody fields of our strife: in Missouri, in Arkansas, in Mississippi—wherever the lurid fires of battle have burned, there sleep the sons of Missouri. Long they guarded the gate to this valley and withstood the advance of the foe; now they fight the battles of the Confederacy on the soil of Mississippi. Brave men!"[22]

On 25 March, Bannon listened to a "terrific firing of Artillery at Vicksburg"—indication that some Federal gunboats had passed Vicksburg's batteries and pushed south. While grayclads contemplated better ways to greet their adversaries, Bannon struggled to save souls. The soldiers' wallowing in the slave whorehouses and drinking and gambling dens continued to cause Bannon trouble.

He began 31 March by offering Mass at 9 o'clock in the morning. The early service consisted of forty-three Communions, and he preached a rousing sermon. After strengthening earthworks and drilling in fields of green, Confederates took care of domestic chores and lounged around camp. Some men smoked pipes, wrote letters for mail-runner Absalom Grimes, and washed clothes around tents. The tranquillity of the encampment broke when word came during the afternoon that Federal gunboats were steaming downriver.[23]

With Bowen's orders to assemble, cannoneers rushed to their pieces. In minutes, Fort Wade was filled with gunners. These artillerymen had more experience than any others in the Confederacy, for they had fought at Carthage, Wilson's Creek, Dry Wood, Lexington, Pea Ridge, Farmington, Corinth, and in dozens of skirmishes.[24] Here, at the lower, or southernmost, earthwork positioned along the flat terrace overlooking the river, Rebel artillerymen of Fort Wade, now awaiting the Union Navy, looked north up the "Father of Waters." Bowen's signal corps upriver at Hard Times Landing would give the alarm by rocket at night or flag by day with the Unionists' appearance.

On the double, the Brigade's infantrymen filled the trenches. Other Missouri regiments took cover in the woods atop the bluffs as a concealed force in case the bluecoats landed. During the entire afternoon, they continued the waiting game for the warships and "pook turtle" ironclads to round the bend above the mouth of Big Black River. Some of these gunboats, ironically, were built in Bowen's hometown of Carondelet.

A spectator eager for the curtain to rise, Bannon wrote of the initial alarm: "Reported craft [at] Warrenton [Mississippi, roughly half-way between Vicksburg and Grand Gulf]."[25] Bannon took a position either in the trenches or in Fort Wade with many of the Brigade's Irish Catholic defenders.[26]

Afternoon passed into evening. No Union ironclads appeared. Darkness fell over Grand Gulf. Graycoat foot-soldiers and artillerymen remained at their posts, resting in position, but they relaxed too much. Most defenders assumed that the enemy warships would not come until the sunrise. Relieved, they enjoyed the breezes sweeping off the Mississippi. After all, the signalmen upriver would launch a rocket as a first warning. Fort Wade's tension finally broke. Gunners leaned against their pieces, talked of home, and told jokes during the pleasant night.[27]

Bannon also felt there would be no attack tonight. He conducted his regularly scheduled Mass at 8 o'clock on the river bluffs. Under the moonlight, he was giving the Communion rite and breaking the bread, when a nearby Rebel sounded the alarm at 8:15. The Mass ended when a soldier screamed that Union warships were practically upon them. Bowen's signalmen had failed to give the warning, and no rockets had blazed across the black sky. Bannon wrote, "The Fed Boats surprised us." The men dashed to their stations. Moving silently with the current down the Mississippi and shielded by the night, the two warships caught Bowen's men unprepared. Almost before the troops reached their positions, the Federal cannon roared, and "the hills rang with the echoes of the sounds of the conflict."[28]

General Bowen hurriedly galvanized a defense. Within minutes after the upper battery at the Point of Rock opened fire, Wade's and Guibor's cannoneers pulled lanyards. Steaming at full speed to run Grand Gulf's forts, the Union warships were riddled with projectiles. Expert Missouri gunners who had shot down Federal flags off Lexington's ramparts, who had pulled cannon along the Bentonville Detour and held off the Union army at Pea Ridge, exploded shells above the gunboat's decks. During the twenty-minute cannonade, bragged one defender, "The enemy didn't kill a man of ours."[29] But ten Southern casualties resulted with the explosion of one of the Confederates' own cannon. In Bannon's words: "One gun [a 20-pound Parrott Rifle] burst in Wade's Batty—2 killed [but] none hurt by the enemy's guns."[30]

The accidental explosion luckily inflicted no harm on Bowen, who stood behind Fort Wade's cannon when the gun burst. Captain Guibor, on the contrary, was not so fortunate. He went down with a bad stomach and arm wound from which he never fully recovered.[31]

Another of Bannon's friends fell, Lt. John Kearny. He was an Ireland-born cannoneer of Wade's battery who had heard many Bannon sermons in St. Louis. The severely wounded Kearny, age thirty-three, now found Bannon's blessings even more comforting. Wade's Battery suffered the highest casualties of any unit, losing six men with the gun's explosion. These losses were in vain, for the Union vessels passed farther down the Mississippi after taking Grand Gulf's punishment. The Federals learned that General Bowen's troops were determined to fight to the end at "the Little Gibraltar."[32]

On the next day, 1 April, Bannon went eight miles to the southeast of Grand Gulf for another burial service. The two cannoneers of Wade's artillery were laid to rest at Port Gibson. During a ceremony attended by many of Port Gibson's citizens, Bannon held services at 4 o'clock and buried the two Confederates from St. Louis, Pvt. Claiborne D. Ferguson, a foreman, and Pvt. John W. Underwood, a Mississippi River boatman. At least one had been a member of St. John's Parish.

Afterward Bannon said Mass at St. Joseph's Catholic Church in Port Gibson. Life at Grand Gulf shortly returned to normal. During the first part of April, Bannon traveled to various locations—such as Port Gibson and Jackson—to attend duties within Catholic communities.[33]

Chaplain Bannon was back at Grand Gulf on 18 April for a festive

Saturday. By now the Emmet Guard's commander from St. Louis—Colonel Wade—had become one of the best artillery leaders in the army. His Missouri militia experience before the war was invaluable for his advancement. Prewar militia duty was one of the most important factors in explaining the Missouri Brigade's elite quality. In antebellum days, Wade had led, in his own words, "a Body of fine Young Irishmen." Not only competent and fiery, the colonel was popular. Bannon reflected the camaraderie between the "long arm" commander and the men of Bowen's Division, by writing of a wild "surprise party at Col Wade's" in his honor.[34]

Colonel Wade had come a long way since a St. Louis woman wrote in 1851: "I don't see why Ma should be horrified at Will Wade's marrying Jane Graham, I think it a very suitable match nothing to boast about on either side."[35] He, nevertheless, had made good, owning his own business in 1861, but had found himself better suited for military adventures than civilian life.[36] Like Bannon, Colonel Wade had been forced to flee St. Louis when the Wade home had been encircled and searched by Federal troops during the summer of 1861. He had slipped away,[37] to rise steadily through the Confederate ranks, gaining more respect and responsibility.[38] General Maury's estimation of Colonel Wade is indicative: "I have never known a more gallant battery commander than he was. He was always cheerful and alert, and never grumbled; kept his men, horses, guns and equippage [sic] in the best possible trim, and always looked after the comfort of his command, and knew how to find for them something good to eat and to drink, when nobody else could. His cheerful voice on the eve of a fight, and his bright face, had a mesmeric effect on all about him. . . . I do not think any man in the army, up to the last, was more respected than Wade."[39]

Father Bannon overlooked the free-flowing whiskey during the party for Colonel Wade. It was Wade who had first requested that Bannon become chaplain of his battery and join his mess during the winter of 1862. He had accepted Wade's offer and started his military career with Wade's Battery. Wade and the clergyman became messmates and friends, and the captain's unit was like a home base for Bannon throughout his service. The artillery command contained some of his best friends as well as his religious paraphernalia, stored with them either in a battery wagon or caisson. The party at the Brigade's encampment was timely. Colonel Wade would be killed in less than two weeks.[40]

Bannon's wishes came true in mid-April when a religious revival swept the Missouri Brigade. Then, the revival caught fire in Green's Second

Brigade. The priest played a prominent role in the increased religious activity. A spring campaign, meanwhile, promising to be brutal, fast approached. As if knowing that about half of the Brigade's twenty-seven hundred members would be killed, wounded, or captured in barely a two-month period, the Missouri Confederates now embraced God as never before.

A Sixth Missouri officer, fated to die in battle, wrote in his diary: "There is a revival of religion going on in the 5th Regiment. There has been a number of conversions, and there is still quite a number of Seekers, the interest continually increasing. We hear that God is reviving His work in the 2nd Brigade, and in the Virginia army. Let men every where praise the Lord." Father Bannon found the receptive atmosphere heaven-sent. Religious leaders, singers, and other citizens from Port Gibson added vigor to the enthusiastic revivals in the encampments.[41]

Outside of camp on 20 April, Bannon "met [General Martin E.] Green's Brigade coming in to Camp" to reinforce Bowen's Grand Gulf garrison to more than four thousand troops. General Bowen now had both brigades of his division, battle-hardened veterans, together once more. But Pemberton had not sent enough units to bolster Grand Gulf adequately, thanks to Union feints north of Vicksburg.

Already the might of the Northern army's muscle was swinging down through Louisiana, hunting for a suitable base from which to cross the Mississippi. Once the blue infantry reached dry ground on the west side of the river, the Union fleet could steam past Vicksburg to transport thousands of Federals from Louisiana to Mississippi. As soon as they were on Mississippi soil, Vicksburg would be negated by a landing below the citadel. Plans to fortify the Louisiana shore to thwart such a scheme, ironically, had been ignored since the first year of the war.[42]

General Grant's plan neared reality when the Union fleet ran Vicksburg's batteries during the darkness of 16 April.[43] Enemy gunboats to Vicksburg's south threatened to cut off a task force in Louisiana under Colonel Cockrell. Only by a narrow margin would these expeditioners, including the Irish of Company F, Fifth Missouri, two guns of Guibor's Battery, and other Missouri infantry units, hurriedly recross the river into Mississippi within sight of the United States Navy. Bannon almost lost a large percentage of his Catholic followers during this scouting expedition. The thirteen-day reconnaissance in Tensas Parish, Louisiana, secured invaluable intelligence, helping to enlighten Bowen of Grant's scheme.[44]

A few days later, Bannon marveled at the spectacle of "5 Fed Gun boats in

Sight."[45] It was now clear that the strike on Grand Gulf was imminent. Reasoning as much, Bowen warned of the threat to the south of Vicksburg, begging for reinforcements, but obsessed with protecting Vicksburg's immediate proximity against decoy feints, Pemberton remained transfixed. The warning from General Bowen went largely unheard.[46]

Confidence, nevertheless, continued to be high for the successful defense of Grand Gulf. As explained by a journalist to the people of Mississippi:

> It may interest our readers to know that we have at that point [Grand Gulf] some of the best troops in the Confederacy. . . . Those veteran bands who stood the shock at Elkhorn, at Shiloh, at Iuka, at Corinth, are there. We know those troops of old. With Bowen a General, and other veteran officers in command; with such soldiers to fight; with equal conditions, and with equal numbers; with God on our side; we have a strong confidence that the invader will be [cut] in two the day he met these men in battle! They might be overpowered—they might all be killed, but they will not be conquered! If they are sacrificed by any unlooked for combination of numbers, it will be to the foe a most costly triumph! Such a disaster, however, we do not anticipate. Our brave men are ready for the fray. They would move in battle with such a shout as only they can give. Memorable will be the field when they are encountered by the Yankees. It is almost certain "somebody will be hurt."[47]

Upcoming events would soon prove the validity of the newspaper's boasts.

The last Sunday of April was busy for Bannon, for he helped dedicate a new church in Port Gibson. He and his comrades had adopted this town as their own. With hard fighting expected soon, the exiled Westerners increased attempts "to get acquainted with some of the damsels of Port Gibson." The Confederates would meet with more success in this pursuit than in winning battlefield victories in Mississippi.

Many Rebels had practically become family members, staying in private homes as much as in camp. Life-long relationships were forged during this quiet period. Mississippi's citizens of Claiborne County placed much of their hopes in the frontiersmen in gray to defend their homeland. Grant, meanwhile, mustered everything he had in preparation to launch one of the greatest offensives of the war.[48]

The beauty of the morning of 29 April broke upon the countryside bordering the Mississippi. Quiet dominated the Brigade's encampment in the bluff's rear. Meanwhile, across the river at Hard Times Landing, Louisiana, above Grand Gulf, Grant's legions piled onto transports. Union gunboats shortly led the armada downriver to destroy Grand Gulf and its garrison.[49]

The invasion had come at last. Redeeming themselves for their earlier negligence, Bowen's signal corps sounded the warning around eight in the morning. Graycoat cannoneers jumped to their guns. Hundreds of Missouri infantrymen spilled into the trenches, Bannon probably entering the works with the defenders. Grant's objective was for the Navy to knock out the Southern cannon and then pour troops ashore, initiating the invasion of Mississippi.[50]

The naval strategy called for the gunboats to swing close to the bank. Then, the warships would remain stationary, while blowing the Rebel fortifications and artillery to bits. As planned, the ironclads swarmed near the upper and lower batteries, Forts Cobun and Wade. Blasting point-blank into the earthen and cottonbale defenses, the seven warships unleashed maximum firepower.

The guns of Captains Wade's and Guibor's batteries and the Louisiana pieces blazed away in return. Cannon smoke almost blocked out the morning sunlight. Now commenced one of the war's longest—more than five hours—and most severe artillery duels to date. With the invasion's success resting upon its performance, the Union Navy hurled twenty-five hundred shells into Bowen's position during "the most terrific firing" most Confederates ever endured.[51]

No one performed better on that day than Colonel Wade. He directed fire and encouraged his gunners to keep pounding the gunboats. But the enemy's overwhelming firepower from seven warships took a heavy toll on Fort Wade. Salvos from naval cannon threw dirt, cotton, and sand in every direction. Much of the parapet was nearly leveled, and Wade's defenders could not maintain a steady fire without protection. Confederate artillerymen fell, killed and wounded, when two heavy guns were dismounted by the incoming barrages.

Fort Wade's return fire grew fainter as more men dropped and ammunition ran low. Wade's and Guibor's cannoneers in Fort Wade had engaged much of the Union fleet on western waters. The higher and less exposed upper battery at Fort Cobun, meanwhile, maintained a steadier defense three quarters of a mile upriver from Fort Wade. But Guibor's red battleflag, torn by projectiles, still waved from the ramparts.[52]

Confederate fire in Fort Wade resumed with a resupply of ammunition, and Fort Wade's defense also was strengthened from an unexpected source.

Led by a determined Irish Catholic, some of Guibor's St. Louisans pushed a fieldpiece by hand to a forward position. From an elevation, the cannon hammered the gunboats at close range.[53] Near the action's conclusion around one o'clock, "Colonel Wade was standing close to my gun, watching the effect of our shells, when a huge one from the enemy exploded in our midst. As the smoke cleared up I noticed Colonel Wade upon the ground. I stepped to his side to assist him, and noticed that about three inches of his skull was carried away by a piece of shell without injuring his brain. He was perfectly conscious, but could not speak. With a bright smile upon his face, he looked at me in the eyes, as I knelt by him, and moved his lips for a few seconds, trying so hard to tell me something, and then gently fell asleep."[54]

Colonel Wade was hit by one of the final shots fired on Fort Wade.[55] (Bannon may have witnessed his friend's death.) The defense of Grand Gulf was the most meaningful success of land-based Confederate artillery over the Union navy up to this time. No Federal infantry landed at Grand Gulf.[56]

The sacrifices were again in vain. Grant knew that Grand Gulf could not be reduced and canceled the landing, but he refused to give up his attempt to cross the river.[57] In summarizing the battle's developments, Bannon wrote in his diary: "Fed Gunboats engaged batteries at Gulf for 5¼ hours from 8 to 1¼ o'clk—Col Wade & [Private Edward] Woods [of Wade's Battery] killed. . . . Fed Boats return [to impede the fortification's restoration in the afternoon] renewed fight & [they] passed with their [infantry] transports southward—2 Gunboats exploded—one transport."[58] General Grant, meanwhile, had quickly readjusted strategy. Gunboats and transports continued south down the Mississippi. Grant now looked for a landing site on Mississippi soil far from Rebel cannon.[59]

None of the Confederate high command, except General Bowen, had correctly ascertained Grant's plan—a brilliant ad hoc strategy adapting to ever-changing circumstances.[60] Bowen's troops expected yet another attack. A Southern newspaper caught the defiance of Bowen's defenders during this period: "Grand Gulf, and the vicinity, seems now to be the point most menaced by the foe. It is by this route, doubtless, he [Grant] means to gain the rear of . . . Vicksburg. With this view, the enemy determines, first, to dispose of the Grand Gulf batteries. Hence the terrible cannonade of yesterday. To thwart this purpose, our artillerists at Grand Gulf are enduring danger and death. Colonel Wade has fallen, and others of his command; but others take their places! Wade 'died at his post,' and the post is now held by his brave comrades!"[61]

The last day of April was especially gloomy, despite the repulse of the invader. Wooden coffins were fashioned for Colonel Wade and Private Woods, one of Bannon's ex-parishioners from St. Louis. Then Bannon escorted Colonel Wade's body to Port Gibson in a solemn funeral procession.[62] Sergeant Hogan wrote in a letter that Private Woods "was taken by myself and Ellen that night [29 April] to Port Gibson in an ambulance; he was carried next morning to church. The funeral services were performed by Bannon, who also preached an eloquent sermon on his virtues. He was buried with military honors, in the cemetery of Port Gibson."[63] Bannon wrote of 30 April, describing how he "buried Woods from Cath[olic] Church in Cath[olic] Graveyard" early in the morning.[64] But a more painful task remained ahead for Bannon.

Large numbers of citizens and soldiers gathered to pay their last respects to Colonel Wade at St. James' Episcopal Church. After making a passionate eulogy, Bannon "buried Wade from the court house at the public graveyard—Large funeral." Once again Bannon said farewell to a companion—one he had laughed with, slept with, and fought beside for almost a year and a half. According to one soldier, Bannon "keenly felt Colonel Wade's death, as they were messmates, and the loss of a faithful friend."

Colonel Wade's body would be transported back to St. Louis by his family in 1865.[65] The list of Bannon's most respected comrades becoming beneficiaries of his burial services would steadily grow. There would be more engagements and more deaths in the days ahead. The seemingly endless cycle of hard luck, ever-higher casualty rates, and tragedies had only begun for the priest and his comrades in Mississippi.

Even as Bannon led the funeral service for Colonel Wade, Grant rushed thousands of troops east into Mississippi. He had discovered a dry road, the Rodney Road, about ten miles below Grand Gulf leading inland to Port Gibson. The Union army made the largest amphibious landing of the war without interference. Division after division of Federals marched through the bottomlands of the Mississippi River, pushing eastward for the high ground. This shelf-like bluff, if gained, was Grant's solid foothold in Mississippi. Only Bowen's small division at Grand Gulf was now close enough to meet the invasion to the south.

Located on Little Bayou Pierre, Port Gibson was now the most important town in the South. After winning a toehold on the elevated terrain without a shot fired, Grant's columns raced east for Port Gibson. The town, built upon a cotton economy, was strategic, with roads leading to Vicksburg, Natchez, and Jackson. Port Gibson's capture would outflank Grand

Gulf. Some twenty-three thousand Unionists swarmed farther into Mississippi in the next few hours, determined to force Grand Gulf's evacuation and outflank Vicksburg.[66]

To meet the crisis brewing to the south, on the evening of 30 April Bowen had hurried portions of Green's Brigade to ascertain enemy intentions. No Confederates yet knew for certain of the invasion.[67] That night Bannon and the Missourians heard skirmishing southward and to Port Gibson's west. Holding the main road that led from the Mississippi to Port Gibson, Arkansas pickets clashed in the darkness with Grant's lead elements. Bowen's worst fears were confirmed. He again called for reinforcements from Pemberton. Some Rebel troops would be dispatched, but in insufficient numbers to stop the blue tide. Facing impossible odds, General Bowen estimated that "it would require from fifteen to twenty thousand men to insure our success."

Grant had caught Pemberton unable to muster an effective resistance. A landing in force south of Grand Gulf, therefore, progressed unmolested. It was now much too late for the Confederacy to react with the energy and troops necessary seriously to impede the invasion. General Grant, now perhaps the best chieftain of the North, had crossed the Mississippi deep in Southern territory without encountering opposition, negating Vicksburg's cannon and garrison in one stroke.[68]

The dawn of 1 May saw the stage set for the actors in blue and gray in the wilderness west of Port Gibson. Vicksburg's existence was at stake. Responsibility fell upon General Bowen to halt the invasion with fewer than seven thousand Rebels. Somehow in the magnolia and oak forests of Claiborne County, he must stop more than twenty-three thousand enemy soldiers. At more than three-to-one odds, General Bowen prepared for an almost impossible bid to hold "off the blue-bellied myrmidons."[69]

To help repel the invaders, the general dispatched orders to Grand Gulf to hurry the Missouri Brigade south.[70] But the slim opportunity to hurl Grant into the river was vanishing rapidly. Bannon was near the action when it broke. After staying the night of 30 April at Port Gibson after the funerals, Bannon evidently felt the excitement of the brewing engagement. The chaplain described the opening phase of the contest: "Green engaged with the Fed forces 4 miles [west] from P[ort] Gibson on the Brewensburg [Bruinsburg] Road—held them in check until my brigade [under Colonel Cockrell]" arrived on the field. Just after noon on 1 May, the Missouri troops reached the scene of strife, after an eight-mile dash in sweltering heat.[71]

With his lines buckling under the blue onslaught, Bowen immediately hurled the Missourians into action. To bolster Bowen's right, Col. Eugene Erwin's Sixth Missouri charged through the woodlands and into the enemy's masses with abandon. Attacking tenaciously, Erwin's Missourians pushed the Yankees back a quarter mile, recapturing artillery of a Virginia battery and taking prisoners. Some pressure was relieved by Erwin's attack, but the Sixth Missouri later would be forced to retire. Erwin's and Green's troops, Gen. Edward D. Tracy's Alabama Brigade, Gen. William E. Baldwin's Brigade of Louisiana, and Mississippi veterans, meanwhile, barely held their own against the might of Grant's army. The frail Southern lines could break at any moment under the relentless pounding.[72]

General Bowen, therefore, was forced to gamble to save his command. A desperate strategy was conceived. The only available units in reserve were the Fifth and Third Missouri. Bowen, nevertheless, led the two small regiments on a flank march to the far left. With the enemy about to gain the Natchez Road that led to Port Gibson and Bowen's rear, the two Missouri regiments tore into Grant's right flank and right-center. Against all odds, the attack achieved considerable success. It took the massed firepower of thirty cannon and almost two full infantry divisions to stop around seven hundred ragged Missouri Rebels. The almost suicidal charge against heavy odds succeeded in blunting the Federals' momentum.[73]

Bannon chronicled the engagement's developments in his diary. The Missouri troops, he wrote, "arrived and held the Yankees in check until night."[74] He stayed close to the front, for "no danger was too great to deter him from administering to a wounded comrade."[75] The fields, canebrakes, and forests of Port Gibson were full of injured Missouri men who needed Bannon's services on 1 May.

Colonel Cockrell's attackers played a key role in stemming the blue onslaught and minimizing Grant's success at the Battle of Port Gibson, but at a cost of more than two hundred Brigade casualties.[76] As one Rebel of another command wrote immediately after the action: "The 1st Missouri brigade, of course, fought well—The gallant charge of two regiments [the Fifth and Third Missouri] of this brigade upon three brigades of the enemy and eight pieces of artillery, through an open field; their success in preventing a further advance, or a flank movement of the enemy [was] one of the most daring deeds of the war."[77] This appraisal was no exaggeration.

General Grant could be slowed on 1 May, but not stopped. In vain the

Brigadier General Francis
Marion Cockrell (Author's
Collection)

"best blood of the land has been again poured out to water afresh the tree of liberty," for more than eight hundred Rebels fell at "Magnolia Hills."[78] The Federals now had implanted a sizable army on the east side of the Mississippi after suffering an almost comparable loss. Vicksburg's destiny would be determined in the stronghold's rear.

The beaten Southerners abandoned the field with approaching darkness, withdrawing north to put the bayou between them and the bluecoats. Bannon retired with the infantry column, trudging onward in the Missourians' ranks. Anguish came with the abandonment of Port Gibson and adopted families left behind to the enemy. But most of all lingered the pain that despite performing "feats of valor almost without a parallel [the Confederate forces again] have failed to accomplish decisive results for want of timely support, or skillful combinations on the part of the head commanders, such as at Elkhorn—such as at Corinth—and such as, we fear, at Grand Gulf [Port Gibson]."[79]

With his troops, Bannon wrote that during the "night . . . we fell [behind] Bayou Pierre"—an effective obstacle before the pursuing Federal army.[80] On the north bank of the bayou, Bowen elected to make a stand. Missouri Confederates dug trenches in the blackness, expecting reinforcements from Vicksburg. With little but audacity, Bowen yet planned to whip Grant on 2 May.[81]

Skirmishing erupted before the morning's mists eased off Bayou Pierre. Grant's forces had arrived in force. Federals inched forward, firing while on the move, to ascertain Confederate numbers and dispositions. Substantial Rebel reinforcements, as on the day before, would not arrive in time. But even worse, Bowen learned that the enemy had crossed Bayou Pierre, outflanking his position along the bayou. Another withdrawal was the only alternative. Bannon wrote of the tactical situation at the Bayou Pierre Line and reflected bitterness with another retrograde movement "because no reinforcements were sent to check Feds who flanked us on both wings—fell into the line of march at midnight."[82]

The race north to reach Big Black River began, in an effort to keep the Yankees from cutting off Bowen's force and a brigade of Loring's Division from the Vicksburg side of the river. Throughout the night, the Confederates retired northward. Soldiers ignored empty stomachs and weariness, as did Bannon, enduring the deprivations like an enlisted man. After learning not to linger too far behind the Brigade as he had done at Pea Ridge and Corinth, he hurried through the maze of wagons, artillery limbers and caissons, and teams of horses clogging the road to Vicksburg. No one had to remind Bannon of the danger. He wrote that the "enemy's cavalry & artillery [were] in pursuit."[83]

Captain Canniff's Irishmen skirmished with the pursuers, keeping them at a distance. The Irish in gray were helping to allow Bowen's force to slip across Big Black River and to enter the safe haven of land near Vicksburg and the bulk of Pemberton's army.[84]

Retiring north was not without risk for Bannon. Duty hastened him to the rear to a point of danger. He was "called back to a tired [and diseased] Mr. [Samuel M.] Kennard [a St. Louisan of Captain Landis's Battery], who fell from wagon & was run over by some." Bannon attended the young lieutenant, who prayed not to be left behind to the Yankees and prison. With Bannon's help, Kennard remained with the army to serve in the

Brigade's next engagement.[85] For more than fifty miles and most of two days, the withdrawal continued north toward Vicksburg and safety.[86]

After gaining the Mississippi River fortress, Brigade members swung east to Big Black River once more. Behind the river, Pemberton patched together a defense to protect Vicksburg on the east. This, ironically, was the last direction the Southern high command had initially expected a strike. Grant, meanwhile, had pushed northeast from Port Gibson, marching roughly parallel to Big Black and toward Jackson. On 6 May Father Bannon and his Missouri troops encamped in the bottoms of Big Black River for a much-needed respite. Within a new defensive line, they rested and reflected on the past disasters and lost comrades.[87] A journalist visited the Rebel encampment along the river and assessed: "There has been no more desperate fighting during the war than was done by Gen. Bowen's men during the two or three days' engagement at Grand Gulf, and the slaughter of Yankees was appalling. Bowen's Missourians are now at Big Black, absolutely used up with fatigue and want of rest. The poor fellows have thrown away their shoes and stockings to relieve their blistered feet."[88]

Bannon had suffered similar discomfort from the recent trials. He would have even less rest than the average soldier, for his services were needed more than ever. He continued religious duties with renewed vigor. On 10 May, he said Mass with the Brigade's First and Fourth Missouri Confederate Infantry (Consolidated), under Col. Amos Camden Riley— destined to die from a sniper's bullet in 1864. On this occasion, Father Bannon gave Communion to twenty-five Confederates.[89]

A fine, experienced command, First Missouri was organized and first led by Bowen. This elite regiment contained many Irishmen. In Company A were Emerald Islanders from New Orleans and Louisiana, and St. Louis Irish of Companies B, D, E, and F.[90] Since the winter of 1861–1862 in Kentucky, the regiment had needed a priest. The void had been only partly filled by a Catholic man of God riding more than sixty miles from Southern Illinois. After the Sunday, 10 May Mass, Father Bannon left the encampment, journeying to Jackson by rail for the afternoon and evening Mass in the main Catholic Church at the capital.[91]

But the return trip to the Brigade was not without incident. That night after services, Bannon entrained "at 12½ [but] a collision at Edward's Station—Walked" the several miles "to Big Black" and the Brigade's camp.[92] Momentous events, meanwhile, were unfolding in mid-Mississippi. On Big Black's opposite, or east, side, Grant demonstrated more ability. He now wanted to get between the two primary Confederate armies—Pemberton's army on Big Black and Gen. Joseph E. Johnston's force at Jackson. General Grant planned to slash farther northeast, disperse Johnston, and capture Jackson. Then he would turn west upon Vicksburg.[93]

Vicksburg stood during the spring of 1863 as the one stronghold that the Confederacy could ill afford to lose. Southern control of the Mississippi meant that Rebel armies on the east side of the river could subsist off the supplies, raw materials, and manpower reserves from Arkansas, Texas, and Louisiana. And for a nation short on almost everything, the Trans-Mississippi West needed to be kept in Southern hands, especially during a struggle of attrition. Vicksburg's loss, as stated in May 1863, would leave "Missouri, Arkansas and Texas at the mercy of the Union forces as shutting out the rebel armies from their usual supply of grain, cattle and war materials, most of which were received through Texas, giving to the control of the United States of more than a million bales of cotton, and large quantities of other productions, securing to the great Northwest the navigation of the Mississippi river, and opening avenues for the advance of the Union armies into the very heart of rebeldom."[94]

For the existence of the infant Southern nation, Vicksburg had to be held. As a Richmond editorial stated: "Thus Vicksburg is at this time a point, not only of strategic, but also of political importance."[95] Further explained the journalist, "The fall of Vicksburg, therefore, cannot fail to be attended with vast moral and political effects."[96] The North's failure to capture Vicksburg and open the Mississippi for additional invasions into the South might break the Union's will to engage in a contest to the death. A Union columnist viewed even worse consequences for the North if Vicksburg survived Grant:

> The rebels could better afford to lose Richmond, Charleston and Mobile, all at one swoop, than to have the key of the Mississippi wrenched from their grasp. . . . If Pemberton holds out, and Grant is not beaten off, Vicksburg promises to be the Sahastopol of the western hemisphere. With the lower Mississippi and a great portion of its western bank in their possession, the Rebels would, if they gain their independence, be a formidable rival and antagonist of the United States. Commanding one or two of the best routes for the Pacific Railroad they would feed their hopes with the prospect of gaining over the Pacific States. . . . We are therefore prepared to see them struggle for the Mississippi with the energy of desperation.[97]

Much would be decided in the upcoming months on the Magnolia State's soil. General Grant continued sending the Confederacy on the road to its extinction on 12 May, when he won another victory at Raymond, Mississippi. But the Union general most of all wanted to hit the railroad lifeline and supply depot of Vicksburg at Jackson. Indeed, the capital continued to pump life into Vicksburg. Before Pemberton realized what had happened, Grant won the battle of Jackson on 14 May and chased off Johnston. To deprive Vicksburg of its base, the bluecoats had destroyed and burned much of the town. Guessing as much, Pemberton led his army east from Big Black's fortifications to meet Grant.[98]

Bannon joined Bowen's column in their push to punish the invader. There was little time for writing, but Bannon described the strategic situation and how the Confederate columns "moved toward Raymond— Yanks in Jackson."[99] With graycoats driving east and Federals swinging west after taking Jackson, the clash to decide Vicksburg's destiny was inevitable. Opposing generals were unaware of the campaign's climactic engagement about to explode in Hinds' County.[100] Father Bannon visited the men of each Missouri regiment on the night of 15 May, sensing death on the horizon.

But at one campfire, he encountered a hard case. During a year and a half of service, he could only count one other Rebel soldier who refused "to avail [himself] of my services." This reluctant Missourian, ironically, was an Irish Catholic. Further, he was a gunner of Captain Guibor's Battery. Bannon realized that the young Irishman "had been long from the Sacraments and was afraid of confession." The chaplain consequently remarked, "Come, man, I know what a soldier's confession is."

But the "dashing, rollicking fellow of the Artillery," only replied, "You have it all there, Sir." Father Bannon, however, refused to be denied and risk losing the man's soul. Pleading for one last confession, Bannon asked once more, "Well then, come and kneel down, and we will finish it off at once." But the cannoneer again declined. Uncharacteristically, Bannon finally gave up, for many other soldiers needed his services on the last night many would ever see. Bannon always remembered this spiritual defeat with the stubborn Irishman, writing, "No, he would not: and as time was precious, I had to leave him, and attend to others."[101]

In the bivouac area among the wet fields and woodlands, Bannon went from man to man. The religious duties continued far into the night so that few soldiers in spiritual need missed Bannon's ministrations on this night in western Mississippi. Physically, spiritually, and psychologically, the Missouri Rebels would be ready to meet the Yankees on 16 May.

Never had the Brigade been in better shape. Before the climactic battle, the Brigade consisted of the First and Fourth [Consolidated], Second,

Third, Fifth, and Sixth Missouri Infantry regiments and Captains Wade's, Guibor's, and Landis's Missouri batteries. It was well that these Confederates were in fighting trim and that Bannon had serviced the boys in gray, for the Brigade would lose six hundred of her sons before the next day's sunset.[102]

The day dawned humid and summer-like. A cessation of the recent rains and cloudless skies promised a hot day. Pemberton's and Grant's armies made contact not long after the sun rose. Sparring continued throughout the agricultural and wooded lands east of Baker's Creek, about halfway between Jackson and Vicksburg. Amid the escalating action, the Brigade hustled into position in the line's center. General Pemberton faced his army to the east for the expected onslaught from Jackson.

But Grant had assembled a strong force to the north on the Rebels' left flank. Hence, the Southern formations aligned to meet an attack from the wrong direction. General Grant soon struck, and enemy legions smashed into the Confederates' vulnerable left flank like a tornado, rolling up the Rebel line. By early afternoon, Pemberton's army was on the verge of destruction. The blue waves crashing from the north had engulfed hundreds of prisoners and several batteries. A full third of the Confederate army was destroyed. The contest to determine Vicksburg's fate had turned into a disaster for the South.[103]

As at Port Gibson, Bowen's fine division was the nearest force to the crisis. Pemberton, fearing the battle already lost, barked to a courier, "Go and tell Gen. Bowen to double quick to that point [the collapsed left] and retake those [captured] guns" and restore the line.[104] With parade ground precision, Cockrell's Brigade raced north to plug the gap before it was too late. Following closely behind Cockrell's onrushing infantrymen came the Brigade's artillery. Captains Guibor's, Wade's, and Landis's caissons and guns bounced behind the surging gray lines. Probably Bannon rode with the St. Louis cannoneers and their bronze pieces and "went with them into action."[105]

Near the shattered left, the Missourians met thousands of panic-stricken Rebels fleeing to the rear.[106] In the midst of the Federal onslaught at this critical sector, General Bowen and Colonel Cockrell deployed their five Missouri regiments to stem the crisis.[107] No doubt Bannon now passed down the gray formations, for much time lapsed before the advance. As customarily before an attack, silent soldiers in soiled uniforms knelt down with bayonets fixed on rifles, while receiving blessings and perhaps the consecrated bread and wine of Holy Communion.[108]

Even such soldiers as "Wild Pat Doolen" may have volunteered suddenly to get closer to God at the last moment. Private Doolen was a hard-drinking and hard-fighting Celt of the First and Fourth Missouri. Like so many others, the twenty-year-old laborer from St. Louis would perish that day in the upcoming action. Bannon in all likelihood spent much time before Colonel Riley's regiment, consisting of many Irish Catholics. This regiment would have eight Ireland-born Confederates killed or wounded on 16 May.[109]

As Bannon hurriedly gave Communion to as many men as possible, a handful of Missouri infantrymen darted before the line to tear down a split-rail fence. The Unionists, meanwhile, poured forward through the fields. A solid wave of bluecoats rolled onward, with hundreds of attackers firing, cheering, and charging forward to complete their victory. Minié balls whistled overhead while Bannon continued his duties and the Yankee masses charged closer. Spitting fire from the Brigade's flanks, the Missouri artillery hurled shot and shell into the blue lines.[110]

The St. Louis Irish gunner who had denied Bannon's services the previous night met with tragedy. He had just rammed down a powder charge into a cannon's barrel when the artillery piece next to his roared. Amid the noise and smoke, he mistook the blast as that of his own gun and rushed before the piece's muzzle to clean it with a sponge-staff. Simultaneously a cannoneer jerked the lanyard of the cannon. The resulting explosion hurled pieces of the sponge-staff into the Irishman with terrific force. He fell mortally wounded with a fractured skull, and broken arms and legs. The dying Confederate gunner could only pray that Father Bannon might appear to save his soul.[111]

The moment of the counterattack came at last. Only a short time before, Green's Brigade arrived to align to the Missouri Brigade's right. Cockrell and Bowen finally screamed, "Charge!" Bowen's Division surged forward to redeem the day. Charging graycoats smashed into the Union onslaught, throwing the Yankees back and stealing the initiative from Grant. The contest swirled with unsurpassed fury beyond the fields of Sid Champion's Plantation and into the forests leading up the slopes to Champion Hill. This elevation was the battlefield's key and the highest terrain in the area. In the magnolia and pine forests, yelling Missourians pushed everything before them. Cockrell's attackers recaptured lost artillery and charged deeper into Grant's center. Wrote a Missouri infantryman in his journal, "we turned the tide, and drove the enemy back a mile."[112]

While attending the Rebel wounded, Father Bannon finally came upon the gunner who had declined his services earlier. Private McGolfe was fatally wounded. The Irish Confederate had been carried to a barn, now a field hospital. Defiant as ever, the dying cannoneer was in a foul mood. The source of his discomfort, besides the painful injuries, was a mortally wounded Federal beside him. Bannon wrote:

> Strange to say, he was in his full senses, and kept roaring out, "Take away this Yankee, boys; I can't lie quiet here with this Yankee by me." I went up and spoke to him; he knew my voice, but his sight was gone; and on my mentioning confession to him, "Oh!" said he, "time enough for that. I'm not so bad as that goes to; I shall be right enough again in a day or two." "No, McGolfe," I replied, "you are dying. Your skull is split open, and your legs and arms are smashed: you cannot live out the day, and you must prepare to meet God's judgment." "Well, take away this Yankee: I can't make my confession with this Yankee close to me. He disturbs my mind: take him away!" [Bannon replied] "Never mind the Yankee; attend to your own soul." The Yankee, I found, was a poor German, who understood no English: so I induced McGolfe to make his confession at once. I then went to the German, and from the few words which I understood, I made out that the poor fellow was a Catholic, and recently enlisted. He was evidently in the best dispositions, kissed fervently the crucifix which I held to him, and seemed intensely grateful at meeting with a Catholic Priest. I did therefore all I could for him, and went to see if any other cases wanted help. . . . [Then on going up to the surgeon in charge, Bannon asked to see more injured men.] "Have you any here for me?" I asked. "Yes," said the surgeon, pointing to one of the wounded. "I think he must be one of yours, for he is an Irishman." I stooped down to the man and asked if he was a Catholic. He was: and of such a regiment, such a company [probably either Company F, Fifth Missouri or one of Colonel Riley's St. Louis companies of First and Fourth Missouri]. He was shot through the bowels, and the bullet had broken his spine. He had not long to live. "Why," I said, "I was with your regiment last night, but I don't remember you. Were you with me, or how was it?" "No, Father," he answered. "I knew you would be coming, and I watched to keep out of your way, for I did not wish to meet you." [Besides Private McGolfe, this Irishman was the only other nonreceptive soldier whom Bannon encountered during the war.] "You unfortunate fellow!" I exclaimed; "Do you see now how the devil deceives you; and how nearly he had you by the throat." "Indeed, I was a fool, Father; and I am sorry for it with all my heart."

He made a good end, poor fellow: and I was careful to take down his name and the address of his family in Ireland, as I always did in similar cases; for I knew how great a consolation it is to Irish fathers and mothers to hear from a Priest that their child died well. He was the son of a small farmer in Meath [a county in mid-eastern Ireland just northwest of Dublin], and his family had heard nothing of him for several years.[113]

Bowen's Division, meanwhile, continued attacking with tremendous force. Onrushing Confederates gained more ground, tearing through multiple lines of resistance. But the cost of winning yardage toward Champion Hill was high. Hundreds of Missouri soldiers lay sprawled under the blossoming magnolias, filling ravines, thickets, and swells.[114] After serving in the infirmary, Bannon moved north, following on the Brigade's heels. Evidently he stayed close to the Missouri artillery units. Sections of guns steadily leapfrogged forward through the smoke-covered woodlands. Moving across the battlefield, Bannon found what he was looking for— piles of wounded and dead Missouri Confederates.

While injured Rebels sent up a chorus of cries and groans, Father Bannon gave the last anointment to mortally wounded men. Some fatally stricken soldiers kissed the silver or gold crucifix before they died. Pleas for water and mercy filled the air, and Bannon went to as many suffering men as possible. He no doubt turned over some good friends and close associates, who now could no longer be helped.[115]

Bannon "was at [the wounded and dying man's side] supporting his head; with the tourniquet he staunched his blood flow; with the spirits [whiskey] he sustained his strength till his confession could be told, or if necessary till he could baptise him from the waters of the nearest brook. Many a short shift was made that day; many lived to feel grateful to the good father for his gallant devotion to his profession and many more to admire his courage and self-sacrifice by which he showed them the chaplain's place was not back among the commissary wagons in time of battle, but among the wounded and dying in the strife."[116]

During a battle claiming six hundred Brigade members, Bannon had plenty of work on 16 May. Dying Rebels were clumped in bloody heaps and scattered over the ground as thickly as the fallen magnolia blossoms.[117] On this hellish field, Bannon took the names and addresses of parents from Brigade members, later writing letters to Irish families, telling of their sons' last moments on earth in struggling for a hilltop in Mississippi.[118]

The Brigade's attack kept surging onward, recapturing artillery and punishing the enemy as never before. Grant's troops were thrown almost a mile to the rear during one of the war's savage counterattacks. Finally, the Missourians overran the all-important crest of Champion Hill, gobbling up more cannon and prisoners. General Grant's army was nearly split in two by the gray tide under Bowen, Cockrell, and Green. It now appeared as if 16 May would become the day of perhaps the South's most spectacular victory. As at Shiloh, Grant's army was in precarious shape because Bowen's sledge-hammer-like blows had driven a wedge into the Union army's midsection. The opportunity now existed for an unprecedented Confederate success in the West.[119]

Father Bannon kept up with the Brigade after covering the three-quarters of a mile the Missourians had gained. During the action, he was "everywhere in the midst of the battle when the fire was heaviest and the bullets thickest."[120] Atop Champion Hill, the victorious Rebels surveyed the scene: no organized body of Federals in sight, heaps of enemy dead, and Grant's supply and munition wagons unguarded before them.

Once more, the Brigade surged forward and down Champion Hill with flags flying. The howling Rebel tide charged farther into Grant's rear and closer to what seemed a decisive victory. A few more minutes and the Union army's vast wagon train would be overrun.[121] Captains Wade's, Guibor's and Landis's batteries galloped forward to unlimber in the fields topping Champion Hill. These guns covered the Missouri infantrymen's advance, while both Cockrell's and Green's veteran brigades and some rallied Southern regiments attacked onward.[122]

But with success in the Confederates' grasp, thousands of Federal reinforcements suddenly arrived to align before them. Seemingly endless numbers of blue reserves spilled out of the forests northward on an adjacent hill. The path to victory was barred. Some Missouri Rebels nevertheless continued attacking, nearly routing the fresh Union troops. But the grayclads' momentum was spent. Cockrell's soldiers fell back to Champion Hill and took cover in a belt of woods cutting across the elevation. Here, the Missourians made their stand.[123]

The struggle raged for hours. Both sides stood up face to face, exchanging volleys in the hot afternoon. Blue and gray fell so rapidly that the bloody elevation became known as "the hill of death." The outnumbered Missourians had little chance for success. Forty rounds in cartridge-boxes were soon expended, and the contest could only continue with the taking of cartridges from Union dead. No Rebel reinforcements or supplies of rounds came to the Brigade's aid.[124]

As the gray infantrymen's fire slackened, the Missouri batteries' role became more crucial than ever before. Only blasts of canister from the guns now kept the Unionists from overrunning Cockrell's position.

Guibor's artillery on the Brigade's left flank and Wade's and Landis's pieces on the right anchored the Brigade's position and held masses of blue infantry from turning both flanks. "It was the artillery saving the infantry," one foot-soldier remarked. Lieutenant Kennard, whom Father Bannon rescued during the Port Gibson withdrawal, now manned one of Captain Landis's guns. He had joined the contest, despite having been ordered by a surgeon to the rear that morning because of sickness.[125]

By this time, Bannon had stopped attending to the wounded. The Brigade's most threatened flank was on the right. Enemy hordes swarmed forward from the east, swinging wide in an "attempt to gain the rear of our right flank." During this emergency—the day's worst crisis—every cannoneer was needed to man the fast-working guns. Enough artillerymen had been shot down that a manpower shortage arose at the most critical moment. Despite being under heavy fire, Bannon joined one of the eight-man gun teams of Guibor's Battery after more gunners fell.

Bannon had served with a gun crew at Pea Ridge and perhaps on other occasions as well. He knew each cannoneer's duties on the gun team as well as he knew the Bible. The priest, therefore, "helped them serve the guns in [the Brigade's most] desperate emergencies," and he worked an artillery piece like a seasoned veteran. To save the foot-soldiers from being smashed under the onslaught, the Missouri cannon now roared at a frantic rate.

Father Bannon's reputation as the Confederacy's "Fighting Chaplain" was further reinforced. While Federal infantrymen concentrated their fire on the grayclad cannoneers and battery horses, "the balls and shells [were] knocking things to pieces" on the hill of death. Again, Bannon would do all in his power to save his graycoats on earth and in heaven.[126]

While bullets whizzed by, he became part of the perfectly timed and precision steps of the artillerymen: swabbing the barrel with a wettened sponge-staff, ramming down a powder charge and canister, and then firing. The mechanics of the gunners flowed like clockwork, allowing the firing of around two shots per minute.[127] Like the fate befalling the Brigade's infantry, the Rebel cannoneers' ammunition ran low. In another Pea Ridge-style dilemma, the Confederate penetration had been so deep into the enemy's line that resupply became a logistical impossibility. But the Missouri artillery had already accomplished much, rescuing the Brigade from being overrun.[128]

Nothing, however, could deny Grant the most decisive success of the Vicksburg campaign on 16 May. The lack of ammunition and reinforcements doomed the Missouri Brigade and Bowen's Division to failure after their initial success. Against tough odds and without support, cartridges, or luck, the Missouri Confederates were forced to retire or die. Stubbornly the Rebels headed back through the blood-stained forests the way they had come. While retiring under fire, they passed the bodies of relatives, friends, and comrades, now stacked like cordwood.

Defeat at Champion Hill sealed Vicksburg's fate. The best chance for reversing the Confederacy's fortunes during the Vicksburg campaign had vanished forever in the woodlands.[129]

But much peril yet remained. The Brigade's survivors back-tracked with Federal intercept columns hovering nearby. Moreover, Union artillery bombarded the withdrawal. Since Cockrell's unit was one of the last brigades off the field, the risky rearguard duty meant Bannon and his comrades were in danger of being cut off. By the narrowest of margins, Cockrell's regiments slipped out of Grant's grasp.

Guibor's, Landis's and Wade's batteries once more provided the necessary protection. The Brigade, now known appropriately as the army's "Old Guard," held the crossing at Baker's Creek, and Green's Brigade performed a similar function. Again Bowen's Division acted as the army's elite troops, despite the unit's great losses. Pemberton's beaten army, meanwhile, retired westward toward Vicksburg, but Colonel Cockrell held his position until the last few stragglers came in.

Under threat of encirclement, the Missourians also finally retired, but only after all Southerners had crossed over Baker's Creek. Here the Brigade found the main road—the avenue of withdrawal—full of bluecoats. Cockrell's troops had to again outrace the Unionists. Brigade members pushed west, making their way through cotton fields, woodlands, and cane brakes in the darkness.[130] Bannon and his comrades struggled throughout the early night hours for the Big Black River's fortifications and, around midnight, reached the defense's safety, the last unit to do so. Many of the men instantly dropped into muddy trenches and went to sleep.

General Bowen was ordered to deploy his division and another Brigade within Big Black's earthworks because a defensive stand in the flat cotton fields and with a river to the rear must be made to slow, somehow, the victorious legions of Grant's Army. Again Bowen's Division received the toughest assignment, for, as General Pemberton reasoned, "I knew that the Missouri troops, under their gallant leaders, could be depended upon."

Skirmishing began with the sunrise on 17 May. Thousands of Unionists were massed before the fortifications. Bannon's diary described how they had taken position: "Mo troops in trenches at Big Black [and the] artillery [firing from the Federals] at 7 o clock—trains ordered to Vicksburg." Bannon departed with the army's wagon trains of supplies, wounded, and equipment.[131]

For the only time during the war, he left the Brigade before an impending battle, retiring with the withdrawing Gray column. The Confederates were able to evacuate many of their wounded. Riding west toward Vicksburg, Bannon encountered the Brigade's ambulance train, a line of wagons with injured men piled together. He discovered Private McGolfe of Guibor's Battery on the morning of 17 May. Bannon attempted to relieve the Irishman's anguish with spiritual uplifting. He wrote the following story about meeting the dying artilleryman once again:

> "Whom have you got in there?" I asked. "McGolfe," was the reply. "What! Is he still alive?" I exclaimed, and rode up to the waggon [sic]. "Ah, Father, is that you!" The wretched man had neither hand nor foot that he could use. I was delighted to find him still sensible, for my heart rather misgave me about his treatment of the poor German, and I was apprehensive that his dispositions yesterday were not as good as they might have been. My delight was increased when McGolfe went on to say; "I can't help thinking of that poor Yankee. I behaved like a brute to him. He died last night, but after you left him he never stopped saying his prayers, and he prayed like a good one. He made me think, I can tell you. I'm just sorry for the way I treated him, and if you can give me any more penance for it, do. Now, if you'll stop by me, I'd like to make my confession again."
>
> And he began to accuse himself out loud before all the men about, so that I expostulated with him, and told him to speak lower.
>
> "No," he said, "I have been a bad man, and they all know it. I have given bad example, and I want to do some penance for it"—and he continued his confession at the top of his voice. When he had finished, I consoled him, telling him I should give him no penance, for he had done enough. I then gave him the last absolution, and in an hour he was a corpse.[132]

In contrast to other Rebels, Bannon could claim a victory of sorts from the Champion Hill defeat. He had saved a good many souls and perhaps some lives on the gory field. In his mind, success could be partially counted by the number of anointments and absolutions given to the Rebel soldiers.

No two cases filled Bannon with more contentment than the two men (Pvt. McGolfe and his hospital mate, both Missourians in gray) who had demonstrated a reluctance to receive the clergyman's services. Wrote a thankful Bannon: "By God's mercy, however, I was in time to give each of them absolution before their death."[133]

Disaster, meanwhile, struck at Big Black River on the morning of 17 May. The Federals overran the Confederate defenses in the line's center. One of the war's shortest and least costly attacks outflanked the Brigade's position on the left. To escape capture, Colonel Cockrell's Missourians fled across the river's floodplain with the Unionists in hot pursuit. Only by a wild sprint over the cotton fields and the slimmest of margins did the Confederates avoid capture.

Many Rebels swam the river or dashed across burning bridges. More than a thousand of Bowen's soldiers were not so lucky, most of them being captured. Nearly all of Captains Wade's, Landis's and Guibor's guns were lost. After the Big Black River debacle the Brigade joined Pemberton's withdrawal toward day's end.[134]

On 18 May, Bannon and his comrades were safely inside Vicksburg's fortifications with Pemberton's command. Grant's victorious legions shortly arrived and invested the Confederacy's Gibraltar. What would eventually become the North's largest army encircled the town on the north, east, and south. The most sizable assemblage of Union warships seen in the war, meanwhile, massed on the city's west side. The stage was set for the siege of Vicksburg, one of the conflict's most important dramas.[135]

SEVEN City on a River

VICKSBURG WAS THE MOST FORMIDABLE BASTION in the Confederacy. Southern engineers had constructed a nine-mile-long network of fortifications
atop ridges encircling the town. The defenses consisted of redans,
lunettes, and redoubts dotting the commanding terrain and protecting the
city's rear. Nature itself had come to the Rebels' aid. The soft loess soil was
gouged by water erosion, cutting gorge-like valleys. These canyons acted
like huge dry moats before the defenses on the heights. An abatis of felled
timber and the ravines' depths guaranteed to fragment attacking enemy
formations. But now Pemberton's thirty-one thousand troops were
trapped inside the citadel on the Mississippi.[1]

The Missouri Brigade and Bowen's Division again upheld their reputation as the army's shock troops by earning the assignment of strategic
reserve, which called for solidifying any threatened sector and ensured
high casualties.[2] A challenge came immediately. The Brigade advanced
outside the works to cover the entry of the last wagons and troops into
Vicksburg on the evening of 18 May. Cockrell's troops held the Unionists at
bay. After the skirmish, Father Bannon recorded that the "Mo. troops
[were] in lines" on Vicksburg's north.[3]

Bannon found a receptive Catholic community at Vicksburg. He was
already familiar with the local Catholics because of his periodic visits in
early 1863. The river town of less than 5,000 people contained a sizable
population of Irish and German immigrants. Most of these new Americans had migrated up the Mississippi from New Orleans to start a new
life. A rarity in Deep South demographics, Vicksburg boasted a Catholic

St. Paul's Catholic Church, Vicksburg, Mississippi, ca. 1900 (Old Court House Museum, Vicksburg)

populace of about seven hundred, a high figure by Southern standards, second only to one other city in Mississippi, Jackson.

St. Paul's Catholic Church, at Crawford and Walnut streets, was well known to Bannon. From now until the conclusion of the siege he worked closely with Father Charles Heuze, in charge of Vicksburg's parish. Heuze was a soldier-chaplain in the Bannon mold. As the St. Louis chaplain, Heuze would serve the injured and save souls in the trenches of Vicksburg.[4]

Grant planned to attack all along the line on 19 May. The Yankee general gambled that the Rebels were demoralized after successive defeats at Port Gibson, Raymond, Jackson, Champion Hill, and Big Black River. Military logic and common sense supported such a decision. A quick strike on 19 May might send blue divisions swarming over the earthworks to capture Vicksburg, and the Confederacy might be delivered a blow from which she could not recover.[5]

Grant's great assault came around two o'clock in the afternoon. Thousands of bluecoats poured from the forests lining the opposing ridges. One of the heaviest strikes fell on the north at the Stockade Redan Complex, a defensive network that guarded the Graveyard Road and was the strongest bastion on the line's left. The strategic position, therefore, was reinforced by the Missouri Brigade during the crisis. Arriving just in time, Cockrell's troops filled the trenches in various sectors of the complex.

General Grant miscalculated. Rebel cannon and infantry volleys slaughtered the attackers. The blue waves were mowed down with ease. Rough terrain and abatis tore regimental alignment to pieces, sapping the assault's impetus.[6] A Fifth Missouri sergeant from St. John's Parish and one of Bannon's ex-parishoners wrote in a letter about the Irish Confederates' determination: "There was no running from them trenches, as every man intended to die rather than surrender, or be driven out of them by any force."[7]

Powder-stained Southerners rapidly loaded and fired into the blue throngs for hours under a blistering sun. In the trenches, the defenders implored God's blessings for success in the holocaust's midst. A Mississippi regimental chaplain reflected that "while this charge was being made no doubt many hearts were lifted to Almighty God that he would defend us & inspire our brave troops with unyielding courage."[8]

Bannon viewed the Unionists' bravery and the deaths of hundreds of Northerners on one hot afternoon and wrote: "Feds press us on left—repulsed 6 times." Then, Bannon concluded, the "assault on left and center [were both] repulsed.'"[9] In fact, the enemy's onslaughts were hurled back at every point. Grant's confidence cost him more than one thousand men, the majority from Illinois, Ohio, Missouri, Indiana, and Iowa.[10]

That night Bannon left the Brigade—now back in reserve—to spend the night at the city's southernmost defenses around South Fort. Along the river, this sector was a bad place to retire for the night. He noted in his diary the next morning that "gun boats shell[ed] South batteries last night." But the worst was yet to come. Bannon soon returned to the Brigade, in reserve behind the front lines on the north.[11]

General Grant, preparing to launch another massive assault, targeted 22 May as the day of decisive success. Indeed, he feared that General Johnston to his rear might assemble a large enough army to attack him from the east.[12] One Southerner promised that "Grant, while attacking our works at Vicksburg, will be assailed fiercely by Johnston in his rear, and we can see no hope for his escape. We predict an early announcement, of the utter cutting to pieces or surrender of the great Yankee Army of the Mississippi."[13] Grant prepared to gamble once more with tactics more suitable for the Mexican War than this first modern war.

On the morning of 22 May, Federal masses again swarmed forward in overwhelming numbers. The Navy pounded the fortifications throughout the morning, trying to draw off Rebel defenders to the west, or toward the river defenses. A weakening of the land-side defenses might allow the attackers to punch a hole in the lines on the east. But outdated tactics of massed infantry assaults against fortifications once more proved obsolete in the face of the technology of rifled cannon and rifles. The poorly coordinated charges were launched with determination but could not overcome the defenders in this new day. Hundreds of young men in blue fell in again proving the futility of headlong assaults against fortifications.[14]

Thousands, nevertheless, continued swarming forward. A hail of lead cut the attackers down in heaps. The killing exceeded that of 19 May. A Northerner wrote, "On our charging, the rebels arose from their pits and entrenchments in thousands, and poured a deliberate and steady fire into the breasts of our advancing columns. They hurled hand grenades by the score into our ranks, and poured grape, canister and shrapnel upon us from batteries hitherto concealed from sight by the treacherous brush and undergrowth, which entangled the feet of our brave lads who fell an easy prey to their deadly sharpshooters. In many instances our regiments were within 50 yards of the rebel works, but the ground was so steep that it required longer time to climb up than to double quick ten times the distance"—a hell on earth for the Federals.[15]

Again the Missouri troops reinforced the Stockade Redan Complex, with Bannon in position in this sector. Brigade members gained revenge by decimating the enemy's ranks, for Cockrell's unit had lost more than a thousand comrades since crossing the Mississippi.[16] Some Missouri defenders realized they were facing Yankees in blue who had captured them at Camp Jackson. Bannon could view the slaughter as God's retribution for the Northerners' alleged "sins" in Missouri.

The Confederate battleflag—the one almost captured at Camp Jackson and rescued by Mrs. John S. Bowen and carried through the lines by her—now waved from the fortifications. Riley's First and Fourth Missouri, now known as the "Camp Jackson Regiment," fought with a special ferocity.[17]

Not far from the Camp Jackson colors, a United States banner was planted on the works. Bluecoats huddled in the deep ditches at the earthwork's base while the fighting escalated around them. A point-blank exchange of gunfire ensued. Some Unionists immediately below the parapet as well as onrushing attackers were those of the Sixth and Eighth Missouri Volunteer Infantry, Federal Missouri units and Camp Jackson's victors. Bannon, consequently, encouraged his Irish defenders to continue "doing an immense business in populating the regions of Pluto" with Yankees. Obligingly the Unionists kept coming, vomiting out of the valley in swarms.[18]

One of Riley's Missourians, a German fated to be killed in 1864, scaled the parapet amid the zipping bullets, snatched the United States colors off the earthwork, and shook the banner at the Federals. He screamed, "Come and get your flag! The Camp Jackson boys are here. Don't you want to take us to the arsenal again! It's our time now." The enraged soldier had to be dragged off the parapet by comrades.[19]

The nature of this fratricidal war was not only represented by Missourians in blue and in gray, but also by divisions among the Irish. Many of the Eighth Missouri attackers were St. Louis Irish. To the right, or south, of Captain Canniff's Company F Irish of the Fifth Missouri, a Federal regiment charged forward with "the green flag of Erin." In a bloody reunion, Ireland's native sons killed one another as rapidly as possible.[20]

The slaughter only ended with nightfall when Unionists trapped below the works escaped. The withdrawing Federals left hundreds of comrades strewn across open ground that had become a vast graveyard.[21] Bannon's reaction to the attack's repulse was comparable to that of a Rebel chaplain's prayer: "Thanks be to the Great Ruler of the Universe, Vicksburg is still safe."[22] More than three thousand Federals were sacrificed on 22 May. General Grant learned another expensive lesson: frontal assaults on fortifications and against modern weaponry could not succeed at Vicksburg. He, therefore, planned to reduce the fortress by siege.[23]

The Rebels gained a new confidence by beating back the onslaught. Almost unsurpassed in the war, the Unionists once again demonstrated remarkable valor during the suicidal attacks against the strongest fortifications they had ever seen. Some Confederates concluded that Grant's soldiers were drunk to show such courage. One Southerner believed as much and prayed: "Let the scoundrels suck rum and die. Let them charge, and shriek, and die, and go to Hell, where they belong." Like Bannon, he believed that God stood on the Confederacy's side.[24]

Siege warfare fell over Vicksburg. Bannon described the deprivations at "the [front] lines of Vicksburg during the siege, where we were under a tremendously hot sun, and a tremendously hot fire, and had to live for six weeks on wretched rations of mule beef."[25] He refused to stay full-time in the city's hospitals as expected of a chaplain.[26] "During the Siege of Vicksburg, Father Bannon was daily at the breastworks and could not be kept away,"[27] wrote one of the men. Despite the dangers, Bannon continued to give the last anointment and absolution to dying Confederates and to inspire hope in the hellish trenches.

Duty never ceased with the non-stop flow of dead and wounded, for Southerners went down each day to the continuous bombardment from land and river. A Louisiana Catholic and Irishman in gray recalled a much repeated role played by Bannon: "In Vicksburg during the siege [he] delivered, at the burial of a Protestant Soldier, of the Missouri Command, a very eloquent and touching address, bringing tears to many of the listeners."[28] As the siege grew, it seemed as if the funerals would never cease.

Union dead, meanwhile, remained unburied. For nearly a week, bluecoat bodies lay before the works, bloating, blackening, and "almost stinking us out of the works." A cessation of hostilities came on 25 May to bury the fallen.[29] Bannon found the day filled with an odd mixture of horror and peace: "Flag of truce [so] forces might bury their dead. . . . Men and officers of both armies advanced and conversed for several hours. . . . No shelling during the night."[30] The truce featured meetings between brothers and other relatives in blue and gray from Missouri.[31]

Vicksburg's deadly routine, thereafter, continued. On 26 May, recorded Bannon, "Sharpshooting resumed next morning. Shelling during the day."[32] The rain of shells came down day and night, from the Navy in front and land batteries on the other three sides. Most feared were the mortar boats, crafts armed with 11,000 pound, 13-inch mortars that threw giant 200-pound projectiles into the surrounded city.[33] A direct hit from one of these mortars could demolish a headquarters, wipe out an infantry company, or ignite an ammunition cache.

General Pemberton's only hope for assistance was from Johnston, who attempted to organize a relief army. With their backs against the river, Rebels cornered in Vicksburg had proved they could rebound from defeats during this tragic May. The common soldiery of the Confederacy demonstrated that Vicksburg could not be carried by storm.

While the South's newspapers and most of her people focused their interest on Lee's second great invasion of the North through Maryland and Pennsylvania, one of the Confederacy's most important contests progressed at Vicksburg in relative obscurity. But the Confederate government understood the strategic implications of losing Vicksburg. In fact, the strike north by the Army of Northern Virginia had been launched in large part to take the pressure off the lower Mississippi Valley and Vicksburg. It was the people of the Deep South who best realized the significance of Vicksburg and were bitter about the rest of the Confederacy's apathy. As a reporter from the *Savannah Republican* explained:

Great columns have been passed upon the Confederate armies in Virginia and Tennessee, and truely do those veteran troops deserve a full measure of credit for the trials and hardships they have gone through. But in point of patriotic determination, bravery, endurance of fatigue, hunger, the heat of the sun, the pelting rain and an abiding faith in their prowess, there is no army in the Confederacy to compare to that which interposes its living breastworks in defence of Vicksburg. . . . No army composed of such material has ever been whipped and never can be. The handful of Spartans who have held an overwhelming force at bay [for weeks] without a murmur, presents a spectacle worthy of the palmiest days of Greece and Rome. . . . The army of Vicksburg now stands among the veteran troops of the world, and it is but just that full credit should be given it by the government and by every portion of the Confederacy. No other army has been placed in such a critical position in this war.[34]

The siege became, in its way, an ally to Bannon in that more Confederates than ever before sought the clergyman and his blessings. Possibilities of imminent death transformed chronic liars, gamblers, and cheaters into near saints. One Sixth Missourian wrote in his journal, "Men were not so wicked during the siege as at other times, there was but verry little card playing, much less swearing than usual, and a great deal more reading the Bible."[35]

Bannon was entertained by some lively action on 27 May. Then the Confederate Water Batteries north of the city crippled the Federal gunboat *Cincinnati*. Bannon, a volunteer gunner himself less than two weeks before, watched as the Southern cannoneers worked their large-caliber siege guns with precision.[36] With the interest of one who could qualify as a veteran artilleryman, Bannon wrote, the: "*Cincinnati* [had been grounded at] the water's edge, sunk by our Northern guns.—The fleet haul off.— Mortars throwing incendiary shells during the evening and night [one] passed over my window [at the City Hospital] . . . fire on the roof of the hospital, which the mortars have shelled incessantly for a week, although we have a flag up and it is visible from the River."[37] Like other Rebels, Bannon was incensed about the infirmaries becoming targets.

The chaplain was now staying some nights with the surgeons and the medical teams at the City Hospital on the Jackson Road, to Vicksburg's northeast edge.[38] The large brick building was as dangerous as the trenches. During the siege, wrote one of Bowen's defenders, the infirmary was "hit over one thousand (1,000) times." Union gunners may have thought the hospital was Pemberton's headquarters and directed their cannon on the structure, but most likely the hits came from random fire.

Multitudes of shells crashing through the building that flew yellow hospital flags caused much bitterness within the garrison. In a Confederate's words, "One constant stream of mortar shells was poured into the devoted city, the enemy exhibiting a refinement of cruelty in throwing their shells at the hospitals particularly, aware that the men who were now well and hearty were perfectly indifferent to the storm of shot and shell poured like hail upon them. They fired into buildings on which the yellow flag waved, killing and wounding several of the inmates."[39]

As ever-increasing numbers of wounded Confederates piled up at the hospitals, Bannon spent more time working with the surgeons and holding Mass at the infirmary. He nevertheless daily visited the Missouri troops in the trenches. The Brigade continued to hold a reserve position, but various units rotated shifts at the front.[40]

Dr. John Leavy, of Green's brigade, wrote in his diary about the siege's horrors and added a tribute to Bannon: "One hundred and fifty thousand (150,000) shells; and nine million (9,000,000) small missles . . . have [been] hurled against us, thus far during this siege. The firing has continued constantly, night and day. I should have mentioned that Father Bannon is here [at the City Hospital], and doing all in his power to benefit our men. He is brave and conscientious and has the respect of all who know him. While talking to me about the urgent necessity for attending to one's religious duties and the uncertainty of life, a large fragment of shell, weighing several pounds, came through the building, and struck a St. Louis boy in the hip, crushing the bones, and imbedding itself in the tissues."[41] Bannon probably attended to the unfortunate young man. His words persuaded the physician to become more religious. Often Bannon found himself in comparable danger, but luck or God, or both, continued to shield the chaplain from injury.

The mutual respect between surgeon and chaplain endured throughout the siege. Each remained dependent upon the other and both had a common goal—saving as many Southerners as possible. In the Confederate army, the bonds between chaplains and physicians were strong.[42] The siege only further cemented the ties. Projectiles were not the only danger. Because of poor diet, hospital patients were beset by scurvy.[43] Day and night in the oven-like infirmaries dying and injured Rebels demanded constant attention during shelling which never ceased.

As Surgeon Leavy indicated, Father Bannon's esteem rose higher during the siege. The priest's reputation transcended the nucleus of Catholic Confederates. He had not only proved himself on the battlefields but had established a camaraderie rare between a man of God and the common soldiers.[44] Most grayclads, for instance, held high admiration for a chaplain of such "character as that of Father Bannon, the Catholic priest who accompanied the artillerymen of Guibor's command [and] who joked and laughed with them in bivouac and went with them into action . . . and who prayed with the dying on the battlefield."[45] Bannon's sense of humor and wit made him a favorite with the troops, especially during the siege.

Indeed, much mutual admiration existed. Bannon respected the hardened Missouri soldiers from the West, who were so long and so far away from families. He wrote that "the Catholic Chaplains were much respected by all the men, whether Catholics or not; for they saw that they did not shrink from danger or labour to assist them. But [most other] Chaplains were frequently objects of derision, always disappearing on the eve of an action, when they would stay behind in some farm house till all was quiet, and then overtake us in a day or two, riding up on their mules with their precious saddle-bags."[46]

Unlike most of the Europeans of Bannon's memory, the rawboned Missouri frontiersmen possessed a spirit of individualism and sense of democracy born of the American experience. Bannon found kindred spirits among the Missouri Confederates, who were self-reliant and thought for themselves in the frontier tradition. These citizen-soldiers often openly questioned orders before West Point-trained generals and frequently vented their displeasure in their presence. With admiration, Bannon revered the common soldier—"these men who from their cradles had been reared in intellectual pride and spiritual independence."[47]

This special relationship between Bannon and the enlisted men and officers remained perhaps the most important factor in explaining his widespread influence. A mutual respect such as that between Bannon and the common soldiers could only have been developed after Bannon proved himself an equal in courage on the battlefield.

But occasionally he encountered anti-Catholic sentiment among the troops. From Ireland after the war he described one such situation.

I went one day to visit the ward for the mortally wounded. This ward was naturally not so well cared for as the others, for the cases were all hopeless as far as nursing and surgery went: but for my purposes they were perhaps more hopeful than many others. On this occasion I noticed a group which struck me more than usual. A wounded man, about forty years of age, lay insensible on one of the beds, and two other soldiers, one about the age of the dying man, the other a lad, but both bronzed with hard service, were standing sad and silent by his side. I went over to them and asked the elder of the two if the wounded man was a relative.

"He is my brother," was the reply, "and this boy's father." They were all three "patriot" soldiers, as the first Southern volunteers were called; they served in the ranks at their own expense, and took not a farthing of pay.

"I fear," I said, "that there is no hope of his life."

"Do you think so?" said the brother anxiously; and turning to the lad he added, "How shall we tell your mother?"

"Well," said I, "perhaps he was prepared for death. Did he profess any religion?" This is the phrase in the States for being a known member of any church.

"No, but he thought a deal about religion, and was fond of hearing preaching."

"Do you know if he was ever baptized?"

"He was not. But I have heard him say quite lately that he wished he had been; and that if God spared him through this war, he would get himself baptized at the end of it."

"Well," I replied "it is a pity that if he wished for it himself, and now cannot help himself. Besides it would be a consolation to his wife and all his family at home to know that he was baptized before he died. It would take off some of the pain of losing him."

After saying so much as this I went away, and left them to talk the matter over between them. It is often well not to seem to push things, but to allow something to come spontaneously from the other side, though it may be in answer to one's own suggestions.

I visited some other cases and came back after an interval. I saw that the two were in some perplexity.

"I am a Catholic Priest," I said, "but if you wish it I will myself offer to baptize your brother; for from what you tell me I find in him all the conditions requisite for me to do so in his present state. Think it over, and let me know."

I then left the ward. It was not long however before the two men came to seek me, and finding me in one of the corridors of the hospital, the elder of them said, "Mister, we think he ought to be baptized. And we should like you to baptize him rather than any body else, for all the boys speak better of the Catholic Priests and the Sisters, than of any other religion at all."

"Very well," I said, "I will keep to my word."

We went back to the bed-side, and taking off the damp cloth that was laid over the dying man's forehead I prepared to baptize him. It was an affecting thing to see those two rough soldiers drop on their knees instinctively, and to see the tears roll down their bronzed cheeks as I administered the Sacrament.

"Minister," said the brother, seizing my hand when I had finished, "I should like to be a Catholic too, if you will have me. If you will only teach me all about it, I will be thankful to you for ever."

The dying man never recovered his senses; and the brother became a Catholic. The younger man did not offer himself at once with his uncle, . . . but I trust his case was only reserved for more worthy hands than mine.[48]

Another active and dangerous day for Father Bannon was 30 May, described by a Vicksburg woman in her diary: "This morning it is comparatively quiet—Trinity Sunday—how like and yet unlike Sunday. All nature wears a Sabbath calm, but the thunder of artillery reminds us that man knows no Sabbath—Yankee man at least." Each day Bannon joined the Missouri troops in the encampments and fortifications. Most often he visited the Stockade Redan Complex or around the Jackson Road sector. Cockrell's Brigade now had the responsibility for filling those sectors north of the Jackson Road (the main east-west avenue leading into the city) and westward to the river. Bannon went to the trenches on a regular basis and often in addition whenever a Confederate had been shot or requested his presence.[49]

The dusty slits dug into the ground became a living nightmare. Grayclads stood atop firing steps to fire through embrasures at an enemy who approached by digging. With the Unionists only a few feet distant in many cases, the sharpshooting was deadly for both sides. Protected from the sun by cane stalks or tree limbs, Rebel snipers stood at portholes for hours, blasting away at the miners in blue. Most casualties came when Federal sharpshooters sent bullets through the firing holes, hitting Confederate faces.

Unionists dug so close to the Southern lines, wrote one Missouri Rebel in his journal, that "the opposing parties [could] enter into conversation, holloring back and forth, being 50 or 100 yards asunder, enquiring of each other who they were and where they were from, and about their acquaintances, sometimes they would meet each other half way, and have a social talk [at night]. They finally got so near each other at some points that they would write on scraps of paper and through [sic] them over to each other."

Federal cannoneers cut shell fuses so that projectiles burst directly over the entrenchments. The resulting explosions propelled iron fragments down on Confederate heads. Bannon's duties at the front lines consequently were risky. Amid the bursting shells and sniper fire, he often gave the last anointing (Extreme Unction) and viaticum (the Eucharist—Communion) to mortally wounded Southerners.[50]

Omnipresent disease was equally the defenders' adversary at Vicksburg. Pneumonia, developing from seemingly endless days and nights of standing in the rain, and typhoid fever were common. These diseases dropped men into shallow graves at a rate equivalent to the enemy's guns. Dysentery was the most fatal.[51]

Sharing the same rations, dangers, and outdoor elements as the troops, Bannon likewise fell victim to disease. After Mass on 5 June, he became "very sick" with "cramp colic [chronic diarrhea]." This bout with dysentery forced him into a bed at a private citizen's residence for recuperation. Bannon was sick for nearly two weeks, lingering near death at one point. Only with nursing, better food, and clean quarters would he recover his health unlike so many other defenders. It seemed as if God had more important work for Bannon to do in the nightmare of Vicksburg.[52]

Father Bannon recovered sufficiently to offer Mass at St. Paul's Church on Sunday, 21 June. His spirits were uplifted this day, when a "courier arrived [from] Johnston [now] 40 miles from Vicksburg on Wednesday [17 June]."[53] But the reinforcements never interrupted the siege. Pemberton's army was abandoned. Vicksburg was on its own, ironically since the river city was the most important bastion in the Confederacy.[54]

Atop one of Vicksburg's highest hills, St. Paul's Church was the only house of worship open in the town. Fathers Bannon and Heuze continued to say Mass each morning at the gothic-style, brick structure.[55] At this spiritual refuge, Captain Canniff, Sergeant Hogan—both destined to die in the same battle—and other Irish Catholics of the Brigade found solace from Vicksburg's storm. The church, as the City Hospital, was a fine target as the second dominant structure on the city's skyline.[56]

Indeed, Bannon had almost lost his life in early June, after he had been removed to the City Hospital during his illness. A gigantic 13-inch shell from the mortar fleet had slammed into the infirmary. The projectile hit the roof around 2:30 A.M., then tore downward through consecutive floors. Additionally, it wrecked the hospital's drug supply storerooms and continued through the building, "smashing up and destroying everything in its path."

John Henry Britts, now the surgeon of the Missouri Brigade, had a close call "when this monster paid us its unwelcome visit." The shell finally halted in Britts's sleeping quarters, "then rolled along the room spitting fire from its angry fuse and then exploded" deep within the hospital's midsection. The tremendous blast rocked the whole structure, ripping down more rooms and floors and blowing out walls.[57]

The projectile narrowly missed Bannon. He had been one of the first at the scene despite being weak from disease. Surgeon Britts was buried by brick and plaster, with a leg nearly severed in two. The physician, age twenty-five, was bleeding to death. One soldier wrote: "Father Bannon was unhurt, and by his quick action he rendered Dr. Britts, saving the doctor's life by stopping the flow of blood until help came." Bannon's assistance allowed Surgeon Britts, who had attended St. Louis University's Medical School, to recover after a successful amputation so that, with an artificial limb, he could continue duty as a physician until the war's end.[58]

Bannon again came close to losing his life on 23 June. On this hot day, he had retired to a command headquarters when a "Parrot [sic] shell passed thru the house about 3 PM 6 feet over my head."[59]

As the siege lengthened, hopes for relief dimmed and losses mounted. In the trenches, Confederate spirits fell to new lows. Vicksburg's doom seemed inevitable by the end of June. Death could come at any moment.

A Southern chaplain summarized the mental anxiety among the garrison's members:

> The night was a solemn night for the soldier. . . . When upon the wings of fond imagination his soul visits the loved ones at home—and while he thinks of a lonely & loving wife whose face he may never look upon again & who may never see his form any more on earth, his heart bleeds & dark forebodings fill his mind. Then when he lies down upon the cold ground & looks up to the shining stars above, the gloomy thought crosses his mind, that it may be the last time he will ever look upon the shining heavens & that those same stars which now look down so quiet upon him, may behold him on the morrow night a lifeless, mangled corpse. If he be a child of God, he will commit his soul to God & implore his protection. If a wicked man he will review the past with remorse & the future with dread & will form a weak resolution to do better from that day if God will spare his life through the [siege].[60]

Under constant danger, Bannon heard more confessions, offered more prayers, and distributed Communion more often during the forty-seven days of siege than at any time in his career. Each day of life in a man-made hell brought the graycoats closer to God. A Missouri Rebel, for example, wrote thanks in his diary: "God has protected me thus far through this trial. May his protection be about me through the siege."[61] Most defenders felt the same, becoming more receptive to Bannon's services.

Grant calculated to break the siege stalemate toward the end of June. For weeks the Unionists dug tunnels beneath the earthworks to implant mines under strategic sectors. One position targeted for mining operations was near the Jackson Road.[62] The entire North held its collective breath for the mines to blow and open the avenue to victory.

In a Northern newspaper, a description of the strategy read: "Sappers and miners are vigorously engaged day and night in making subterranean passages to and under those fortifications. When their work is completed, as it very soon must be, probably two or four mines will be sprung at once, and the faces of the doomed fortifications will be torn off by as many earthquakes, opening the way for a tremendous rush of our troops into the city."[63]

The primary target for the mine work was the Third Louisiana Redan. This fortification at the city's northeast protected the Jackson Road, and the Missouri troops were positioned behind the fort for the anticipated explosion. Nothing could stop the enemy's mine activity. Finally, on the afternoon of 25 June, more than two thousand pounds of powder exploded under the Third Louisiana Redan.[64]

The blast erupted like a volcano. Part of the fort and much of the surrounding ground were hurled skyward. One Rebel wrote how the Unionists "blew it up, the blast shocked the whole hill, they then commenced fireing more rapidly." The defenders quickly rallied with the arrival of reinforcing Missourians. In forming a defense and attempting to lead a counterattack, Colonel Erwin, the grandson of Henry Clay, was killed. Blue and gray met in a hand-to-hand contest at the crater.[65] Bannon later recorded the assault's outcome, writing how the Yankee troops mounted a "charge on our lines after blowing up positions [but the] Feds driven back with great loss."[66]

When the mine blew, Bannon was in the sector below, or south of, the Jackson Road. During the attack an officer had been mortally wounded and requested to see the priest from St. Louis. Bannon, therefore, received word that his services were urgently needed far northward in the Jackson Road sector. He mounted his "magnificent black horse" and even "before the firing had ceased started to gallop more than a mile to the position in which the officer was stationed. His commanding figure, of course, enabled him to be recognized, and the troops on both sides, Federal and Confederate, struck by his heroism started up from their trenches, ceased firing, and cheered him loudly."

During this incident, possibly one of the war's most unforgettable, Rebels and Yankees paid Bannon the ultimate compliment. Hundreds of soldiers in blue and gray waved hats and cheered at the spectacle of the chaplain riding wildly atop the ridges in full view.[67] His prestige grew greater, but not so much among the army's generals as among the common soldiers, North and South.

The following day after attending to the injured officer, he returned to infirmary duty. Once again, another large "shell [tore] thru Hospital." He escaped injury,[68] but another old friend died that day. While surveying the Federals' position, General Green was "killed this morning," wrote Bannon, when he was "shot in the head." Green was the only general slain during the siege. A blueclad sharpshooter dropped the gray-haired general who had once been "a terror in North Missouri." Green lived by a personal creed that became true at Vicksburg: "Final victory or an honorable grave."

Later Bannon labored in the infirmary beside Mrs. Green, the general's wife from northeast Missouri. She gave heroic service like so many of Vicksburg's women. Indeed, as one of Bowen's surgeons wrote: "The southern women are especially brave. I knew that some women were courageous, but had no faint idea of its universality until I saw it so conspicuously displayed in Vicksburg."[69]

Sunday 28 June dawned bright and warm, the siege's forty-first day. As usual on Sunday, Father Bannon went to St. Paul's Church to celebrate Mass.[70] Sergeant Hogan's wound healed enough for him to go "to six o'clock mass in the Cathedral."[71] Many townspeople gathered at the only open church in town and on the final Sunday in an unconquered Vicksburg. One Confederate described how "the Arguseyed enemy across the river discovered the unusual number of people in the streets, and instantly opened on them with a Parrott gun. As the shells came screaming wickedly through the streets, exploding . . . men, women and children hastily sought shelter to escape the danger. Several persons were struck by fragments of shells, but, fortunately, no one killed. Such an unheard of, ruthless and barbarous method of warfare as training a battery of rifled cannon upon an assembly of unarmed men and worshiping women, is unparalleled in the annals of history."[72] Once again the conflict disrupted Bannon's hope for a safe Sunday service in Vicksburg.

As shells exploded outside St. Paul's Church, Bannon continued Mass preparations.[73] Sergeant Hogan, the former St. John parishioner, struggled up the steep hill. He "had just gotten inside the door when a 132-pound parrot shell, from the batteries on the [DeSoto] peninsula, struck the railing outside the church, taking off the arm of a citizen [Michael Donovan] who was coming in."[74]

More shells, meanwhile, burst outside, as the bombardment intensified. The priest later noted in his diary the tragedy on 28 June, writing that "Mr. Donovan [had his] arm shot off . . . by a parrott shell from the point [of the peninsula]."[75] But the worst was yet to come. "When I was about to go on the altar another shell passed thru the church [but] no one hurt." Roaring like a freight train, the huge mortar shell tore through the church from end to end. The projectile passed several feet above the crowded pews and just inches over the head of Father Bannon, who was higher behind the altar. It exploded almost directly above the altar of the Blessed Virgin as Bannon was about to speak. Plaster and bricks were hurled around the room and covered the altar with debris. Choking dust and smoke enveloped the church and women and children screamed. Most parishioners jumped from their seats and raced for the door. It appeared that Bannon's Mass of 28 June was over.[76]

But he shouted to restore the calm, imploring the congregation to remain, and the panic subsided. Despite the barrage, he said Mass as usual. As one Confederate wrote: "The congregation [had risen] to rush out, but Father Bannon continued the services as though nothing unusual had happened. Thus assured, the people resumed their seats. After the service he addressed them and called their attention to be prepared at all times for death. After thanking God for preserving their lives, he dismissed them with a blessing." The Irish chaplain from faraway St. Louis celebrated a Mass that Vicksburg's residents never forgot.[77]

Bannon worked closely throughout the siege with eight nuns of the Sisters of Mercy. Much to his delight, two of these women were from Ireland. The Sisters of Mercy were seemingly sent by God to serve hundreds of ailing Southerners. Vicksburg's Sisters of Mercy had been established in late 1859 by a Baltimore-based order. Indeed, the effort to eliminate sinful elements common to a Mississippi River port was timely. The order survived despite a hostile Know-Nothing climate. Nowhere in the South was the need for Sisters of Mercy now greater than at Vicksburg.

Only a few blocks from St. Paul's Church, the convent and school of the Sisters of Mercy were turned into hospitals. In addition, the eight nuns also serviced the infirmaries with Father Bannon and visited many private houses—now hospitals—deserted by the town's citizens. Most of Vicksburg's townspeople were living in cave shelters.[78] Bannon held the Sisters of Mercy in high esteem. Summarizing their influence during the war, he wrote:

> The four years' civil war has done more to advance the cause of Catholicity in the States, both North and South, than the hundred years that preceded. And perhaps the principal cause of this advance has been the charity shown by the Religious Sisters who tended the sick and wounded in both armies. Thousands of men who either knew nothing of the Catholic Church, or only such lies concerning it as are to be found in the periodicals and fictions of the day, were brought into intimate contact with it in its most energetic work, in its most winning character. In the Confederate army, and I believe also in the Northern, any religious community who chose to volunteer for the work had transport, lodging, and rations supplied to it by the Government, with a Chaplain for the Sisters. Some had the care of stationary hospitals; others

followed the different armies in charge of the camp hospitals. More than eighty per cent of the Protestants who entered the Sisters' hospitals became Catholics; and scarcely a man died among them whom they did not win over before his death. Their tender care and charity was the talk of the army: the soldiers swore by them, so to speak; and no man who had been in one of their hospitals would ever willingly go to any other. I have often witnessed a scene of this kind. A soldier ill, or wounded, but able to walk, would come and hand his billet to the Sister in charge.

"But this billet is not for our hospital," said the Sister.

"Oh, now, look here, Sister! I'm not going to any other place. I'm going to stop here."

"Well, but there is not room for you."

"There's room in the passage," was the reply, "and I won't give any trouble, indeed."

And the man would spread his blanket in the corridor, or by the door, and lie down; well knowing that he would not be turned away. I have seen the corridors so full, that it was difficult to make one's way along, without treading on the men. They looked on the Sisters almost as superior beings, and it is something incredible how they submitted their will and their reason to them.[79]

None of the eight Sisters of Mercy was injured during the siege. While Bannon no doubt often "was filled with anxiety about their welfare and the city was ablaze with the brilliant horror of shot and shell of the siege of Vicksburg, the Sisters, as if by a miracle, remained unhurt while thousands of wounded filled the air with their cries of distress." These nuns were often admonished with the warning, "Sisters, do not go out all together, for I do not want you all killed. Divide, and work in different directions so that some of you may escape."

The services of the Sisters of Mercy earned them the title of the "Nuns of the Battlefield." These heroines were Mother Mary de Sales Browne, Sister Mary Vincent Browne, Sister Mary Philomena Farmer, Sister Mary Agnes Madigan (Wexford County, Ireland), Sister Mary Teresa Newman, Sister Mary Xavier Poursine, Sister Mary Agnatia Sumner, and Sister Mary Stephana Warde (Carlow County, Ireland).[80]

General Grant, meanwhile, refused to give up hope of breaking the siege stalemate. The Federals gambled once more on blowing a hole in the Confederate line. During the afternoon of 1 July, another mine exploded beside the Jackson Road near the 25 June blast site. A number of Sixth Missouri soldiers were blown up in the blast and buried alive. Performing another rescue mission at Vicksburg, the Missouri troops raced for the breach to meet the expected infantry attack.

But Grant, recalling the repulse of 25 June, did not send his regiments through the crater. Heavy fighting, nevertheless, erupted around it, and all the while, the Union cannon pounded the area. Not knowing that the bluecoats were not attacking, Cockrell's defenders remained in position while a torrent of shells tumbled down.[81]

The struggle at the Third Louisiana Redan continued far into the night, and Bannon remained near the front. He wrote on 2 July: "Col [Pembroke S.] Senteny [of the Second Missouri] killed yesterday when the enemy [attacked] at the Jackson Road—Several of the 6th Mo and 3rd La killed."[82] More men on both sides died without altering the strategic situation.

July brought more of the familiar routine—night and day shelling, death at any moment, and more casualties. Bannon's brushes with death were frequent and well known. According to a St. Louis officer, "the Rev. Father Bannon had many narrow escapes" throughout the siege.[83] Such close calls failed to deter him in his duties, however. At the Sisters of Mercy hospital, an incident occurred with a Protestant soldier during the siege, and Bannon described it at length.

> One of [the] Sisters told me one day that she had a patient willing to become a Catholic, that she had given him some instruction, but that it would be better if I would see him at once. I went to his bed-side, and after a few introductory questions, I asked if he had ever professed any religion.
>
> "No," he said, "I have not: but I have made arrangements about that now; I have settled it all with the Sisters."
>
> "Quite right," I replied, "but it will be well for me to have a little talk with you."
>
> "Now, I tell you what it is, Mister," replied the patient, "it's no use any of you coming talking to me. I belong to the Sisters' religion, and that's enough."
>
> "Exactly, and so do I. I am a Priest of their religion—the Catholic religion: and I have come to see what I can do for you."
>
> He would not however be satisfied until he had called the Sister and learnt from her that all was right and proper. While I was instructing him, something or other I told him seemed too much for his good will.
>
> "Oh, come now," he said, "you don't expect me to believe that!"
>
> "Yes," I said, "that is what the Catholic Church teaches, and we are bound to believe it."
>
> "Well," he replied, "we'll see. Here, Sister!"

The Sister came, and the patient addressing her said, "Sister, this man tells me so and so. Is that true?"

"Oh yes," said the Sister smiling, "quite true."

"Do you believe it, Sister?"

"Yes certainly; we all believe it."

"Very well," he said, turning to me, "all right, I believe it. Go a-head, Mister; what next?"

The man's language may seem flippant and off-hand; but he was thoroughly in earnest, and received everything I told him: it was however necessary to make a few appeals to the Sister now and then, and when she confirmed what I said, he accepted it at once and finally. He only remarked once, "He says some very hard things, Sister!" But he took all the hard things in directly he had the Sister's word. In the end I baptized him; though it might be said perhaps to be rather in fidem Sororum, than in fidem Ecclesice.[84]

The Vicksburg garrison within "Grant's Bull Pen" was running out of time. Some ten thousand of Pemberton's Rebels were now casualties to disease, bullets, and shells.[85] Conditions became so bad that Bannon and his comrades were eating mule meat by July.[86] In addition, wrote one defender, "Rats, under the name of 'ground squirrels,' are said to command two dollars a piece."[87] Another crisis was the shortage of percussion caps for muskets.[88] Because of limited supplies, according to one Unionist, "had another assault been made, the garrison could not have held out an hour, except at the point of the bayonet."[89] There were no more attacks on Vicksburg, however.

On the afternoon of 3 July near the Jackson Road, Bannon recorded his worst dream-come-true when: "Pemberton & Bowen went out on a flag of truce—Vicksburg to be surrendered tomorrow."[90] During a conference with his top lieutenants, General Pemberton had learned that his command was unable to fight or cut its way out. Capitulation seemed the only alternative against an army numbering more than seventy-five thousand. The surrender was scheduled on the Union's great national holiday, the Fourth of July.[91] No one was more angry over the citadel's fall than Bannon.[92]

In a final scene of Vicksburg's forty-seven-day siege, the priest saved the battleflag of Guibor's Battery. He considered this task as sacred as a religious ceremony. The cannoneers wanted desperately to keep the flag out of Yankee hands, and Bannon was a most suitable choice to perform the honor. After all, he had served Guibor's cannon in action with these St. Louis gunners and had been the artillery unit's first chaplain.

Members of Captain Henry Guibor's First Missouri Light Artillery. Father Bannon is in upper left; Captain Guibor is the middle figure in the top row. (Missouri Historical Society, St. Louis)

Since the onset of the siege, the battery's red banner had been "conspic-uous on the heights of Vicksburg, while [Guibor's] brazen guns hurled tons of shells at the ranks of Union infantry encircling the city for forty-seven days." Captain Guibor and Bannon folded the flag, decorated with white letters spelling "Guibor's Battery," "Carthage," "Dry Wood," "Oak Hill," "Lexington," "Elk Horn," and "Corinth." Then the colors were placed in a box for safekeeping.

After walking to the city's commercial district along the river, Bannon handed the box over to an Italian merchant, probably a St. Paul's Church parishioner. The Catholic businessman would hold the flag throughout the years of Union occupation. After the war's end Captain Guibor returned to Vicksburg and brought the unit's colors to St. Louis.[93] But unlike his comrades, Father Bannon would never see the cherished flag again.

Finally the dreaded surrender ceremony came.[94] Bannon entered nothing of his thoughts in his diary,[95] but a soldier recorded in his journal that during this capitulation ordeal, "Father Bannon . . . was in a very bad humor." He watched the surrender to the assembled troops, among them hundreds of Irishmen of the Seventh Missouri, U.S.A., standing in line and under green banners.[96]

Many of Vicksburg's defenders "lived to feel grateful to the good father for his gallant devotion to his profession and many more to admire his courage, and self-sacrifice by which he showed them the chaplain's place was not back among the commissary wagons in time of battle, but among the wounded and dying in the strike."[97]

Father Bannon watched the surrender near the Jackson Road and wrote of the last scenes at Vicksburg: "Surrendered at 10 [o'] clock. [I] went out to see our men stack arms—Genl Grant entered [Vicksburg] at 10½ o'clk—Yankee troops & officers scattered thru town—Several Brigades marching in at noon—Yankee flag over [the Warren County] Court House—122 Guns . . . fired salutes . . . answered [by the Union Navy's] batteries."[98] The end of a dream came at last. The strategic Jackson Road, ironically, was the road for which so many Missouri troops had died. With the only consolation that of saving the flag of Guibor's Battery, Bannon had to watch his comrades lay down arms and surrender Confederate flags.

Appropriately for Bannon's tastes, these Missouri battleflags were dis-tinguished by white Latin Crosses on a blue field. So distinctively religious were the crosses that Price's Missouri troops in the Trans-Mississippi ini-tially refused to fight under them because they appeared to be Catholic banners. Bannon must have taken much pleasure in the fact that he and his comrades struggled under these Crosses of God. General Grant, at the Jackson Road surrender site, was again nearby when Bannon became a prisoner of war for the second time in two years. As he had been after Camp Jackson's fall, he was once again in the enemy's hands.[99]

The North was now ensured control of the Mississippi River. Port Hudson, Louisiana, would shortly fall. Combined with other reversals in the Mississippi Valley, the South suffered an irreversible blow in Vicksburg's loss. Split in half, the Confederacy was left wide open to further invasions, and in the future, Union thrusts would be deeper and more penetrating than ever before. While Pemberton's army capitulated, meanwhile, the Army of Northern Virginia limped toward the South after taking a beating at Gettysburg. Neither the expected victory on northern soil in the East nor the relieving of pressure in the West was gained from the invasion. The Confederacy's hopes for survival faded further away with the twin defeats at Vicksburg and Gettysburg.[100]

Apparently Bannon was not required to sign a parole with other Confederates, for his parole record does not exist.[101] Most Southerners took parole instead of prison. Bowen would not live to see his men take the field again. Dysentery brought the brilliant general closer to death by the siege's end. General Bowen had been a key player in the siege and in the surrender negotiations with his old St. Louis neighbor and friend, Grant. One of the South's rising stars in the West, Bowen's brightness would soon be extinguished.[102]

While the Southern troops would not march to parole camp for nearly a week, Bannon prepared to leave Vicksburg immediately. He wrote of getting ready to "move out to-night at 3 o'clock PM."[103] Finally on 6 July, he left the city and the many comrades buried on Vicksburg's hillsides. With General Bowen and his wife, Father Bannon "Marched out at 6 AM . . . Gen Bowen sick."[104]

Perhaps at the request of Mary Kennerly-Bowen, Father Bannon accompanied the dying general and his wife in an army ambulance. A man of God needed to be available, for the general's condition worsened. Bowen had refused offers by Union officers to remain with Federal surgeons at a Vicksburg hospital. Also hidden in the ambulance were two Missouri battleflags, which Mrs. Bowen smuggled out of the fallen citadel.[105]

The ambulance jolted toward parole camp around Demopolis, Alabama. For six days, the more than one-hundred-fifty-mile trip east through Mississippi proceeded in the hot, muggy weather of a Deep South summer. "Marched to Mrs. Watson's beyond 14 mile Creek," wrote Bannon on 12

July. Here, two miles west of Raymond and on the tributary of Big Black River, the party spent the night. Bowen would never leave the house alive. The next day was General Bowen's last, for the attention of Mrs. Bowen and local women and Father Bannon's prayers were not enough to save him.[106] As Bannon had written in his diary shortly before the general's death: "Gen. Bowen too sick to move any further."

The general died far from his Carondelet home and the troops he commanded brilliantly.[107] A Southern newspaper during the past winter had prayed: "May [Bowen] live to see his country free, and, once more repose securely in his pretty mansion at Carondelet!" Bannon, being in the correct place at the proper time, helped bury the Confederate general and friend in Mississippi soil.

The task was eerily similar to a comparable act performed less than a year before for another high-ranking Rebel commander, General Little. No doubt Bannon's service for the exceptional general of his same age, thirty-two, on 13 July 1863, matched in dignity the funeral for General Little in September of 1862 at Iuka.[108] He had now attended to three Missouri Confederate generals at or shortly before their deaths—Generals Slack, Little, and Bowen.

The Confederacy lost one of its best leaders in General Bowen. "It appeared like a reversal of the decree of Providence," one Confederate wrote. "To them [the Southern troops] he was the one general in that army who could not be replaced."[109] Bowen's death and Vicksburg's surrender may have shaken the faith even of Bannon. His prayers for victory had gone unanswered once again.

The next day, Bannon "overtook my Brigade at Pearl River," farther east toward Alabama.[110] Brigade survivors were uplifted with Bannon's arrival, but the journey east became a death-march, many diseased Southerners falling out of column by the roadside. The trek ended on 17 July near Enterprise, Mississippi—eventual headquarters for the paroled prisoners.[111] As if to wash away Vicksburg's horrors and the pain of losing General Bowen and so many others, Bannon took a refreshing "swim in [Chickasawhay] river" and contemplated his uncertain destiny.[112]

He now gained strength in body and soul. As he had done throughout the war, Sergeant Hogan kept his St. John's Parish family up-dated on the founding father of their church, writing on 22 July: "Father Bannon is in good health and spirits."[113] It was well that Bannon recuperated after one of the longest and most brutal sieges in American history, for even more challenging duty awaited the Irish chaplain in the months ahead.

EIGHT Diplomatic Mission for the Confederacy

FATHER BANNON STAYED WITH THE BRIGADE for less than a week. Hundreds of other Rebels were leaving, deserting to recross the Mississippi River to link with General Price and try to reclaim Missouri. Large numbers of parolees also departed to private homes of relatives and new-found friends throughout the South. Many had never reached Alabama, falling sick or dying beside the road. Only a skeleton brigade of Missourians remained in Alabama, and much of Pemberton's army likewise had disintegrated.[1]

On 21 July, therefore, Bannon entrained for Mobile. The city was a haven for exiled Missourians, the clergy, and a large Irish Catholic population. After regaining health and spirit, Bannon journeyed north to rejoin his command, encamped around Demopolis. He reached the parole rendezvous site on 1 August. As usual, the chaplain was ever-ready for more field service with the eventual exchange of the Missouri troops. Bannon now worked on saving souls while waiting, as he wrote, "for the muster of the Missouri troops at the end of the two months furlough, stipulated for [them] at Vicksburg."[2]

Unlike many of the soldiers, Bannon elected not to forsake the Brigade.[3] In September of 1863, the Missouri Brigade would be exchanged and reactivated to embark on even more arduous campaigns during 1863–1865. During these trials in Mississippi, Georgia, Tennessee, and Alabama, it earned more fame as containing "the most heroic and the best fighters in the service."[4] The distinguished record was summarized by Capt. Francis Von Phul after four years of conflict: "Truly the 1st Mo

Brigade covered itself with glory and I flatter myself at one time I was a member of that body of most gallant men."[5] Bannon shared his pride.

The priest would not be with General Cockrell's Brigade during its 1864 and 1865 campaigns. Bannon, although he did not realize it at the time, left the Missourians forever on 4 August 1863.[6] He would never again see his comrades in service. Since a month remained before the Missouri troops would be exchanged and with the parole encampment nearly empty, he left for Mobile, and once on the Gulf of Mexico coast, welcomed the respite from the war.[7]

In mid-August, Bannon entrained for the Confederacy's capital at Richmond. This was his first visit to a Catholic community in the east. The trip by rail took the chaplain northeast to Atlanta, then east for Augusta, then toward the Atlantic coast and Wilmington, North Carolina. Before reaching Richmond, he stopped briefly at Petersburg, Virginia, where he met Father Benjamin J. Keiley.

Once at Richmond, Bannon became acquainted with some of the top political, religious, and military leaders of the Confederacy. His winning qualities made favorable impressions upon those he met. Indicating that his reputation had preceded him, the chaplain's arrival in late August became a much-heralded affair in the nation's capital on the James River. President Jefferson Davis shortly learned about the presence of the much talked about Catholic priest from the Western army, who was known as "the Fighting Chaplain."[8]

Since the Missourians had yet to re-enter active service, Bannon was now officially "a chaplain without a command."[9] Consequently, he told the Bishop of Richmond, Father John McGill, "that he would gladly perform any duty assigned him."[10] He wrote that he "was content to remain and do duty in Richmond" if necessary.[11] President Davis received the news that an Irish Catholic priest noted for bravery on the battleground had arrived in Richmond when a critical void in the Confederate diplomatic field needed filling in Ireland. Father Bannon's sudden appearance in his country's seat of government could not have been more opportune.[12]

A serious crisis for the Confederacy existed by 1863 with the sudden and drastic increase in foreign immigration to the North, after a lull during the first half of the war. New York City, for instance, now received about a thousand European immigrants per day. During 1863, Irish immigration almost tripled in comparison to the previous year.[13] Such additions of foreign manpower to resupply Northern armies resulted in a grim statistic for Confederate fortunes. One out of every four or five Federal soldiers in

1864 would be a recent immigrant.[14] The law of averages stacked up on the Union's side with the addition of foreign volunteers, almost making the defeat of Southern armies inevitable. As one astute Rebel noted: "We are breaking our heads against a stone wall. We are bound to be conquered. We cannot keep it up much longer, against so powerful a nation as the U.S. of America. Crowds of Irish, Dutch, Scotch are pouring in to swell their armies."

The Confederacy's brilliant Secretary of State, Judah P. Benjamin, understood the implications of the ledger's imbalance.[15] One indignant Southerner made the historical analogy between the North's utilization of foreign-born troops with the British employment of mercenary allies during the American Revolution and War of 1812. He wrote that the North and "England will never hear the last of the 'Hessians,' nor of [the British] incitement of the Indians in 1812 on the Northwestern frontier."[16]

The Lincoln administration realized how Union victory rested upon the rapid replacement with immigrants of casualties suffered at Fredericksburg, Vicksburg, and Gettysburg. Many Federal units were decimated at the conflict's halfway point. Desertions were increasing; the three-year enlistments of most Federal troops would expire in 1864; a manpower crisis was imminent. Hence, the importance of Ireland's sons. The Green Isle was the Lincoln Government's largest potential manpower pool. Because of crop failures in the early 1860s, America's historic promises of a better life, and free passage to the New World in return for enlistment in the Union Army, Irish immigration to the North jumped dramatically in 1863. This exodus coincided with the highest depletion of Union armies.

Although exact figures are unknown, at least several hundred thousand Europeans served in Federal blue, a supplement that perhaps was the decisive factor eventually bringing Union victory. William H. Seward, Lincoln's Secretary of State, realized the critical importance of foreign recruits, writing that, "this civil war must be a trial between the two parties to exhaust each other. The immigration of a large mass from Europe would of itself decide it."[17] While the North had a healthy lifeline to Irish manpower, the South could only draw from a reserve of boys and elderly gentlemen. Union recruitment by agents, therefore, was pursued with a zeal in Ireland during 1863.[18]

This upsurge in Irish immigration to the North would prove crucial in the political field as well. The Union desperately needed battlefield victories during the military campaigns of 1864 to uplift a sagging morale. Success was necessary for Lincoln's reelection in late 1864 and a guaranteed prosecution of the war to the end. Secretary of State Benjamin, "the brains of the Confederacy," and President Davis understood the significance of the active Union solicitation and recruitment of immigrants in causing the "mysterious repletion" of Federal armies. President Davis, therefore, sought to combat this serious threat to the Confederacy during the pending decisive campaigns of 1864.[19]

Benjamin's efforts to stem the accelerated Union activity to secure "mercenary soldiers" in Ireland increased during the summer of 1863.[20] Twin Rebel defeats at Vicksburg and Gettysburg brought a new realism to Southern leadership. Benjamin, consequently, dispatched the Confederacy's first secret agent for Ireland service, Lt. James L. Capston. Lieutenant Capston's duty was to enlighten the Irish masses upon their future status as cannon fodder if they emigrated and accepted the lucrative enlistment bounties for military service. But an unknown military officer, while competent and an Ireland native, could not extensively reach the lower classes or the common Irish people.[21] To win the contest of high stakes for Irish manpower, the farmers, laborers, and workers needed to be convinced. These were the folk most likely to come to America and grab $500 cash inducements for Union Army service.[22]

To assist Capston and increase the Confederacy's chances for survival in this critical and little-known arena, a resourceful individual with an intimate understanding of Ireland's common folk was necessary for the increasingly vital "Irish mission." This candidate needed to have an extensive background in Ireland, a thorough knowledge of the everyday people, and must be highly respected by the populace to win the battle for hearts and minds.

Few men in all the South better met this unique set of requirements at such a critical moment in the Confederacy's lifetime than Chaplain Bannon, and this perfectly qualified priest from St. Louis was in Richmond without an assignment at this crucial time. Bannon, who knew intimately the Irish folk's deepest hopes and fears and how to reach them, was now available for duty in his native land. President Davis would not pass up the opportunity.[23]

After his arrival in Richmond, Father Bannon celebrated a late Sunday Mass on 30 August at the capital's Catholic cathedral, St. Peter's Church. His friend, Secretary of the Navy Mallory, was in attendance, and afterward Mallory met Bannon for the first time since he had assisted in securing his Confederate chaplain's commission the previous winter. This service by the Secretary of the Navy had allowed Bannon to remain in the army. Mallory asked Bannon and Bishop McGill to join him for tea that evening at his home on the city's northeast side. But before leaving the Bishop's residence for Mallory's house, Bannon was astounded to receive "a message from President Davis requesting him to come to the President's house."[24]

The priest traveled alone through the city to Richmond's eastern edge, the "Court End" district. Here, in a neighborhood of fine old homes on the bluffs above the James River, he went to the end of Clay Street and then entered the executive mansion for a meeting with President Davis. During the conference at the White House of the Confederacy, the President offered Bannon an important mission.

The new assignment called for going to Ireland alone to convince the Irish immigrants not to migrate to the North and enlist in the Union army. On this duty, Bannon would work undercover as a special secret agent of the Confederacy. The crisis was immediate. A Confederate Department of State order had stated: "Recent advices from the North indicate that the U.S. Government is about to make fresh efforts to induce the Irish laborers to emigrate to New York, the ostensible purpose being to get them as recruits for the Federal Army. It has, therefore, been deemed prudent to send Father Bannon" to the Emerald Isle in this critical endeavor to help stop the immigrant tide, which had swelled to seventy-five thousand Irishmen, for Mr. Lincoln's armies.[25]

During conversations with Davis and Benjamin in the next few days, Bannon brought up a brilliant strategy to enhance foreign recognition— the Confederacy's goal since the war's beginning. He proposed to the President that the South should attempt to gain recognition from Pope Pius IX. As Bannon later specified to Benjamin in writing of the missed opportunity, "The C.S.A. have neglected to enlist in their favor the sympathies of a power exerting a great moral influence on the peoples & governments of Europe."

Father Bannon's knowledge of the Irish masses provided him with a clear understanding of the mentality and psychology of the average Irishman. He had a keener awareness of the potential impact of the pope's influence than anyone else in the Richmond government. Where the Davis administration saw no major opportunity, Bannon spied an untapped gold mine.[26]

Bannon's formative years in Ireland and the priesthood and Confederate Service made him aware of what President Davis and Secretary of State Benjamin failed to fully understand—that the pope's recognition held infinite possibilities. By this means, the Confederacy could take the "moral" high ground that the North had garnered with the Emancipation Proclamation. In a liberal versus conservative clash, world opinion supported the human rights struggle for an oppressed minority rather than the self-determination of a majority in the South.

With much of the Confederacy's existence contingent upon foreign recognition, attempts to gain the approval of the head of the Catholic church should have been made in early 1861. This Vatican strategy employed in conjunction with the Confederacy's early initiatives toward securing recognition from Catholic Mexico might well have led to recognition from European powers. Even by the autumn of 1863, official moral support by the pope would draw Catholic nations closer to proclaiming the Confederacy a legitimate nation among the countries of the world. Catholic leaders and peoples of Europe could be turned, perhaps decisively, in favor of the South. Father Bannon felt that the pope's influence "may not only direct the opinion of the masses but influence the policy of governments." If only one of Europe's smallest Catholic countries, such as Belgium, could be swayed to offering recognition in response to the pope's recognition, then other nations might follow suit. As one Southerner predicted, "the very fact of Belgium stepping forward in the first instance to recognize the Southern Confederacy, would, if she did so, argue that the measure had been agreed upon as one of general European policy, and that it would be concurred in and supported by the joint policy and by the action, if necessary, of all. A recognition in this manner would be the most desirable that could be expected. It would not fail to be followed up at once by that of every considerable power in Europe."[27]

Perhaps only an intellectual soldier-chaplain of the Catholic faith could have understood the important possibilities in the pope's recognition. Overly pragmatic and provincial Southern statesmen, diplomats, and military leaders often overlooked the power of the emotional and psychological appeal of religion, especially in foreign countries. Missed opportunities were nothing new to the Confederate diplomatic corps. While the South won repeated victories on the battlefield, she suffered setbacks for years from ineffective statesmanship and diplomacy on the international front. Hence, Bannon's insightful and penetrating arguments convinced President Davis and Secretary of State Benjamin. Because Benjamin was sympathetic to Catholicism and open-minded to new ideas, Bannon was granted permission to go to Rome, on a mission to the pope before his Ireland assignment.[28]

His proposal seemed to hold almost limitless potential. Securing the pope's recognition for the new Southern republic could push France, the most likely large Catholic power to grant recognition, and other Catholic nations closer to bestowing legitimacy on the Confederacy. France was the key, for "without France," wrote one Southerner, even "[General George] Washington could not have done it [secure independence]." If France granted recognition, then Britain would follow, for they acted in harmony toward America's fratricidal conflict. With one diplomatic stroke at the Vatican, perhaps the young Southern nation might win the support of Spaniards, Bavarians, Frenchmen, Austrians, Prussians, and Portuguese and influence the opinions of other Catholics throughout the world, or so the suppositions went. By the midway point in the war, it was felt that Bannon's strategy was now the best chance to win foreign recognition and secure foreign aid.[29]

Since the "Principal Chambers of Commerce of France had memorialized the Emperor to recognize the Southern Confederacy," France might repeat its performance of the American Revolution by supplying decisive assistance to Americans in revolt.[30] According to the *Mobile Register*: "It is to France that we have reason to look for the first demonstration of right feeling toward us. As in the first revolution France was the friend of the wronged, so in this it would seem that she is to be the first to show justice, if not friendliness to the cause of right."[31]

Despite the mission's extreme importance, Bannon had not given President Davis and Secretary of State Benjamin an instant agreement to become a secret agent. Questions about the morality of a clandestine mission, forsaking his Missouri troops, and rigid religious dogma left Bannon with some doubt. "The Irish mission was altogether unexpected and accepted only after Dr. McGill's approval and advice," he wrote. After much personal debate, he accepted both confidential diplomatic ventures and transferred from the Confederate Army to special, or secret, service in the State Department.[32]

While at Richmond and before departing for his twin missions, Bannon met another exiled Missouri priest, Father T. J. M. Donnelly of St. Joseph. Besides his "Southern sympathies," Donnelly had been banished from Missouri for writing in behalf of two sisters, evidently of his congregation. The women were imprisoned "for shouting for Jeff Davis, and for sporting rebel colors at parties and in the streets" of the town. Word had leaked out in northwest Missouri that Father Donnelly was preaching against the United States. After banishment, Donnelly traveled from St. Louis to Mobile and subsequently to Richmond.[33]

Bannon found in him a kindred spirit. Both priests were persecuted by

Crayon portrait of Father
Bannon by Scholten, 1889
(Eleanor S. Brockenbrough
Library, The Museum of the
Confederacy, Richmond,
Virginia)

the government for their political beliefs.[34] After learning that the Missouri Brigade finally was exchanged in September of 1863, Bannon informed Donnelly of the Brigade chaplain vacancy, and Donnelly agreed to take Bannon's place with the Missourians. He would serve as the Brigade's chaplain during the Atlanta campaign.[35]

Bannon made his last preparations to embark upon his new career, reporting to Benjamin and Mallory for final instructions. Then, on the day before departure, the new agent drew money from the quartermaster department. He left Richmond on 9 September 1863, taking the railroad south. As if chary of writing that he had become a secret agent, Bannon's diary included few notations during the Richmond visit. Going with Bannon deeper into Dixie was the Missouri Brigade's new Catholic chaplain, Father Donnelly. Bannon and Donnelly parted company at Petersburg to pursue their respective new assignments, and Bannon continued his journey alone, heading south for the North Carolina coast.[36]

After a lengthy trip through Virginia and much of North Carolina, he finally reached his destination at Wilmington on 10 September. The Atlantic port city had been transformed from a quiet coastal community to a booming haven for Confederate blockade-runners. Wilmington was now a major port, receiving tons of arms and munitions run past Union warships to resupply the Confederacy. Like any bustling commercial town during a conflict, Wilmington was a rough-and-tumble port, and it, therefore, was with some risk that Bannon arrived in Wilmington with $1,500 in gold. This money was President Davis' payment to sustain the clergyman during his two missions.[37]

At Wilmington, Bannon prepared for his overseas duty. He carried with him Benjamin's orders dated 5 September 1863 to his superior, Henry Hotze. These orders specified the objectives of Bannon's diplomatic missions as secret agent.

> This letter will be handed to you by the Reverend John Bannon, who has been in service in our cause as the Chaplain of the gallant Missourians under General Price, and who, at my solicitation, has consented to proceed to Ireland and there endeavor to enlighten his fellow-countrymen as to the true nature of our struggle, and to satisfy them, if possible, how shocking to all the dictates of justice and humanity is the conduct of those who leave a distant country for the purpose of imbruing their hands in the blood of a people that has ever received the Irish emigrant with kindness and hospitality. Recent advices from the North indicate that the U.S. Government is about to make fresh efforts to induce the Irish laborers to emigrate to New York, the ostensible purpose being to employ them in railroad works, but the real object to get them as recruits for the Federal Army. It has, therefore, been deemed prudent to send Father Bannon. . . . If Father Bannon desires to go to Rome for the purpose of obtaining from the head of the Catholic Church such sanction of his purpose as may be deemed necessary to secure him a welcome among the Catholic clergy and laity of Ireland [he could do so].[38]

Bannon may have continued to have reservations about the mission's legitimate and moral nature. Benjamin was concerned about the quick transformation of a man of God to a secret agent engaged in undercover work and wrote to Bannon to alleviate troubles of conscience, "Your mission is, although secret, honorable." Benjamin informed the new agent that there could be no "room whatever for doubt or cavil."[39] But Secretary of State Benjamin had underestimated the resolve of Father Bannon and had no need to worry about his steadfastness.

After saying Mass and giving a sermon on Sunday, 13 September, in Wilmington, Bannon fell sick, the illness lingering apparently from the siege of Vicksburg. His remaining bedridden for the next several days placed the Ireland and Vatican missions in jeopardy. But two weeks later, on Sunday, 27 September, Bannon had recovered sufficiently to say Mass at Wilmington's main Catholic church. On the final day of September, he met with Patrick N. Lynch, bishop of Charleston and a native Irishman. Lynch, ironically, would later be named a special Confederate envoy to the Vatican after Bannon had made the initial contact with the pope.

By this time, Bannon may well have had in his possession a letter from President Davis to the pope, the first communication from the Confederate president to the Vatican. Bannon had not only proposed such a letter from Davis on 2 September but offered the ideas that became its contents. He had initiated these position points to "set forth the claims of the Southern States to the special sympathy of the Holy See, . . . because I know such sentiments & statements would not be without their weight & influence on the mind of the Sovereign Pontiff and that their reflection from such a center on the minds of the people of Ireland thro [through] the Bishops & priests of the Irish church would facilitate my mission" and win support from "the Catholic nations & peoples of the continent of Europe." Despite questionable health, the priest prepared for running the blockade and leaving America forever on a moonless night in early October of 1863.[40]

The dash through the blockade would be made on the *Robert E. Lee*, a famous blockade runner that had successfully run past the ring of Union vessels more than twenty times. In compiling a record as one of the South's most successful blockade runners, the "white painted, birdlike looking steamer" had transported black powder from the British West Indies and the Azores Islands into Wilmington. Bannon was assigned to a vessel appropriate to his mission's importance.[41]

Midnight on 3 October was chosen as the date of departure. The *Robert E. Lee* raced south down the coast and beside the reefs for Cape Fear, North Carolina, about twenty miles south of Wilmington, the jumping off point for slipping through the North's blockade of warships. During this trip along the North Carolina shoreline, Bannon met John Banister Tabb, a Virginia teen-ager and crewman of the *Robert E. Lee*. Bannon influenced the young man, causing him eventually to become a priest. Father Tabb later wrote that he had "learned of a few of the doctrines and practices of the Church . . . from Father Bannon, who went aboard with us on our trip to England."[42]

The *Robert E. Lee* steamed east from Cape Fear and into the Atlantic, making for the Bermuda Islands, neutral British territory. Upon reaching the town of Hamilton, directly east of Wilmington, Bannon and the crew relaxed. After replenishing stores, the Confederate ship steamed across the ocean toward Liverpool, accompanied by constant danger. A Union warship pursued the *Robert E. Lee* during a nervous ordeal for the Confederacy's newest secret agent. Capture would have been serious for Bannon, who now carried his orders, perhaps President Davis's letter, and other correspondence to the pope. Ironically, this would be the *Robert E. Lee's* last escape. She would be captured, along with the future Father Tabb, on the return journey to Wilmington.[43]

Father Bannon decided not to go directly to Ireland. As Benjamin's orders specified, Bannon had this discretion, the Secretary of State having allowed the priest an unusual amount of individual initiative. In a 4 September directive, Benjamin had stated: "If, in order fully to carry out the objects of the Government . . . you should deem it advisable to go to Rome for the purpose of obtaining such sanction from the sovereign pontiff as will strengthen your hands and give efficiency to your action, you are at liberty to do so."

Looming as an outside possibility, the more important mission of securing the pope's recognition of the Confederacy was absent from these orders. The secret nature of this enterprise confined the mission's orders to only a verbal directive from President Davis and Secretary of State Benjamin. To maintain secrecy, Bannon was not going as an official envoy to the Vatican.

Realizing diplomatic assistance now might better serve the Confederacy than altering the balances of manpower on the battlefield, Bannon promptly journeyed for Italy. Indeed "it was easy enough to get to Rome as he had been provided with money and letters of credit by the Confederate Government." The trip overland to Rome was difficult. Exact circumstances are not known, but on this journey Bannon "saved the life of a woman in danger" in the mountains of Italy. If the rescue resulted from an encounter with highwaymen, an Irish soldier-chaplain recently from the battlefields of America would not have been an easy victim.[44]

Bannon now became the first representative of the Confederate government to visit the Vatican and Pope Pius IX. During the long audiences with the pope, Bannon expounded arguments outlined by President Davis and Secretary of State Benjamin about the righteousness of the Confederate experiment in rebellion and the unscrupulous recruiting methods of the North. He supplemented these statements with many of his own opinions as well. In addition, he could have given Davis's letter to the pope. This written correspondence would be a means to open up further communications between the Confederate government and the Vatican. If Bannon did not now deliver Davis's letter, then it would later be forthcoming from another agent.

As no one else had, he succeeded in unlocking this potentially important diplomatic channel, and he left the Vatican with high hopes. He received "much encouragement" from Pope Pius IX regarding the recognition of the Confederacy. Bannon who "came away from his last meeting very much encouraged, was led to believe that if France would recognize the Confederate States that the Pope would join in." By meeting with the Pope Bannon also gained more legitimacy toward influencing the Celtic clergy and people of Ireland during his upcoming mission in his homeland. After more than a ten-year absence, and after surviving some of the most sanguinary battles of the war, Father Bannon was finally returning to the land of his birth.[45]

NINE Confederate Secret Agent in Ireland

AFTER HIS VATICAN MISSION, Bannon reported to Hotze in London during late October, his stay in England brief because the Ireland mission beckoned.[1] He at last set foot upon Irish soil at the end of October 1863. Upon arriving in Dublin, his boyhood home, he lodged with his brother. Evidently he made this decision to visit his relatives for the safety of more than $1,000 on his person, but he soon moved into the Angel Hotel in central Dublin. At this popular inn near the farmers' market, he could gauge sentiment among the middle class and clergy and gain their views on the fratricidal war in America.[2]

One of Father Bannon's first activities was to attend to a matter that took precedence over the Irish mission. He carried a small notebook containing the names of fifty or sixty native Irishmen of the Missouri Brigade who had died. Beside each name was listed his family's address, information that Bannon had taken down from the dying Confederates on the battlefields and in hospitals. He now wrote long letters to the farm families throughout the island.

In writing to Private McGolfe's family, for instance, Bannon told the artilleryman's mother how "her son had been mortally wounded at the battle of [Champion Hill], that I had attended him at his last moments, and could give her the consolation of knowing that he died happily." Later, he met with some of these families, expressing his condolences to the relatives.[3]

As an undercover agent, Bannon pursued his mission with enthusiasm. He recalled, "there was nothing in my dress to indicate my Priesthood."[4]

Ironically, when a civilian with the army he had worn a Rebel uniform, but now while a Confederate agent he wore the common clothes of his countrymen. Bannon would not work alone. Lieutenant Capston was still on assignment in Ireland.[5]

The priest soon learned the reality of the situation. More than the efforts of Federal recruiters, economic hard times were causing the exodus from the Emerald Isle, the same reason which caused the flight during the 1840s. Crop failures during 1861 and 1862 meant that thousands of poor Irish would continue pouring into the North for a better life.

Unfortunately for the Confederacy, social and economic conditions were the explanations for the mass migrations. Bannon, therefore, initially felt pessimistic about the chances for success in stemming the tide. As early as November, for instance, he reported to the Confederate State Department, "Every day proves the futility of the efforts made by clergy and laity, that this emigration cannot be stayed."[6]

But despite the gloomy assessment, Bannon embarked on his mission with a passion. If the overall exodus could not be stopped, then at least the numbers of immigrants headed into the Federal ranks could be slowed. By the third week in November, Bannon went "to the country to reconnoitre & avail myself of such occasions as may present of making [contacts] amongst the men of influence, clerics & laymen." Clearly, he understood his impact as a Celtic man of God among the masses.

One crucial ingredient to enhance his position further was still missing, however. If the Irish mission were to succeed, a latent Irish nationalism needed to be stimulated and then identified with Bannon's efforts. He discovered a solution by soliciting the aid of leaders of the "Young Ireland Movement" and shortly had these invaluable nationalist allies, "the Irish rebels of 1848," influencing the Irish people by a newspaper writing campaign. He understood how the "reliable leaders of the patriotic party [all] have the confidence of the country." According to Bannon, the two top pro-Southern "patriotic" leaders were "the Moses & Aaron of the Irish at home and abroad." He himself also produced editorials for periodicals under the pen name of "Sacerdos"—a name denoting the priesthood. In them he warned his people of the perils of enlistment in the Union army.[7]

The usefulness of his Vatican mission now manifested itself in two ways. First, his credibility among the Irish clergy and populace had been greatly increased. And, second, he could well employ the fact that the pope had indicated support toward the Confederacy's struggle during his two interviews, which were given much consideration by the pope.

Thanks to Bannon's overtures, Pope Pius IX reflected more on the American conflict. Throughout November and early December, the pope contemplated Bannon's statements and Davis's letter, which had been brought either by Bannon or by a new Confederate agent, A. Dudley Mann. Or perhaps both agents brought copies of the Davis letter to the pope to ensure its delivery.

In this remarkable communication of late September 1863, President Davis wrote that the Southern "people at whose hearthstones the enemy is now pressing the threats of dire oppression and merciless carnage are now and ever have been earnestly desirous that this wicked war shall cease, that we have offered at the footstool of Our Father who is in heaven prayers inspired by the same feelings which animated your Holiness; that we desire, no evil to our enemies, nor do we covet any of their possessions; but are only struggling to the end that they shall cease to devastate our land and inflict useless and cruel slaughter upon our people." These were desperate appeals to win the pope's support and recognition.[8]

The new official representative of the Confederacy to the Vatican was sent at Bannon's insistence that he should be dispatched to follow up on the priest's earlier success. Agent Mann gained an 11 November 1863 interview with Pope Pius IX.[9] Like Bannon, Mann felt that the Confederacy was "amply justified by the great American principles of self government proclaimed by their ancestors in 1776."[10] During the first meeting between Mann and the pope, the pontiff reiterated his pro-Southern leanings, first expressed to Bannon.[11] Again the pope proclaimed an "unbounded admiration of the wonderful powers which we had exhibited in the field of resistance to a war which had been prosecuted with an energy, aided by the employment of all the recent improvements in the instruments for the destruction of life and property, unparalleled, perhaps, in the world's history."[12] This tantalizing expression of support seemed to lean toward recognition.

Mann's discussions with the pope continued throughout November. The interviews caused the agent to declare to the Secretary of War: "Thus I am exceedingly hopeful that before [the] spring [of 1864] our independence will be generally acknowledged" by the pope, then by Europe. Father Bannon was elated by such a possibility.[13]

The Catholic Church flirted with the recognition of the Confederacy in early December 1863, when the pope responded to Davis's September letter and the initiatives of Bannon and Mann. Pope Pius IX addressed this communication "to the Illustrious and Honorable Jefferson Davis, President of the Confederate States of America." The first line of his letter, in Latin, alluded to Father Bannon: "We have lately received with all kindness, as was meet, the gentlemen [Father Bannon and Mann] sent by your Excellency to present to us your letter dated on the 23d of last September. . . . And it has been gratifying to us to recognize . . . that you and your people are animated by the same desire for [a settled] peace and tranquillity. . . . We indeed shall not cease with most fervent prayer to beseech God, the best and highest, and to implore Him to pour out the spirit of Christian love and peace upon all the people of America, and to rescue them from the great calamities with which they are afflicted." The pope, leader of the Holy Roman Church, had addressed Davis as the President of the Confederate States of America.[14]

Because the South went down in defeat, modern historians have underestimated the potential opportunities for the Confederacy with the Vatican connection. Many Southerners equated the pope's letter with an official acknowledgment of the Davis government. Mann wrote a letter to Richmond, reporting: "Thus we are acknowledged, by as high an authority as this world contains, to be an independent power of the earth."[15] He later recorded from London: "In all intelligent British circles our recognition by the sovereign Pontiff is considered as formal and complete."[16]

The Union was enraged by the pope's letter. One Northern journalist wrote: "There is a tone in it that will not win the Pope favor with loyal Americans . . . in fact he betrays a sympathy which he, of all foreign rulers, ought to be the last to entertain." Bannon gained comfort from knowing that he had helped mastermind a strategy that enhanced the prospects of foreign recognition, but the Emancipation Proclamation had strengthened the ties between the pope and the Lincoln administration. The North had stolen the moral high ground from the South's concept of self-determination by espousing a crusade for human rights by 1863. Perhaps more important was the Confederacy's inability to win a decisive battlefield victory, which eliminated any real chance for foreign recognition.

In Ireland, meanwhile, Bannon stressed how young Irishmen were tricked by the promise of jobs in America; instead they were destined for the Northern armies and perhaps deaths on Southern battlefields. But he needed a broader medium than personal talks by which to spread his message. He understood by late 1863 that all the editorials by him and the popular nationalist leaders could never reach the lower class—those people for the large part illiterate and most likely to migrate to America. Only the upper and middle classes could afford newspapers and periodicals.[17] Thus, he altered his role to meet circumstances. He quit his passive strategy of remaining largely behind the scenes by writing under the sobriquet of "Sacerdos" and took a much more active role, planning an extensive information blitz. He duplicated his arguments made in public on "broadsheets . . . for circulation among leaders & broadsheets for posting at church doors and elsewhere."[18] In addition, some two thousand circulars, or handbills, were distributed at Ireland's most important ports of departure.[19] Hundreds of these delivered to "only the young able bodied emigrant" as he stood on the docks before the journey to America would have a wide impact. In addition, the handbills would be posted on "the boarding houses usually occupied by expectant emigrants." His handbill read:

> It is well authenticated that many an Irish Emigrant on landing at the other side of the Atlantic, is set up, cajoled, and enticed away, to swell the ranks of the Federal Army. The moment that an Emigrant Ship reaches the port of America, the unpretending Emigrant, full of warm and friendly feelings to the Country, is persuaded by interested Agents to declare his intention to become a Citizen (as they term it, a REAL AMERICAN); after his declaration being made, according to the late Act of Congress, he comes under the CONSCRIPTION LAW [the Enrollment Act of March 1862].
>
> And no alternative is left. He becomes a SOLDIER. In 48 hours he is landed in the Swamps of Carolinas, or on the Sand Bars of Charleston. There to imbrue his hands in THE BLOOD OF HIS COUNTRYMEN, and fight for a People that has the greatest antipathy to his birth and creed.
>
> Let Irishmen remember the fate of MEAGHER's Brigade, on the bloody field of Fredericksburg, 5,000 strong! now no more; and were refused permission to reorganize; some of the New York Papers stating that they could afford to lose a few thousand of the scum of the Irish.[20]

The Battle of Fredericksburg, Virginia, in December of 1862, provided Bannon with his best example of the slaughter of the Irish. Gen. Thomas Francis Meagher had led his Irish brigade against Confederate fortifications on Marye's Heights, where they had charged magnificently up the slopes with green banners flying. But courage had not been enough at bloody Fredericksburg. The Irish, primarily from New York City, were cut to pieces, more than five hundred of them being lost during the suicidal attacks. Bannon's success in propagandizing this debacle was important in shaping public opinion.[21]

Some one thousand of the handbills were hurried to his co-agent, Capston, who would distribute them throughout Queenstown. Another five hundred, went to Galway, on Ireland's west coast. These were circulated among those Irish ready to embark to the United States. Bannon himself passed around the remaining five hundred in Dublin and other locations.[22]

So widespread was the knowledge that the immigrant Irish were bolstering the Union armies that a Southern newspaperman decried their fate. The editorial appealed to Ireland's dormant independence movement, which was losing its revolutionary manpower to Rebel bullets: "And the green flags lie torn on many a battle-field, and the bones of those who were to liberate Ireland whiten the plains of the continent from Galveston to the Potomac. It is pity to them; yet; they deserved their fate. They were prompt to carry fire and sword into the peaceful abodes of a people who had never wronged them, and to make an Ireland of these Confederate States. . . . It was a crime sure to bring its own punishment."[23]

This editorial echoed Bannon's views. Since Irishmen in blue were engaged in an aggressive, "HOLY AND CRUEL WAR" of invasion, he felt that he was saving Irish souls by keeping them out of such a devil's scheme to crush the Southern people.[24] He was also motivated by the desire to continue helping the comrades in gray he had left behind. Consequently, he tried desperately to stop the immigrant exodus to the North.

Besides the handbills, Bannon's other strategy to reach the lower classes about to emigrate was to utilize the large posters, which could be read aloud to the illiterate. These broadsheets were nailed up on the boarding houses of perhaps such western Ireland seaports as Mal Bay, Kerry Head, Bertraghboy Bay, and Bantry and, in addition, were put upon the doors of Dublin's churches. Across the poster, Bannon printed the words of the Irish nationalists whom he had cultivated. This was a masterful stroke, for the common people looked upon these revolutionaries as their nation's saviors, who would deliver the Irish country from the British yoke.

His most effective poster was conceived in late 1863 but was not completed until January of 1864, for it was contingent upon the success of Bannon's earlier efforts. To Bannon, it seemed that Pope Pius IX had given his full support to the Confederacy, and now the pope's sympathies further justified Bannon's Ireland mission. This poster was his masterpiece. It included the pope's letter, President Davis's letter, and a Bannon letter all in one large poster almost three feet square.

To catch the immigrant's attention, the poster was entitled in bold print, "The Letters of Pope Pius IX on the War in America." Such a combined political, psychological, and religious punch made the average

Irishman think again about the wisdom of going to America. Bannon had fused Irish nationalism and religion with the South's interests. So convincing was the new poster that twelve thousand were printed.[25]

Because of the inroads that he had made with the Celtic clergy, he now developed a sound strategy to spread the poster's message beyond the thousands of Irish gathered at the seaports. To reach the most people possible by the most effective means, he decided to send the poster to "each parish priest in Ireland." The target consisted of three thousand clergymen from all across the island, a means by which to get the word to the most obscure rural peoples, who were those most likely to go to America.

By this time, Bannon had discovered that the upper and middle classes were "all with us," but the common people remained "ignorant" of the nature of the war in America. An intensive educational campaign, therefore, needed to be conducted. So completely did Bannon believe in this stratagem of appealing directly to a powerful moral force to influence the common people that he used his own money to send not one, but two, copies to each of "the priests of the Kingdom."[26] He also gave each parish priest a personal letter emphasizing the potential dangers for their parishioners in America. The letter was composed by Bannon apparently during his trip across the Atlantic and given to Pope Pius IX in Rome.

Each Irish priest could now verify the truthfulness of Bannon's claims, for they were magnified in importance by the pope himself. Bannon added further credence to the letter by visiting many of Ireland's priests to stress his opinions and tell them of the pope's pro-Southern sympathy as expressed to him at the Vatican.[27] By this method, he hoped to educate each cleric who would then inform his congregation about Bannon's views of the American war: the immoral recruiting practices; the death awaiting Ireland's sons across the South; the unholy war to destroy the South against the pope's will; the facing of other Irishmen while they were in blue uniforms, perhaps even relatives, in Confederate gray.

The impact of hearing this message from the priests would have a great effect on the Irish people because this strategy would circulate the arguments of his "Address to the Catholic Clergy and People of Ireland" among a rural, religious population.[28]

In the poster, Bannon emphasized the historic analogies to the American Revolution of the Confederacy's struggle. He stressed how the last "remnant of Christian civilization [was] yet dominant in the South," for in his view, true Christianity had disappeared throughout the remainder of

America. To support his position, he cited examples that he personally knew to be true: the Nativist riots against the Irish people in St. Louis that he had witnessed; and the May morning in 1861, when Federal soldiers felled nearly one hundred civilians during the Camp Jackson shooting. He and fellow priests were persecuted during the Nativist Movement, and he had become a target of Union authorities because of his Southern sympathies in 1861. Further, Southern Catholic churches had been wrecked by Protestant bluecoats, he wrote, including those houses of worship at Vicksburg and Jackson where he had preached.

After listing proof, he thought, of the Union's alleged infidelity, he then delivered his masterstroke. "As a priest of the Catholic Church, I am anxious to see the desires of the Holy Father realized speedily, and therefore have taken this means [the poster] to lay before you the expression of his sentiments on the subject of the American War, knowing that no Catholic will persevere in the advocacy of an aggression condemned by his Holiness."[29]

As projected, Bannon's poster hit Ireland like a bombshell. Even he was shocked with the amazing "results of my circular . . . throughout the country." An enlightenment, or "a great revolution" wrote Bannon, swept the island. Now fewer Irishmen would be vulnerable to Northern recruitment because the sympathies of the common people had swung toward the Confederacy. His and the pope's words, moreover, were successful in winning over not only most of the parish priests, but also the bishops.[30]

Hotze was astounded by the effectiveness of Bannon's efforts and heaped praise upon the priest. In addition, Hotze sent money to cover his personal expenditures for the posters. In Hotze's words, Father Bannon "has certainly proved himself admirably well qualified for his duties; he has tempered a noiseless industry and devoted zeal with sound discretion."[31]

Secretary of State Benjamin also wrote a tribute to Bannon for his accomplishments: "I am much gratified with the zeal, discretion, and ability displayed by the Rev. Mr. Bannon in the service undertaken by him."

Bannon's accomplishments represent the most important diplomatic success achieved by the Confederacy in Ireland. More than ever before, the common Irishman gained an awareness about the fate of many Irish immigrants who joined the Federal army. To the young men of County Kerry and Cork, the Union fiasco at Fredericksburg had new meaning—a symbol of God's retribution and an example of the United States government's employment of Irish bodies as cannon fodder. Fewer Irish immigrants would wear Federal blue in the future.[32]

Winning over the Irish clergy to his cause had been no easy task, for pro-Northern sentiment had dominated the island since the beginning of the war.[33] Now thousands of the all-important middle men, the Irish clergy, with the strongest ties to the people's hearts and minds, convinced by Bannon, became his megaphones. These enthusiastic recruits in vestments broadcasted Bannon's agenda. "With only few exceptions the Parish Priests had complied with my suggestions and explained to their people" the situation, Bannon wrote. Only a Catholic priest originally from Ireland could have tapped such a heretofore unexploited resource and achieved such a difficult goal.

With the success of the poster, Bannon established himself as the most capable and successful Confederate secret agent not only in Ireland, but in Europe as well. The exact extent of his success cannot accurately be ascertained—no measurements can be made of the number of people who had stayed in Ireland because of his efforts. It is impossible also to tally the exact numbers of Irishmen who refused to join the Union Army after Bannon's educational campaign. But many fewer Irishmen were now acquired by Federal recruiters in Dublin and at other locations. Indeed Hotze claimed that the annual average of sixty-five thousand Irish recruits for Union armies dropped by two-thirds from December 1863 to May 1864.

The main struggle to influence European sentiment and stem the exodus to America had been contested in Ireland. Bannon had accomplished perhaps as much as had been possible in keeping Irishmen from becoming clogs in the North's military machine. Additionally, even though the Confederacy was not recognized by any foreign power, Bannon's efforts to win recognition through his Vatican initiatives brought that possibility closer to reality than at any other time after Antietam, the Emancipation Proclamation, and Gettysburg.

Most significantly, this original strategy had been conceived and initiated by Father Bannon. An Irish chaplain from the battlefields of the West had orchestrated an innovative effort to secure foreign recognition at a time when the Confederacy had run out of initiatives. Perhaps the South might have gained the foreign recognition necessary for independence from Bannon's brilliant strategy had he conducted his diplomatic mission in 1861 instead of in 1863–1864. Previous historians have underestimated the significance of Bannon's contribution to the Confederacy's diplomatic effort and have ignored his role as an architect of a masterful strategy to secure foreign recognition for the Southern nation.

But despite his slowing of the Irish tide to America, the flood of Irishmen would continue, largely for reasons beyond the control of Confederate secret agents. His success, nevertheless, seems more remarkable because comparable Union efforts to increase Irish migrations were part of a superior organization with more personnel, experience, and money.[34]

Reflecting the poster's success, members of the Irish clergy now sought out Bannon, verifying that one of his most important objectives had been achieved. For the first time, Ireland's most respected priests made overtures to Bannon, imploring him to come to their churches and speak to the people himself. These clergymen saw the urgent need to have their parishioners enlightened by the ex-Confederate chaplain from across the sea. Naturally he accepted all such invitations and embarked upon a lengthy tour throughout Ireland during February of 1864.[35]

Father Bannon's efforts brought about a transformation of thought that caused a slowdown of the numbers of Irishmen bound for the Union armies.[36] During an interview on Bannon's tour, a common Irishman explained the shift in public opinion: "We who were all praying for the North at the opening of the war, would willingly fight for the South if we could get there."[37] An alerted Irish clergy now complained loudly to the pope that the Lincoln government was rapidly "using up the Irish in the war like dogs."[38] By April of 1864, Bannon felt confident that the youth of Ireland had been educated on the realities of Union recruitment and the war in America—that he had sparked a revolution in popular opinion. On 9 March 1864, less than six months since beginning his Ireland mission, he reported his success. "The people [now] sympathize with the South, the priesthood advocated the Southern cause, and little more is required than to allow the leaven to work, and should the Federal and Confederate recruiting officers be allowed to enter the field of competition for recruits within a month from now the Southern cause would attract four-fifths of the material."[39]

But the Confederacy would never utilize the Irish resource that Bannon had cultivated. Unlike the North, the South did not exploit this Irish resource in manpower to fill her decimated ranks during a war of attrition. For the all-important 1864 campaigns that would determine the war's course, the Confederacy could muster only a third of the enemy force that invaded her territory.[40]

Even though Bannon realized that he had succeeded in his mission, he continued to work as hard as ever. Another poster campaign, some seven thousand more, and a tour throughout the countryside to talk to additional people and priests began in March.[41] His continued efforts helped ignite in the British Parliament further debates on the righteousness of the Confederate nation's struggle. Supplied with information from Bannon, these pro-Southern House of Commons members raised the emotional, moral, and legal issue of Northern recruitment on Irish soil.

Additionally he was instrumental in exposing a Boston-based recruiting agent in Dublin, an agent who had long lured Irishmen into Federal service with false promises of railroad work in America. By publicizing the story, Bannon influenced more young Irishmen not to fall victim to the Northern recruiters.[42]

Clearly, by this time, he had accomplished nearly all that one man could do. Now another mission and another phase of his life were finished. Bannon realized that "the object of my mission had been successfully accomplished, and a great change wrought in the sentiments of the Irish clergy & people regarding the merits of the southern question." Then, on 28 May 1864, Bannon reported to the Confederate Secretary of State Benjamin: "I see not what remains for me to accomplish in Ireland— Priests and Bishops are instructed on the social and moral evils awaiting the emigrant in America, they are opposed to the emigration and laboring to check it. They are informed of the mode of Federal enlistment and disgusted with the details, are warning and cautioning their people against the knavery of prigs and primps. They are the most influencing class in Ireland, and have assumed the task of counteracting any future emissaries of the Federal government. My money is exhausted—my mission accomplished."[43]

Father Bannon left his work in capable hands after having erected a sturdy foundation. With his duty completed, he was joined by Bishop Lynch in Dublin near the end of May. Lynch, now a Confederate commissioner to the Vatican, linked with Bannon because of his earlier initiatives to the pope. The two planned a visit to the pope, and Bannon's return to the Vatican probably occurred in June 1864. Once again, the Confederacy's recognition was sought, but nothing developed from this visit. The Lincoln Administration's threat to wage war on France or England if either recognized the Confederacy, and the inevitability of Southern defeat in addition to the effect of the Emancipation Proclamation had established

Father Bannon after the war in the Jesuit Order in Ireland (Father
William Barnaby Faherty Collection, St. Louis, Missouri)

an insurmountable barrier against the pope's recognition. Bannon's initiative had been too late to help rescue the Confederacy from destruction.[44]

Because of the ever-tightening Federal naval blockade, Bannon never
returned to the Confederacy. After his second trip to Rome, he returned to
his native Ireland. Since the Missouri Brigade had Father Donnelly and
Ireland had an informed clergyman to carry on his work, he now devoted
his life completely to God once more. There would be no more wars,
adventures or secret missions for Bannon. Since 1861, Father Bannon, now
age thirty-five, had packed a lifetime of experiences in only two and a half
years.

He joined the Jesuit Order at Milltown Park, Ireland, on 26 August 1864. While at the Jesuit institution and unknown to him, "the Confederate Congress [enacted] a vote of thanks for my success in stopping the recruiting in Ireland, & voted me $3,000 as a bonus." This acknowledgment was appropriate, because Father Bannon's Vatican and Ireland missions were as distinguished as any in Confederate diplomatic history.[45]

While he studied theology and learned of Jesuit life, his adopted Southern nation finally succumbed in the spring of 1865. The Confederacy was no more, and Bannon's life in the United States had ended forever. Because of his Confederate service, he was banned by law from preaching at his St. John the Apostle and Evangelist Church. No doubt he would have refused to take the oath of allegiance in order to return to the pulpit in St. Louis. "Thus was lost to Saint Louis this heroic and goodly Priest," lamented one St. Louisan. Bannon elected to remain in Dublin to stay close to his surviving relatives, his father and brother.[46]

For decades, he would find a spiritual home with the Jesuit Order, enjoying a new-found contentment far away from the horrors of war. He lived most of the remainder of his life at the St. Francis Xavier Parish Rectory. As much as he tried to avoid it, Bannon continued to garner fame. In 1869, he formed a Missionary team, which toured Ireland to spread the word of God. For a year and a half, he made a continuous circuit, preaching at every parish in Ireland for two-week periods. He became "one of the best-known Jesuits in the Ireland of his time and his pastoral influence was enormous."

Throughout the 1870s, Bannon won renown as the "greatest preacher" in Ireland. Hard work and dedication led to his appointment as Superior of St. Francis Xavier's at Dublin in 1884. He held this position through 1889. In addition, he served more than forty years as a Director of a spiritual organization for the leading businessmen of Dublin.[47] He had easily reentered and thrived in the religious community and academic environment that he loved so much. The Civil War years had been only a brief interlude.

But those turbulent war days in America would never be forgotten. Consequently, the deeds of Bannon's Confederate comrades at Pea Ridge, Farmington, Iuka, Corinth, Grand Gulf, Port Gibson, Champion Hill, and Vicksburg would be told and retold with much relish to the young students destined for the priesthood. These exciting narratives generated so much enthusiasm that Father Bannon's superior demanded that the story-telling cease. From that day, lamented one Novice, the reminiscences of the "Fighting Chaplain" were "not to be repeated."[48]

When his stories ended, Bannon kept the emotions of his war days bottled up deep inside. But the battlefield, camp, and religious episodes enacted in Missouri, Arkansas, Tennessee, Mississippi, and Alabama could not be dismissed from his mind as the years passed. Often upon viewing the green, rolling countryside of Ireland, the former Rebel envisioned the martial sights of a past saga in faraway America. Too many never-to-be-forgotten scenes and the faces of deceased comrades flooded emotions, transforming the memory of his chaplain years into an obsession as sacred as Christianity. Like many combat veterans, he tried hard to block out the pain, sacrifice, and passion of the 1860s.

The individuals and events of the war years had an even greater impact on him than his religious experiences. The reality that America's sectional war was the high point in his life was perhaps a disturbing realization for a man who had devoted his existence to religion. After being sent 1880s newspaper clippings of the memoirs of Missouri Confederates, Father Bannon wrote, "So vividly, so sensibly did the details narrated bring back the scenes before my mind that I often started from a revery, relieved to find it was only a dread reality." Haunted by the War for Southern independence, Bannon wrote near his life's end an emotional letter to an ex-Brigade member:

> I often wander back in thought to St. Louis and the South and all the friends of days gone by. General Bowen and the First Missouri, General Little of the [First] Missouri Brigade, Wade's Artillery, Guibor's, Mc-Donald's, Landis', and Bledsoe's Batteries and all the officers, yourself too, with many others I shall never see again, until we meet in [the after life].
>
> Tis a sad memory that "Lost Cause" and all its varied incidents. Yet, tho' sad I would not blot it from my memory or expunge it from my life, for it made me acquainted with brave and honorable men, of high spirit, great endurance and generous natures, whom I am proud to remember as companions and friends. Many of them are passed away, and the few who remain are scattered so far apart and so seldom meet, that a note or a paper or other message from an old companion in arms is to me like a message from another world, so long ago does it seem last we met and interchanged a greeting.
>
> A few years more and we too will have passed away and become a memory, only like others have gone before. To make use of the present as men about to die, whose only passport to Paradise shall be the record of their virtues is true wisdom. Praying you may be judged by its teachings is the wish of
>
> Faithfully yours,
> John Bannon, S.J.[49]

Lamenting the many lost opportunities of the war, Father Bannon wrote in 1895 of recalling the many old "comrades and friends, brave, faithful and generous, whose cherished names are still enshrined in my heart." And he was not forgotten by the soldiers who stood by his side in battle. He "was still fresh in the hearts of his comrades after twenty years of peace," wrote one Rebel. Because his mission to Ireland was secret, few Brigade members knew of Bannon's life after he departed parole camp in Alabama during the summer of 1863. One Confederate officer, Joseph Boyce, for instance, wrote that "right after the siege of Vicksburg Father Bannon disappeared; and, it was a long time before we could find out what had become of him."[50]

A Confederate veterans' organization in St. Louis sent an ex-Brigade member and Irishman to "convey to the Rev. John Bannon, now of Dublin, Ireland, the compliments of this association, and to assure that distinguished clergyman that we still hold in grateful remembrance his bravery in the field and his unselfish devotion to Christian duty, both on the field of battle and in the camp."[51]

Whenever a former Missouri Brigade veteran was in Europe, he sought out Father Bannon. These occasional visitors may have expected him to be yet leading as adventurous a life as during the war years, but Bannon was no longer the same man in body, soul, or spirit. Compared to his religious peers, there now seemed a greater wisdom, a lost innocence, and fatalism about the Civil War veteran, who had once been known as the Confederacy's "Fighting Chaplain."

Something incalculable had left Bannon forever—an intangible quality which could not be ascertained or replaced. With the demise of so much that he once held so dear: his Southern nation, Generals Little and Bowen, Captains Clark and Wade, Colonel Rives, Lieutenant Farrington, and so many others, those days could not be severed from Bannon's mind and soul, anymore than could religion.

During these visits from comrades, however, the old fire last seen in the American conflict could be briefly rekindled. On these occasions Bannon and a visiting ex-Missouri Brigade member often "talked for hours, and the old brigades and regiments and batteries passed before us like a panorama."[52] Then upon separating for the final time, Bannon emotionally blessed each old friend, whom he knew he would never see again for a fatal disease, no doubt from the war years, was slowly killing him. When he knew the end was near, Father Bannon unexpectedly gave his Civil War diary, Confederate chaplain's commission, and other war-related items to a visiting American scholar with his blessings.

Perhaps when by himself and lonely on a cold winter night in Ireland toward the end of his life, the aged and sickly priest might have allowed himself to wonder how the Confederate experiment in nationhood might have fared had he been more successful in his dual missions to save the South in 1863–1864. Could the South have been rescued from destruction by foreign recognition initiated by the Vatican in early 1864? If so, then the efforts of Father Bannon would have catapulted him out of obscurity and into a gallery of founding fathers of an independent and democratic nation. Staying true to his Southern beliefs to the end, Bannon died in Dublin on the morning of 14 July 1913. As could be expected, "he never lost his admiration for the confederacy which he had served" so faithfully.[53]

His death sent a pall of gloom over much of Ireland. More than eighty priests of all orders and dioceses throughout Ireland attended his funeral Mass. A fellow Jesuit wrote one of seemingly countless tributes forthcoming from America and Ireland: "Many will have cause to regret in his loss a true friend, a generous benefactor, a wise and comforting adviser. But to his brothers in religion, to those who knew him in the intimacy of his daily life, his memory will remain as that of a man of deeply religious feeling, of profound humility and simplicity of character and, added to great strength of will, a heart as tender as a mother's."

In St. Louis, a requiem Mass for Father Bannon was offered on the sweltering morning of 14 August at St. John the Apostle and Evangelist. Many old Confederate comrades paid their last respects to the priest they loved as a brother. Bannon's death on the eve of World War I was felt deeply on both sides of the Atlantic. He had written his last words to his ex-Rebel comrades in honesty, love, and respect. In the peaceful years after the conflict, he had longed for one last opportunity to make a final sacrifice, despite a life dedicated to God and a world without war: "Yet, for the same men, for their spiritual consolation and salvation, would I again face the same weary marches, vigils and privations, persuaded I would be discharging a duty acceptable to God; religion and humanity, whether ministering to federal or confederate; but surely so when tending to the devoted men of Missouri and St. Louis, whose kindly smile and warm grasp, generous welcome and friendly co-operation so constantly and unfailingly aided me in my ministrations."[54]

NOTES

ONE An Irish Priest in America

1. "A Famous Chaplain Was Rev. John Bannon," in Billon Scrapbook, vol. 2, Missouri Historical Society, St. Louis (hereafter MHS); John Bannon Sketch, Confederate Museum, Richmond.

2. Albert Castel, *General Sterling Price and the Civil War in the West* (Baton Rouge: Louisiana State University Press, 1968), 139; "Rev. John Bannon," *Confederate Veteran* 21 (September 1913):451; *New Orleans Picayune*, 11 Aug. 1901; Ephraim McDowell Anderson, *Memoirs: Historical and Personal; Including the Campaigns of the First Missouri Confederate Brigade*, ed. Edwin Cole Bearss (1868; reprint ed., Dayton: Morningside, 1972), ix–x; Compiled Service Records of Confederate General and Staff Officers and Nonregimental Enlisted Men, National Archives, Washington, D.C. (hereafter Service Records); "A Famous Chaplain," Billon Scrapbook; Bannon Sketch, Confederate Museum, Richmond; "The Restoration of St. John's," *Bulletin of the Missouri Historical Society* 13 (April 1957):336.

3. Sidney J. Romero, *The Rebel Chaplain: Religion in the Rebel Ranks* (Lanham, Md.: University Press of America, 1983), 28; Reverend Benjamin J. Blied, *Catholics in the Civil War* (Milwaukee: private printing, 1945), 110; Bell Irvin Wiley, *The Life of Johnny Reb: The Common Soldier in the Confederacy* (Baton Rouge: Louisiana State University Press, 1978), 234–35; Charles F. Pitts, *Chaplains in Gray: The Confederate Chaplains' Story* (Nashville: Broadman Press, 1957), 2.

4. Joseph Boyce, "Rev. John Bannon—Chaplain Price's Missouri Confederate Division" (Paper Read 8 Mar. 1914 at Confederate Veteran Meeting, Camp 731, St. Louis, United Confederate Veterans), MHS, n.p. (hereafter Boyce 1914 Paper); *Mobile Daily Advertiser and Register*, 19, 23, and 24 Jan. 1864; Robert S. Bevier,

History of the First and Second Missouri Confederate Brigades, 1861–1865 and From Wakarusa to Appomattox, a Military Anagraph (St. Louis: Bryan, Brand and Co., 1879), 107, 130, 136, 145; *Weekly Mississippian* (Jackson), 17 and 20 Nov. 1862, 4 Jan. 1863; *Mobile Register and Advertiser*, 9, 19, and 24 Jan. 1864; Walter A. Roher, "Confederate Generals: The View from Below," *Civil War Times Illustrated* (Harrisburg, Pa.: July 1979), 13.

5. Boyce 1914 Paper, MHS; Rev. Laurence J. Kenny and Joseph P. Morrissey, "Father John Bannon, S.J.," *Historical Records and Studies of the United States Historical Society* 26 (1936):93–94.

6. Mark Wyman, *Immigrants in the Valley: Irish, Germans, and Americans in the Upper Mississippi Country, 1830–1860* (Chicago: Nelson-Hall, 1983), 20–23, 31; Gearold O'Tuathaigh, *Ireland Before the Famine 1798–1848* (Dublin: Gill and Macmillan, 1972), 130–33; Edward Norman, *A History of Modern Ireland* (London: Allen Lane, 1971), 23–25; Theodore William Moody and F. Martin, eds., *The Course of Irish History* (Cork: Mercier Press, 1967), 189–93, 218–19, 248–49; Erich Strauss, *Irish Nationalism and British Democracy* (New York: Columbia University Press, 1951), 2–15.

7. Boyce 1914 Paper, MHS; *St. Louis Missouri Republican*, 1 Aug. 1913; Daisy E. LaGrave, "The Artist Unknown and a Missing Diary: A Report Presenting Certain Selected Data in the History of St. John's Church, St. Louis, Missouri, October 1960," St. John's Church Archives, St. Louis; Fergus O'Donoghure, S. J., Dublin, Ireland, to author, 23 Mar. 1990; Collection of John Bannon material from William and Sarah Fetherston, County Dublin, Ireland.

8. Kenny and Morrissey, "Father John Bannon, S.J.," 96; Wyman, *Immigrants in the Valley*, 20; William Barnaby Faherty, *The Catholic Ancestry of Saint Louis* (St. Louis: Bureau of Information, Archdiocese of Saint Louis, 1965), 27; Norman, *History of Modern Ireland*, 13, 47–51, 76–78; Moody and Martin, eds., *Course of Irish History*, 217–18, 249–50; Strauss, *Irish Nationalism and British Democracy*, 2–15, 38–46, 133–34; Daniel J. O'Neil, *Three Perennial Themes of Anti-Colonialism: The Irish Case* (Denver: University of Denver Press, 1976), 3–5, 18–20; R. V. Comerford, "Nation, Nationalism, and the Irish Language," in Thomas H. Hackey and Lawrence J. McCaffrey, eds., *Perspectives on Irish Nationalism* (Lexington: University of Kentucky, 1989), 20–24.

9. Boyce 1914 Paper, MHS.

10. Kenny and Morrissey, "Father John Bannon, S. J.," 93; Norman, *History of Modern Ireland*, 104; Deirdre Hamill, Trinity College Library, Dublin, Ireland, to author, 5 Mar. 1990.

11. Ibid.

12. Wyman, *Immigrants in the Valley*, 20–25; Strauss, *Irish Nationalism*, 80–82; Richard Davis, *The Young Ireland Movement* (Dublin: Gill and Macmillan, 1987), 230–64; Moody and Martin, *Course of Irish History*, 263–74; O'Tuathaigh, *Ireland Before the Famine*, 203–27, 135–39; Norman, *History of Modern Ireland*, 108–37.

13. Kenny and Morrissey, "Father John Bannon, S.J.," 96; Martin G. Towey, "Kerry Patch Revisited: Irish Americans in St. Louis in the Turn of the Century Era," in Timothy J. Meagher, ed., *From Paddy to Studs: Irish-American Communities in the Turn of the Century Era* (Westport, Conn.: Greenwood Press, 1986), 139; Fergus O'Donoghue, S.J., Dublin, Ireland, to author, 23 Mar. 1990; Deirdre Hamill to author, 5 Mar. 1990.

14. Boyce 1914 Paper, MHS.

15. Towey, "Kerry Patch Revisited," 139–41; *From Kerry Patch to Little Paderborn: A Visit in the Irish-German Communities of Nineteenth Century St. Louis* (St. Louis: Landmarks Association of St. Louis, 1966), 4–6; *St. Louis Missouri Republican*, 22 Oct. 1911; Miscellaneous Papers and Newspaper 1949 Articles about Kerry Patch, Frank O'Hare Papers, MHS; 1953 Reminiscences of William G. Eliot, Jr., William G. Eliot Papers, MHS; Dorothy Breen Neuman, "Kerry Patch—A Changing Neighborhood," undated typescript, MHS; John T. Scharf, *History of St. Louis City and County from the Earliest Period to the Present Day*, 2 vols. (Philadelphia: Louis H. Everts and Co., 1883), 1:166; James Neal Primm, *Lion of the Valley: St. Louis, Missouri* (Boulder: Pruett Publishing Co., 1981), 357–58; *St. Louis Missouri Republican*, 16 May 1849 and 21 Oct. 1875.

16. Boyce 1914 Paper, MHS.

17. Primm, *Lion of the Valley*, 171–80; George Engelmann to Benjamin Soulard, 24 Nov. 1854, in Antoine P. Soulard Papers, MHS; John C. Schneider, "Riot and Reaction in St. Louis," *Missouri Historical Review* 68 (January 1974):171–85; William Barnaby Faherty, *Better the Dream, St. Louis: University and Community 1818–1968* (St. Louis: St. Louis University, 1968), 95–98, 101–103.

18. John Bannon to Judah P. Benjamin, 19 Jan. 1864, Division of Manuscripts, Library of Congress, Washington, D.C.; Norman, *History of Modern Ireland*, 13; Faherty, *Better the Dream*, 98, 101–103.

19. Boyce 1914 Paper, MHS.

20. John Bannon Obituary, *Dublin Telegraph*, 14 July 1913; Faherty, *Better the Dream*, 102–103.

21. Boyce 1914 Paper, MHS.

22. Ernest Kirschten, *Catfish and Crystal* (New York: Doubleday, 1960), 288.

23. John O'Hanlon, *Life and Scenery in Missouri: Reminiscence of a Missionary* (Dublin: J. Duffy and Co., 1890), 144; Primm, *Lion of the Valley*, 174, 180–81.

24. O'Hanlon, *Life and Scenery*, 141, 144; Interview with Marjorie Evans, Lincoln County, Missouri, Historical Society, at Troy, Missouri, 20 Nov. 1987; *History of Lincoln County, Missouri* (Chicago: Goodspeed Publishing Co., 1881), 586–87, 591.

25. Boyce 1914 Paper, MHS; Fifth Ward, Census Records of the Eighth Census of the United States, City of St. Louis, Missouri, 1860; Kenny and Morrissey, "Father John Bannon, S.J.," 97.

26. Boyce 1914 Paper, MHS; Kennedy's 1860 St. Louis City Directory, Appendix 11.

27. John Rothensteiner, *History of the Archdiocese of St. Louis*, 2 vols. (St. Louis: Press of Blackwell Wielandy Co., 1928), 2:99; La Grave, "Artist Unknown"; Boyce 1914 Paper, MHS.

28. Rothensteiner, *History of the Archdiocese of St. Louis*, 2:99.

29. Ibid.; Kennedy's 1860 Directory, Appendix 11.

30. Rothensteiner, *History of the Archdiocese of St. Louis*, 2:99.

31. Faherty, *Catholic Ancestry of Saint Louis*, 26; Scharf, *History of Saint Louis City and County*, 2:1662; La Grave, "Artist Unknown."

32. La Grave, "Artist Unknown"; Rothensteiner, *History of the Archdiocese of St. Louis*, 2:100.

33. La Grave, "Artist Unknown"; Rothensteiner, *History of the Archdiocese of St. Louis*, 2:100.

34. Ibid.; "The Restoration of St. John's," 335.

35. Faherty, *Better the Dream*, 101–104; Kennedy's 1859 St. Louis Directory, 47.

36. Brian P. Burnes, *If These Towers Could Talk* (St. Louis: private printing, 1947).

37. *St. Louis Post-Dispatch*, 6 June 1957; William R. Babcock Scrapbook, MHS.

38. Babcock Scrapbook, MHS; Martin G. Towey and Margaret L. Sullivan, "The Knights of Father Mathew: Parallel Ethnic Reform," *Missouri Historical Review* 75 (January 1981):171–72; Basil Duke, *Reminiscences of General Basil W. Duke* (Garden City: Doubleday, Page and Co., 1911), 52; Billon Scrapbook, vol. 2, MHS; Joseph Boyce, St. Louis Military Organizations Manuscript, MHS; Kennedy's 1859 St. Louis City Directory, 38; William Hyde and Howard L. Conrad, *Encyclopedia of the History of St. Louis*, 4 vols. (St. Louis: Southern Historical Co., 1899), 2:1766; Michael McEnnis to Joseph Boyce, July 22, 1907, in Camp Jackson Papers, MHS.

39. Babcock Scrapbook, MHS.

40. Kennedy's 1859 St. Louis City Directory, 38; Billon Scrapbook, vol. 2, MHS; Boyce, "St. Louis Military Organizations Manuscript," 22, 59, 68, MHS; Service Records, NA; Towey and Sullivan, "Knights of Father Mathew," 171–72; Kennedy's 1856 St. Louis Directory, 38; Michael McEnnis to Joseph Boyce, 22 July 1907, Camp Jackson Papers, MHS.

41. La Grave, "Artist Unknown."

42. Ibid.; Boyce 1914 Paper, MHS; *St. Louis Post-Dispatch*, 16 June 1957; Scharf, *History of St. Louis City and County*, 2:1662; Kenny and Morrissey, "Father John Bannon, S.J.," 92.

43. *St. Louis Post-Dispatch*, 16 June 1957.

44. Babcock Scrapbook, MHS.

45. Ibid.

46. Cass County, Missouri, Petition to Governor Sterling Price, 20 Aug. 1856, Missouri Militia Collection, MHS; State of Missouri House of Representatives Journal, Twenty-First Assembly, First Session, 9; Michael Fellman, *Inside War: The Guerrilla Conflict in Missouri During the American Civil War* (New York: Oxford University Press, 1989), 11–22.

47. J. B. Johnson, *History of Vernon County, Missouri* (Chicago: C. F. Cooper, 1911), 2:240–42.

48. Ibid., 241; Babcock Scrapbook, MHS.

49. Babcock Scrapbook, MHS; Boyce, St. Louis Military Organizations Manuscript, 71, MHS.

50. Babcock Scrapbook, MHS; William Streeter Reminiscences, 26 July 1908 newspaper clipping, Camp Jackson Collection, MHS.

51. William P. Barlow Manuscript, 10, Missouri Militia Collection, MHS.

52. Robert J. Rombauer, *The Union Cause in St. Louis in 1861* (Chicago: Nixon-Jones Printing Co., 1909), 127; Service Records, NA; St. John's Archives Records, St. John's Church, St. Louis.

53. *Daily Missouri Democrat*, 29 Nov. 1860; Babcock Scrapbook, MHS.

54. *Daily Missouri Democrat*, 29 Nov. 1860 and 3 Dec. 1860.

55. Johnson, *History of Vernon County, Missouri*, 2:250.

56. Ibid.; St. John's Church Archives Records; *St. Louis Missouri Republican*, 29 Nov. 1860.

57. St. John's Church Archives Records; *St. Louis Missouri Republican*, 29 Nov. and 16 Dec. 1860; *Daily Missouri Republican*, 1, 8, and 10 Dec. 1860; *St. Louis Daily Evening News*, 27 Nov. 1860.

58. St. John's Church Archives Records.

59. Kennedy's 1860 St. Louis City Directory, 36.

60. *St. Louis Daily Evening News*, 17 Dec. 1860; Service Records, NA.

61. Billon Scrapbook, vol. 2, MHS; Boyce, St. Louis Military Organizations Manuscript, 72–73, MHS; James Neal Primm and Steven Rowan, eds., *Germans for a Free Missouri: Translations from the St. Louis Radical Press 1857–1862* (Columbia: University of Missouri Press, 1983), 210; Fellman, *Inside War*, 11–22; Christopher Phillips, *Damned Yankee: The Life of General Nathaniel Lyon* (Columbia: University of Missouri Press, 1990), 140.

62. Kenny and Morrissey, "Father John Bannon, S.J.," 96.

63. Boyce 1914 Paper, MHS; Rothensteiner, *History of the Archdiocese of St. Louis*, 1:212.

64. Walter Harrington Ruyle, *Missouri: Union or Secession* (Nashville: George Peabody College for Teaching, 1931), 155, 166; William H. Lyon, "Claiborne Fox Jackson and the Secession Crisis in Missouri," *Missouri Historical Review* 58 (July 1964):422–23, 433.

65. Faherty, *Better the Dream*, 142; Horton O'Neil, "The Story of Joseph O'Neil 1817–1893," Manuscript, 201, MHS.

66. John McElroy, *The Struggle for Missouri* (Washington, D.C.: National Tribune Co., 1909), 38; Primm and Rowan, eds., *Germans for a Free Missouri*, 172–73, 228; Towey and Sullivan, "Knights of Father Mathew," 171; Jason H. Silverman, "Stars, Bars, and Foreigners: The Immigrant and the Making of the Confederacy," *Journal of Confederate History* 1 (Fall 1988):272–73; Towey, "Kerry Patch Revisited," 139–42; Faherty, *Better the Dream*, 101, 134, 149.

TWO   War in the West

1. Lyon, "Claiborne Fox Jackson," 433–34; Robert V. Johnson and C. C. Buel, eds., *Battles and Leaders of the Civil War*, 4 vols. (New York: Thomas Yoseloff, 1956), 1:262–64; Phillips, *Damned Yankee*, 47–48, 104–28, 132–38, 156–57.

2. *Memphis Daily Appeal*, 14 May 1861; Arthur Roy Kirkpatrick, "Missouri in the Early Months of the Civil War," *Missouri Historical Review* 55 (April 1961):235–39; James W. Covington, "The Camp Jackson Affair: 1861," *Missouri Historical Review* 55 (April 1961):200–201; Deborah Isaac, "Confederate Days in St. Louis," newspaper clippings, MHS; Phillips, *Damned Yankee*, 156–57, 177–78.

3. O'Neil, "Story of Joseph O'Neil 1817–1893," 201–202, MHS.

4. Covington, "The Camp Jackson Affair: 1861," 197–98; *Weekly Mississippian*, 8 Jan. 1860; Stanley F. Horn, *The Army of Tennessee* (Norman: University of Oklahoma Press, 1952), 18; Phillips, *Damned Yankee*, 157.

5. McElroy, *Struggle for Missouri*, 39–40; Hans Christian Adamson, *Rebellion in Missouri 1861* (New York: Chilton Co., 1961), 45–46; Phillips, *Damned Yankee*, 144; Faherty, *Better the Dream*, 143.

6. Isaac, "Confederate Days in St. Louis," MHS; "Camp Jackson Clippings," MHS; Phillips, *Damned Yankee*, 133, 138, 144; Horn, *Army of Tennessee*, 18; *Memphis Daily Appeal*, 14 May 1861.

7. Daniel Frost Papers, MHS; Camp Jackson Clippings, MHS; Horn, *Army of Tennessee*, 18–19.

8. Primm and Rowan, eds., *Germans for a Free Missouri*, 209; Eben (Richards) to Mrs. E. Richards, 13 May 1861, Camp Jackson Papers, MHS; Horn, *Army of Tennessee*, 18–19; Phillips, *Damned Yankee*, 166–67.

9. Camp Jackson Clippings, MHS; Streeter Reminiscences, MHS; Horn, *Army of Tennessee*, 18–19; Faherty, *Better the Dream*, 135; *Memphis Daily Appeal*, 14 May 1861; Phillips, *Damned Yankee*, 181–87.

10. Streeter Reminiscences, MHS.

11. Franklin P. Cole, Introduction to *They Preached Liberty* (Indianapolis: Liberty Press, n.d.), 11–44; Thomas O'Brien Hanley, *The American Revolution and Religion, Maryland 1770–1800* (Washington, D.C.: Catholic University of America Press, 1971), 36, 43–44.

12. *Memphis Daily Appeal*, 14 May 1861; Streeter Reminiscences, MHS.

13. *Memphis Daily Appeal*, 14 May 1861; Ebsen to Mrs. Richards, 13 May 1861, MHS; Camp Jackson Clippings, MHS; Phillips, *Damned Yankee*, 188–90.

14. Isaac, "Confederate Days in St. Louis," MHS; Streeter Reminiscences, MHS; Breckenridge Scrapbook, vol. 2, MHS; Camp Jackson Collection, MHS; *Memphis Daily Appeal*, 14 May 1861.

15. Walter Williams, *History of Northeast Missouri*, 3 vols. (Chicago: Lewis Publishing Co., 1913), 2:1018; Boyce, "St. Louis Military Organizations Manuscript," 26, MHS.

16. *St. Louis Missouri Republican*, 11 May 1885; Lois Stanley Wilson, George F. Wilson, and Mary Helen Wilson, eds., *Death Records From Missouri Newspapers: The Civil War Years, January 1861–December 1865* (Decorah: Anundsen Printing Co., 1983), 46; *Memphis Daily Appeal*, 14 May 1861.

17. Horn, *Army of Tennessee*, 18–19; List of Exchanged Camp Jackson Prisoners, 1, Camp Jackson Papers, MHS; Phillips, *Damned Yankee*, 190.

18. Streeter Reminiscences, MHS.

19. Ibid.; Camp Jackson Clippings, MHS; Ebsen to Mrs. Richards, 13 May 1861; Hyde and Conrad, *Encyclopedia of the History of St. Louis*, 4:2435; *Memphis Daily Appeal*, 14 May 1861; Phillips, *Damned Yankee*, 190–92.

20. William Lane Carr to William Glasgow, Jr., 14 April 1862, William Carr Lane Collection, MHS; William Clark Breckinridge to S. B. Laughlin, 15 April 1921, William Clark Breckinridge Papers, MHS; Johnson and Buel, *Battles and Leaders of the Civil War*, 1:265–66; Phillips, *Damned Yankee*, 192–94, 197–99, 214, 262–64.

21. Streeter Reminiscences, MHS; Galusha Anderson, *The Story of a Border City during the Civil War* (Boston: Little, Brown and Co., 1908), 98; Rombauer, *Union Cause in St. Louis in 1861*, 236; Kenny and Morrissey, "Father John Bannon, S.J.," 96; Camp Jackson Clippings, MHS; *Memphis Daily Appeal*, 14 and 15 May 1861.

22. Streeter Reminiscences, MHS; Camp Jackson Clippings, MHS; *Memphis Daily Appeal*, 14, 16, and 17 May 1861.

23. William F. Switzler, *Switzler's Illustrated History of Missouri from 1541 to 1877* (St. Louis: C. R. Barns, 1879), 355.

24. Streeter Reminiscences, MHS; *Memphis Daily Appeal*, 15 May 1861; Phillips, *Damned Yankee*, 195.

25. Castel, *General Sterling Price*, 13–14, 25–26; *Daily Journal of Commerce*, 21 June 1861; J. C. McNamara, "Sketch of the Sixth Division, Missouri State Guard," 6–7, Monroe Mosby Parsons Papers, MHS; *Memphis Daily Appeal*, 15 May, 19 and 22 June, 13 July 1861; Phillips, *Damned Yankee*, 197–99, 206–22, 262–64.

26. Rothensteiner, *History of the Archdiocese of St. Louis*, 2:100; Billon Scrapbook, vol. 2, MHS; Bannon Confederate Service Record, NA; Scharf, *History of St. Louis City and County*, 2:1766; *Memphis Daily Appeal*, 15 June 1861.

27. Castel, *General Sterling Price*, 27; McNamara, "Sketch of the Sixth Division," 8–13, MHS; *Memphis Daily Appeal*, 14 and 24 July 1861.

28. Scharf, *History of St. Louis City and County*, 2:1766; McNamara, "Sketch of the Sixth Division," 2–3, MHS.

29. Burnes, *If These Towers Could Talk*, n.p., MHS.

30. Primm and Rowan, *Germans for a Free Missouri*, 224.

31. Burnes, *If These Towers Could Talk*, n.p., MHS; Billon Scrapbook, vol. 2, MHS; Rothensteiner, *History of the Archdiocese of St. Louis*, 2:213; *Weekly Mississippian*, 5 Nov. 1861; Faherty, *Better the Dream*, 143.

32. McNamara, "Sketch of the Sixth Division," 16–25, MHS; Boyce Scrapbook, MHS; L. E. Schroeder, "The Battle of Wilson's Creek and Its Effect upon Missouri," *Missouri Historical Review* 71 (January 1977):156, 172–73; R. I. Holcombe and F. W. Adams, *An Account of the Battle of Wilson's Creek, or Oak Hills* (Springfield: Dow and Adams, 1883), 70–75; *Weekly Mississippian*, 16 Aug. and 8, 9, and 11 Oct. 1861; *New York Daily Tribune*, 13 Sept. 1861; *Memphis Daily Appeal*, 10, 14, 15, 16, 17, and 24 Aug. 1861; Phillips, *Damned Yankee*, 245–57.

33. McNamara, "Sketch of the Sixth Division," 26–32, MHS; *Western Journal of Commerce*, 20 Aug. 1861; Castel, *General Sterling Price*, 57–61; Johnson and Buel, *Battles and Leaders of the Civil War*, 1:273; *Richmond (Virginia) Enquirer*, 1 and 10 Oct. 1861; *Organization and Status of Missouri Troops in Service During the Civil War* (Washington, D.C.: U.S. Government Printing Office, 1902), 269–70; *Weekly Mississippian*, 8 Oct. 1861; *Memphis Daily Appeal*, 26 and 27 Oct., 1 Nov., and 10, 11, and 17 Dec. 1861.

34. Richard H. Musser, "The War in Missouri," *Southern Bivouac* 2 (1886):45; *Memphis Daily Appeal*, 10, 11, and 17 Dec. 1861.

35. Bannon Confederate Service Record, NA; John Bannon Diary, Yates Snowden Collection, South Caroliniana Library, University of South Carolina, Columbia; List of Exchanged Camp Jackson Prisoners, 1, MHS.

36. Rothensteiner, *History of the Archdiocese of St. Louis*, 2:100.

37. Bannon Diary, SCL.

38. Billon Scrapbook, vol. 2, MHS.

39. Bannon Diary, SCL; Boyce 1914 Paper, MHS.

40. Kennedy's 1859 St. Louis City Directory, 44; Kennedy's 1860 St. Louis City Directory, 13; Walter Stevens, *St. Louis, The Fourth City*, 3 vols. (St. Louis: S. J. Clarke, 1909), 2:994–96; Boyce 1914 Paper, MHS; List of Exchanged Camp Jackson Prisoners, 2, MHS; Dorthy Garesche Holland, *The Garesche, De Bauduy and Des Chapelles Families: History and Genealogy* (St. Louis: Schneider Printing Co., 1963), 122, 166–72; *The War of the Rebellion: A Compilation of the Official Records of the Union and Confederate Armies*, 130 vols. (Washington, D.C.: U.S. Government Printing Office, 1880–1901), ser. 2, 1:554 (hereafter *OR*); James E. Love to Molly, James E. Love Papers, MHS; Garesche Family Papers, MHS; C. Gibson to Governor Hamilton R. Gamble, Hamilton R. Gamble Papers, MHS.

41. Father William Barnaby Faherty Collection of Father John B. Bannon Material, St. Louis.

42. Warren R. Guibor Collection of Captain Henry Guibor material, Manchester, Missouri.

43. Bannon Diary, SCL; Boyce 1914 Paper, MHS.

44. Billon Scrapbook, vol. 2, MHS; Faherty, *Dream by the River*, 89, 143.

45. William G. B. Carson, "Secesh," *Bulletin of the Missouri Historical Society* 23 (January 1967):124.

46. William Barnaby Faherty, *Rebels or Reformers? Dissenting Priests in American Life* (Chicago: Loyola University Press, 1987), 14.

47. Bannon Diary, SCL.

48. Ibid.; Brauckman Scrapbook, MHS; Samuel Churchill Clark to Aunt, 25 Jan. 1862, Clark Family Papers, MHS.

49. Bannon Diary, SCL; *Richmond Enquirer*, 10 Oct. 1861.

50. Kenny and Morrissey, "Father John Bannon, S.J.," 94.

51. Anderson, *Memoirs*, 161; Bannon Diary, SCL; Brauckman Scrapbook, MHS; Sidney J. Romero, "The Confederate Chaplain," *Civil War History* 1 (January 1955):131.

52. Bannon Diary, SCL; Compiled Missouri Service Records, War Record Group 109, Microcopy 322, Rolls 81, 90, NA, Washington, D.C.

53. Warren Guibor Collection; Compiled Missouri Service Records, Roll 81, NA; Boyce, St. Louis Military Organizations Manuscript, 12, 65, 69, MHS; Brauckman Scrapbook, MHS; Boyce Scrapbook, MHS; William Wade to Gov. Robert M. Stewart, 23 Feb. 1860, Western Historical Manuscript Collections, State Historical Society of Missouri, Columbia.

54. Bannon Diary, SCL.

55. Ibid.; Boyce, St. Louis Military Organizations Manuscript, 65, MHS; Warren Guibor Collection; Asa M. Payne, "Story of the Battle of Pea Ridge," Pea Ridge National Military Park Archives, Pea Ridge, Ark.; Robert St. Peters, *Memorial Volume of the Diamond Jubilee of St. Louis University, 1829–1904* (St. Louis: St. Louis University Press, 1904), 262.

56. Billon Scrapbook, vol. 2, MHS.

57. Ibid.

58. Ibid.; Bannon Diary, SLC.

59. Compiled Service Records, NA; Thomas Hogan to Father, 1 May 1864, Civil War Papers, MHS; Henry Little Diary, United States Army Military History Institute, Carlisle Barracks. Pa. (hereafter USAMHI).

60. Compiled Service Records, NA.

61. Brauckman Scrapbook, MHS.

62. Boyce 1914 Paper, MHS.

63. Little Diary, USAMHI; Bannon Diary, SCL; Billon Scrapbook, vol. 2, MHS; Hyde and Conrad, *Encyclopedia of the History of St. Louis*, 4:2440.

64. Hyde and Conrad, *Encyclopedia of the History of St. Louis*, 4:2440; Historic Homes of Missouri, vol. 2, MHS; Compiled Service Records, NA; Bannon Diary, SCL; *St. Louis Missouri Republican*, 14 Sept. 1838 and 26 Nov. 1874; Scharf, *History of St. Louis*, 1:657–58; Hyde and Conrad, *Encyclopedia of the History of St. Louis*, 4:2381–84.

65. Bannon Diary, SCL.

66. Little Diary, USAMHI; Johnson and Buel, *Battles and Leaders of the Civil*

War, 2:733; *Richmond Enquirer*, 10 Oct. 1861; Maryland General Assembly (Laws) 1849–1850, Resolution 15, "Resolution in Favor of Captain Henry Little," 29 Jan. 1850, Maryland State Archives, Annapolis, Md.; Ezra J. Warner, *Generals in Gray: Lives of the Confederate Commanders* (Baton Rouge: Louisiana State University Press, 1959), 188–89.

67. *Richmond Enquirer*, 10 Oct. 1861.

68. Little Diary, USAMHI; Bannon Diary, SCL; Bevier, *History of the First and Second Missouri Confederate Brigades*, 78, 130, 136, 333; Anderson, *Memoirs*, 114, 227; Henry Little Biographical Sketch, Maryland Historical Society, Baltimore.

69. *St. Louis Missouri Republican*, 19 Aug. 1887.

70. Billon Scrapbook, vol. 2, MHS.

71. Hyde and Conrad, *Encyclopedia of the History of St. Louis*, 4:2440.

72. Anderson, *Memoirs*, 133; Richard M. Hubble, "Personal Reminiscences and Fragments of Old Settlers," 56–57, MHS.

73. Billon Scrapbook, vol. 2, MHS.

74. Johnson and Buel, *Battles and Leaders of the Civil War*, 1:314–16; *OR*, 8 (ser. 1):503–506, 526, 540–42.

75. Bannon Diary, SCL; Glenn W. Sunderland, *Five Days to Glory* (New York: A. S. Barnes, 1970), 26.

76. Bannon Diary SCL; Joseph R. Mothershead Journal 1862, 1–2, Tennessee State Library and Archives, Nashville, Tenn.; Isaac Vincent Smith Memoir, 13, Western Historical Manuscript Collection, State Historical Society of Missouri; *St. Louis Missouri Republican*, 21 Nov. 1885; William Kavanaugh Memoir and Papers, 11, Western Historical Manuscript Collection, State Historical Society of Missouri.

77. Bannon Diary, SCL.

78. Ibid.; Benjamin Avery Rives Sketch, MHS; Compiled Missouri Service Records, War Record Group 109, Microcopy 322, Roll 119, NA; *St. Joseph (Missouri) Gazette Extra*, MHS; *OR*, 8 (ser. 1):427–28; Michael A. Mullins, *The Fremont Rifles: A History of the 37th Illinois Veteran Volunteer Infantry* (Wilmington: Broadfoot Publishing Co., 1990), 53.

79. Bannon Diary, SCL; Mothershead Journal, 3, TSLA.

80. Bannon Diary, SCL; Mothershead Journal, 3, TSLA; Smith Memoir, 13, WHMC-SHSM.

81. Johnson and Buel, *Battles and Leaders of the Civil War*, 1:316–17.

82. Mothershead Journal, 3, TSLA.

83. Bannon Diary, SCL.

84. Ibid.; Mothershead Journal, 3, TSLA; Smith Memoir, 13, WHMC-SHSM; Anderson, *Memoirs*, 144–45; *OR*, 8 (ser. 1):757; Homer L. Calkins, ed., "Elkhorn to Vicksburg: James H. Fauntleroy's Diary for the Year 1862," *Civil War History* 2 (January 1956):12.

85. Bannon Diary, SCL; Mothershead Journal, 3, TSLA; Anderson, *Memoirs*, 144–46; Smith Memoir, 13, WHMC-SHSM; Calkins, "Elkhorn to Vicksburg," 12.

86. Bannon Diary, SCL; Mothershead Journal, 3–4, TSLA; Kavanaugh Memoir, 11, WHMC-SHSM; Smith Memoir, 13–14, WHMC-SHSM; Anderson, *Memoirs*, 146–47.

87. Bannon Diary, SCL; Smith Memoir, 13–14, WHMC-SHSM; Mothershead Journal, 3–4, TSLA.

88. Smith Memoir, 13–14, WHMC-SHSM; Anderson, *Memoirs*, 146–48; Bannon Diary, SCL; Mothershead Journal, 3–4, TSLA; Edwin C. Bearss, "From Rolla to Fayetteville with General Curtis," *Arkansas Historical Quarterly* 19 (Autumn 1960):248–49; *Memphis Daily Appeal*, 8, 9, 11, and 12 Feb. 1862.

89. Bannon Diary, SCL; Anderson, *Memoirs*, 148–50; Bearss, "From Rolla to Fayetteville," 250; Mothershead Journal, 4, TSLA; *OR*, 8 (ser. 1):757.

90. St. Peters, *Memorial Volume of the Diamond Jubilee of St. Louis University*, 236; Anderson, *Memoirs*, 149; Compiled Missouri Service Records, Roll 87, NA; Samuel Churchill Clark to Aunt, 25 Jan. 1862 and 5 Nov. 1861 to Father, Clark Family Papers, MHS; Smith Memoir, 14, WHMC-SHSM; *The Intelligencer*, 11 April 1862.

91. Clark to Aunt, 25 Jan. 1862, Clark Family Papers, MHS; Bevier, *History of the First and Second Missouri Confederate Brigades*, 101; Kavanaugh Memoir, 9, WHMC-SHSM; Henry Howe, *The Times of the Rebellion in the West* (Cincinnati: private printing, 1867), 219.

92. Kavanaugh Memoir, 11, WHMC-SHSM; Brauckman Scrapbook, MHS; Smith Memoir, 13, WHMC-SHSM.

93. Brauckman Scrapbook, MHS; Anderson, *Memoirs*, 151; Mothershead Journal, 5, TSLA; Bearss, "From Rolla to Fayetteville," 250–51; Bannon Diary, SCL.

94. Bannon Diary, SCL.

95. Brauckman Scrapbook, MHS.

96. Ibid.; Bannon Diary, SCL; Anderson, *Memoirs*, 151; Mothershead Journal, 5, TSLA; Bearss, "From Rolla to Fayetteville," 250–51.

97. Kavanaugh Memoir, 13, WHMC-SHSM; Brauckman Scrapbook, MHS; Johnson and Buel, *Battles and Leaders of the Civil War*, 1:337; Mothershead Journal, 4, TSLA.

98. *OR*, 8 (ser. 1):757; Brauckman Scrapbook, MHS.

99. Calkins, "Elkhorn to Vicksburg," 12; Mothershead Journal, 3–4, TSLA; Anderson, *Memoirs*, 144–48.

100. Bannon Diary, SCL; Mothershead Journal, 4–5, TSLA; Johnson and Buel, *Battles and Leaders of the Civil War*, 1:317; Anderson, *Memoirs*, 152–53; Kavanaugh, 11, WHMC-SHSM; Bearss, "From Rolla to Fayetteville," 251–52.

101. Mothershead Journal, 4–5, TSLA; Anderson, *Memoirs*, 152–53; Kavanaugh Memoir, 11, WHMC-SHSM; Typescript of Diary of H. P. Greene, Washington County, Ark., Historical Society, Fayetteville, Ark.; L. G. Bennett and William M. Haigh, *History of the Thirty-Sixth Regiment Illinois Volunteers: During the War of the Rebellion* (Aurora: Knickerbocker and Hodder, 1876), 119–20; Mullins, *Fremont Rifles*, 54.

102. Bannon Diary, SCL; Mothershead Journal, 5, TSLA; *St. Louis Missouri Republican*, 21 Nov. 1885; Anderson, *Memoirs*, 150; Kavanaugh Memoir, 11, WHMC-SHSM; Horn, *Army of Tennessee*, 23, 29–30, 34–35.

103. Mothershead Journal, 6, TSLA; Bannon Diary, SCL; Brauckman Scrapbook, MHS; Kavanaugh Memoir, 11, WHMC-SHSM.

104. Bannon Diary, SCL; *St. Louis Missouri Republican*, 21 Nov. 1885; Johnson and Buel, *Battles and Leaders of the Civil War*, 1:270, 273–74, 318.

105. Bannon Diary, SCL; William H. Tunnard, *A Southern Record: The History of the Third Regiment Louisiana Infantry* (Dayton: Morningside repr., 1970), 50–65; Edward A. Pollard, *Southern History of the War: The First Year of the War*, 2 vols. (London: Philip and Son, 1863), 1:275; Robert G. Hartje, *Van Dorn: The Life and Times of a Confederate General* (Nashville: Vanderbilt University Press, 1967), 103–18; *Weekly Mississippian*, 25 Sept. 1861.

106. Brauckman Scrapbook, MHS; Bannon Diary, SCL.

107. H. C. Burbridge Papers, Jacksonville, Fla.; John Gerber, "Twain's Private Campaign," *Civil War History* 1 (March 1955):40–41; *St. Louis Missouri Republican*, 18 July 1885; St. Peters, *Memorial Volume of the Diamond Jubilee of St. Louis University*, 229; Compiled Missouri Service Records, Roll 104, NA.

108. Walter L. Brown, "Pea Ridge: Gettysburg of the West," *Arkansas Historical Quarterly* 15 (Spring 1956):3–4.

THREE   A Tavern Called Elkhorn

1. Brown, "Pea Ridge: Gettysburg of the West," 3–4; Kavanaugh Memoir, 13, WHMC-SHSM; *Mobile Register and Advertiser*, 5 Mar. 1862; Johnson and Buel, *Battles and Leaders of the Civil War*, 1:319; *St. Louis Missouri Republican*, 5 June 1886; Sterling Price to Earl Van Dorn, 9 Feb. 1862, Mesker Collection, MHS; James J. Hamilton, *The Battle of Fort Donelson* (New York: Thomas Yoseloff, 1968), 18–23; Benjamin Franklin Cooling, *Forts Henry and Donelson: The Key to the Confederate Heartland* (Knoxville: University of Tennessee Press, 1987), 67–80.

2. Bannon Diary, SCL; *St. Louis Missouri Republican*, 21 Nov. 1885; Kavanaugh Memoir, 15, WHMC-SHSM; Anderson, *Memoirs*, 162; Brauckman Scrapbook, MHS.

3. Bannon Diary, SCL; Brauckman Scrapbook, MHS; Mothershead Journal, 7, TSLA; McElroy, *The Struggle for Missouri*, 320; Boyce 1914 Paper, MHS; Calkins, "Elkhorn to Vicksburg," 12; *OR*, 8 (ser. 1):307.

4. Brauckman Scrapbook, MHS.

5. Johnson and Buel, *Battles and Leaders of the Civil War*, 1:337; Bannon Diary, SCL; Mothershead Journal, 8, TSLA; Sterling Price to Earl Van Dorn, 9 Feb. 1862, MHS.

6. Bannon Diary, SCL; *St. Louis Missouri Republican*, 21 Nov. 1885; Mothershead Journal, 8, TSLA; *OR*, 8 (ser. 1):307.

7. Johnson and Buel, *Battles and Leaders of the Civil War*, 1:319–21; *St. Louis Missouri Republican*, 19 Dec. and 7 Mar. 1885; Albert Castel, "A New View of the Battle of Pea Ridge," *Missouri Historical Review* 62 (January 1968):139; Henry Voelkner to Family, 18 Mar. 1862, MHS; Mullins, *Fremont Rifles*, 57.

8. Henry Voelkner to Family, 18 Mar. 1862, MHS; Anderson, *Memoirs*, 164–66; *St. Louis Missouri Republican*, 21 Nov. and 19 Dec. 1885; Mothershead Journal, 8, TSLA; Calkins, "Elkhorn to Vicksburg," 12–13; *OR*, 8 (ser. 1):305, 307; Junius Henri Browne, *Four Years in Secessia* (Hartford: O. D. Case and Co., 1865), 93–96; Dabney H. Maury, "Recollections of the Elkhorn Campaign," *Southern Historical Society Papers* 2 (1876):186; Robert E. Shalhope, *Sterling Price: Portrait of a Southerner* (Columbia: University of Missouri Press, 1971), 204–205; Thomas W. Knox, *Camp-Fire and Cotton-Field: Southern Adventure in Time of War* (Philadelphia: Jones Brothers, 1865), 134; Edwin C. Bearss, "The Battle of Pea Ridge," *Arkansas Historical Quarterly* 20 (Spring 1961):89–93.

9. Castel, "New View of Pea Ridge," 140–41.

10. Bannon Diary, SCL; Shalhope, *Sterling Price*, 202; *OR*, 8 (ser. 1):307.

11. Shalhope, *Sterling Price*, 201; Hartje, *Van Dorn*, 157; Castel, *General Sterling Price*, 72; Johnson and Buel, *Battles and Leaders of the Civil War*, 1:320; Maury, "Recollections of the Elkhorn Campaign," 187; *St. Louis Missouri Republican*, 21 Nov. 1885.

12. Johnson and Buel, *Battles and Leaders of the Civil War*, 1:320; Castel, *General Sterling Price*, 72; Maury, "Recollections of the Elkhorn Campaign," 187; *St. Louis Missouri Republican*, 7 Mar., 4 July, 21 Nov., 19 Dec. 1885; Edwin C. Bearss, "The Battle of Pea Ridge," *Annals of Iowa* 36 (Spring 1963):572.

13. Castel, *General Sterling Price*, 72; Maury, "Recollections of the Elkhorn Campaign," 187; *St. Louis Missouri Republican*, 4 July 1885; Pea Ridge National Military Park Centennial Committee, *The Battle of Pea Ridge* (Rogers, 1963), 3; Topographical Map, Pea Ridge Quadrangle, U.S. Department of the Interior, Geological Survey.

14. Castel, *General Sterling Price*, 72–73; Mothershead Journal, 9, TSLA; *St. Louis Missouri Republican*, 21 Nov. 1885; Maury, "Recollections of the Elkhorn Campaign," 187; *Battlefield of Pea Ridge, Arkansas, Battlefield Folklore* (Fayetteville: Washington County Historical Society, 1958), 9–10.

15. Bannon Diary, SCL; Mothershead Journal, 9, TSLA; *OR*, 8 (ser. 1):307.

16. William Baxter, *Pea Ridge and Prairie Grove or Scenes and Incidents of the War in Arkansas* (Cincinnati: Poe and Hitchcock, 1864), 59.

17. Anderson, *Memoirs*, 166–67; Bannon Diary, SCL; James E. Payne, "The Test of Missourians," *Confederate Veteran* 37 (February 1929):64; Edwin C. Bearss, "The First Day at Pea Ridge," *Arkansas Historical Quarterly* 17 (Spring 1958):133;

Bearss, "Battle of Pea Ridge," 577; Payne, "Story of the Battle of Pea Ridge," PRNMP; Hartje, *Van Dorn*, 135.

18. Payne, "Test of Missourians," 64; Anderson, *Memoirs*, 166–68; Bearss, "The Battle of Pea Ridge," 577; Samuel Baldwin Dunlap Diary, Western Historical Manuscript Collections, State Historical Society of Missouri, 67.

19. John T. Wickersham, *The Gray and the Blue* (Berkeley, 1915), 50; *St. Louis Missouri Republican*, 21 Nov. 1885; Pea Ridge National Park Association, Battle of Pea Ridge, Arkansas, Arkansas History Commission; *Battlefield of Pea Ridge, Arkansas: Battlefield Folklore*, 4, AHC; Mothershead Journal, 9, TSLA; Hartje, *Van Dorn*, 135; Bevier, *History of the First and Second Missouri Confederate Brigades*, 317; Michael Hughes, "The Battle of Pea Ridge or Elkhorn Tavern," *Blue & Gray Magazine* 5 (January 1988):18; Payne, "Test of Missourians," 64–65; Pea Ridge Quadrangle Topographical Map; Anderson, *Memoirs*, 166–67; *St. Louis Missouri Republican*, 4 July 1885; Pea Ridge Memorial Association, *Reports on the Historic Marker Program, March 10, 1963* (Rogers, 1963), n.p.

20. Alden McLellan to Albert C. Danner, 18 May 1919, MHS.

21. Anderson, *Memoirs*, 167–68.

22. *OR*, 8 (ser. 1):307.

23. Robert A. Lynch to Yates Snowden, 28 Dec. 1916, Yates Snowden Collection, South Caroliniana Library, University of South Carolina, Columbia.

24. Bannon Diary, SCL; Payne, "Test of Missourians," 64–65; Mothershead Journal, 9, TSLA; Payne, "Story of the Battle of Pea Ridge," PRNMP; Wiley Britton, *The Civil War on the Border*, 2 vols. (New York: G. P. Putnam's, 1899), 1:221; Thomas Depp, "Personal Experience at Pea Ridge," *Confederate Veteran* 20 (January 1912):17; Anderson, *Memoirs*, 167–68; Claire N. Moody, *Battle of Pea Ridge or Elkhorn Tavern* (Little Rock: Arkansas Valley Printing Co., 1956), 27.

25. Hughes, "The Battle of Pea Ridge or Elkhorn Tavern," 19, 48; Bannon Diary, SCL; *OR*, 8 (ser. 1):307.

26. *OR*, 8 (ser.1):307; *St. Louis Missouri Republican*, 7 Mar. and 19 Dec. 1885.

27. Bannon Diary, SCL.

28. Ibid.; *OR*, 8 (ser. 1):307; *St. Louis Missouri Republican*, 7 Mar. and 19 Dec. 1885.

29. Payne, "Story of the Battle of Pea Ridge," PRNMP.

30. Hartje, *Van Dorn*, 135; *OR*, 8 (ser. 1):307; *St. Louis Missouri Republican*, 7 Mar. and 9 Dec. 1885.

31. Bannon Diary, SCL; Anderson, *Memoirs*, 166–67; Johnson and Buel, *Battles and Leaders of the Civil War*, 1:337; Hughes, "Battle of Pea Ridge or Elkhorn Tavern," 48; Bearss, "Battle of Pea Ridge," 577; *OR*, 8 (ser. 1):307.

32. Bannon Diary, SCL; Britton, *Civil War on the Border*, 1:221; *OR*, 8 (ser. 1):307.

33. Hartje, *Van Dorn*, 135; *OR*, 8 (ser. 1):307.

34. Noble L. Prentis, *Kansas Miscellanies* (Topeka: Kansas Publishing Co., 1889),

51; Mothershead Journal, 9, TSLA; Anderson, *Memoirs*, 164; Alden McLellan to Albert C. Danner, 18 May 1919, MHS.

35. *OR*, 8 (ser. 1):307; Bannon Diary, SCL.

36. Bannon Diary, SCL; Mothershead Journal, 9, TLSA; *OR*, 8 (ser. 1):307.

37. Maury, "Recollections of the Elkhorn Campaign," 187; Bannon Diary, SCL; *OR*, 8 (ser. 1):305–307; Anderson, *Memoirs*, 167; Mothershead Journal, 9, TSLA; *St. Louis Missouri Republican*, 11 July, 21 Nov., and 19 Dec. 1885; Britton, *Civil War on the Border*, 1:221; Payne, "Story of the Battle of Pea Ridge," PRNMP; Dallas T. Herndon, "Traditions of the Battle of Pea Ridge and Elkhorn Tavern," Arkansas History Commission; *New York Herald*, 21 Mar. 1862; *Northwest Arkansas (Fayetteville) Times*, 9 Mar. 1962; John W. Bond, "The History of Elkhorn Tavern," *Arkansas Historical Quarterly* 21 (Spring 1962):4; Frances H. Kennedy, ed., *The Civil War Battlefield Guide* (Boston: Houghton Mifflin, 1990), 21.

38. Bearss, "First Day at Pea Ridge," 133; Bearss, "Battle of Pea Ridge," 573; *Mobile Register and Advertiser*, 29 Mar. 1862; Johnson and Buel, *Battles and Leaders of the Civil War*, 1:337; Maury, "Recollections of the Elkhorn Campaign," 187; *St. Louis Missouri Republican*, 4 July and 21 Nov. 1885; Castel, *General Sterling Price*, 72–74; Brauckman Scrapbook, MHS.

39. Bond, "History of Elkhorn Tavern," 4; *OR*, 8 (ser. 1):307; *St. Louis Missouri Republican*, 4 July 1885.

40. Pitts, *Chaplains in Gray*, 93–94; Bannon Diary, SCL; "Rev. John Bannon," 451; Wiley, *Life of Johnny Reb*, 188–89; John Bannon, "Experiences of a Confederate Army Chaplain," *Letters and Notices of the English Jesuit Province* 34 (1866–1868):202.

41. Bannon, "Experiences of a Confederate Army Chaplain," 202; Wiley, *Life of Johnny Reb*, 188–90; Pitts, *Chaplains in Gray*, 93–94; "Rev. John Bannon," 451.

42. Brauckman Scrapbook, MHS; "Rev. John Bannon," 451; Father Bannon Sketch and depiction in Wilson P. Hunt Painting of the Battle of Pea Ridge, Confederate Museum, Richmond.

43. Bearss, "First Day at Pea Ridge," 137; Bannon Diary, SCL; *OR*, 8 (ser. 1):305–307; Maury, "Recollections of the Elkhorn Campaign," 187; Payne, "Story of the Battle of Pea Ridge," PRNMP; Mothershead Journal, 9, TSLA; *St. Louis Missouri Republican*, 4 July 1885.

44. *St. Louis Missouri Republican*, 4 July 1885; Dunlap Diary, 69, WHMC-SHSM.

45. Bannon Diary, SCL; Bevier, *History of the First and Second Missouri Confederate Brigades*, 154; Dunlap Diary, 69, WHMC-SHSM; *New York Herald*, 9 Mar. 1862; Mothershead Journal, 9, TSLA; *OR*, 8 (ser. 1):307; Hyde and Conrad, *Encyclopedia of the History of St. Louis*, 4:2440; Bearss, "First Day at Pea Ridge," 137–38; *St. Louis Missouri Republican*, 4 July and 19 Dec. 1885; Compiled Missouri Service Records, Roll 90, NA.

46. Bannon Diary, SCL; Compiled Service Records, NA; Dunlap Diary, 69,

WHMC-SHSM; Mothershead Journal, 9, TSLA; "Rev. John Bannon," 451; *OR*, 8 (ser. 1):307; *St. Louis Missouri Republican*, 4 July and 19 Dec. 1885.

47. Bannon Diary, SCL; *OR*, 8 (ser. 1):307; Bearss, "First Day at Pea Ridge," 138; *New York Herald*, 9 Mar. 1862; *St. Louis Missouri Republican*, 4 July and 19 Dec. 1885.

48. Bannon Diary, SCL.

49. Ibid.; Bearss, "First Day at Pea Ridge," 139; *OR*, 8 (ser. 1):307.

50. Bearss, "First Day at Pea Ridge," 139–40; Mothershead Journal, 9–10, TSLA; *OR*, 8 (ser. 1):307.

51. Compiled Service Records, NA; Brauckman Scrapbook, MHS; Bannon Diary, SCL.

52. Bannon Diary, SCL; Brauckman Scrapbook, MHS.

53. Compiled Service Records, NA.

54. "Rev. John Bannon," 451.

55. *OR*, 8 (ser. 1):307–308; Bannon Diary, SCL; Mothershead Journal, 9–11, TSLA; Bearss, "First Day at Pea Ridge," 138–40.

56. Bannon Diary, SCL; Brauckman Scrapbook, MHS; Payne, "Story of the Battle of Pea Ridge," PRNMP; *OR*, 8 (ser. 1):308; *St. Louis Missouri Republican*, 4 July 1885.

57. *OR*, 8 (ser. 1):308; Bannon Diary, SCL; Bearss, "First Day at Pea Ridge," 144.

58. Bannon Diary, SCL; *OR*, 8 (ser. 1):308; Anderson, *Memoirs*, 170; *Richmond Enquirer*, 14 Mar. 1862; *Mobile Register and Advertiser*, 16 and 27 Mar. 1862.

59. Payne, "Story of the Battle of Pea Ridge," PRNMP; Bannon Diary, SCL; Bearss, "First Day at Pea Ridge," 138–42; Anderson, *Memoirs*, 171; Mothershead Journal, 9–10, TSLA; Kavanaugh Memoir, 13–14, WHMC-SHSM; *OR*, 8 (ser. 1):308; *St. Louis Missouri Republican*, 4 July and 19 Dec. 1885; Bennett and Haigh, *Thirty-Sixth Regiment Illinois Volunteers*, 156–58.

60. Payne, "Story of the Battle of Pea Ridge," PRNMP; Bannon Diary, SCL; *OR*, 8 (ser. 1):308; Mothershead Journal, 10, TSLA; Kavanaugh Memoir, 13–14, WHMC-SHSM.

61. *Mobile Register and Advertiser*, 12, 13, 16, 27, 29, and 30 Mar. 1862; Bannon Diary, SCL; Brauckman Scrapbook, MHS; *St. Louis Missouri Republican*, 4 July 1885; Mothershead Journal, 12, TSLA; Henry Voelkner to Family, 18 Mar. 1862, MHS; Brown, "Pea Ridge: Gettysburg of the West," 13–14; Britton, *Civil War on the Border*, 1:259–61; *The Intelligencer*, 23 March 1862; *Memphis Daily Appeal*, 4, 6, and 8 April 1862.

62. Bannon Diary, SCL.

63. Bevier, *History of the First and Second Missouri Confederate Brigades*, 105; Anderson, *Memoirs*, 178; Mothershead Journal, 13–14, TSLA.

64. Mothershead Journal, 10, TSLA; Bearss, "First Day at Pea Ridge," 138–39; Payne, "Story of the Battle of Pea Ridge," PRNMP.

65. Boyce 1914 Paper, MHS; "Rev. John Bannon," 451; Kenny and Morrissey, "Father John Bannon, S.J.," 98.

66. Boyce 1914 Paper, MHS; "Rev. John Bannon," 451.

67. Kenny and Morrissey, "Father John Bannon, S.J.," 98.

68. James T. King, *A Life of General Eugene A. Carr* (Lincoln: University of Nebraska Press, 1963), 46–49; Bannon Diary, SCL; Bearss, "First Day at Pea Ridge," 144–45; Mothershead Journal, 10, TSLA; *OR*, 8 (ser. 1):308.

69. Mothershead Journal, 10, TSLA; Bannon Diary, SCL; *St. Louis Missouri Republican*, 4 July 1885.

70. Bannon Diary, SCL; Mothershead Journal, 10–11, TSLA; King, *Life of General Eugene A. Carr*, 49; Anderson, *Memoirs*, 171–72; *New York Herald*, 9 Mar. 1862; Calkins, "Elkhorn to Vicksburg," 13; Bearss, "First Day at Pea Ridge," 146; *OR*, 8 (ser. 1):307–308; Smith Memoir, 16–17, WHMC-SHSM; Brauckman Scrapbook, MHS; *St. Louis Missouri Republican*, 4 and 11 July 1885; Jay Monaghan, *Civil War on the Western Border 1854–1865* (New York: Bonanza Books, n.d.), 244.

71. Bannon Diary, SCL; *St. Louis Missouri Republican*, 19 Dec. 1885; Mothershead Journal, 11, TSLA; Johnson and Buel, *Battles and Leaders of the Civil War*, 1:337; *OR*, 8 (ser. 1):308–309.

72. Bannon Diary, SCL; Breckinridge Scrapbook, vol. 1 (1893), MHS; Anderson, *Memoirs*, 172–75; *St. Louis Missouri Republican*, 11 July 1885; *Battlefield of Pea Ridge, Arkansas: Battlefield Folklore*, 8, AHC; Herndon, "Traditions of the Battle of Pea Ridge or Elkhorn Tavern," AHC; *Northwest Arkansas Times*, 9 Mar. 1862; Bond, "History of Elkhorn Tavern," 4–6.

73. Nathan C. Harwood, *The Pea Ridge Campaign, Civil War Sketches and Incidents Read Before the Nebraska Commandery, Nebraska Military Order of the Loyal Legion* (Omaha: Ackerman Brothers and Heintze Printers, 1887):17; Bannon Diary, SCL; Payne, "Story of the Battle of Pea Ridge," PRNMP; Mothershead Journal, 12, TSLA; Anderson, *Memoirs*, 172; *OR*, 8 (ser. 1):309; *Mobile Register and Advertiser*, 22 Mar. 1862.

74. Payne, "Story of the Battle of Pea Ridge," PRNMP; *OR*, 8 (ser. 1):309; Smith Memoir, 18, WHMC-SHSM; Brauckman Scrapbook, MHS.

75. Voelkner to Family, 18 Mar. 1862, MHS; *St. Louis Missouri Republican*, 11 July 1885; *New York Herald*, 9 Mar. 1862; Bannon Diary, SCL; Brauckman Scrapbook, MHS; Brown, "Pea Ridge: Gettysburg of the West," 14–15; Maury, "Recollections of the Elkhorn Campaign," 188; Castel, "New View of the Battle of Pea Ridge," 145; Bennett and Haigh, *History of the Thirty-Sixth Illinois Volunteers*, 161; Alwyn Barr, "Confederate Artillery in Arkansas," *Arkansas Historical Quarterly* 22 (Autumn 1963):243–44, 249.

76. Bannon Diary, SCL; Smith Memoir, 18, WHMC-SHSM; Mothershead Journal, 12–13, TSLA; Anderson, *Memoirs*, 176–77; Maury, "Recollections of the Elkhorn Campaign," 188–89; *OR*, 8 (ser. 1):309–10; Prentis, *Kansas Miscellanies*, 48; Voelkner to Family, 18 Mar. 1862, MHS.

77. *OR*, 8 (ser. 1):309-10; Mothershead Journal, 12-13, TSLA; *New York Herald*, 9 Mar. 1862; Anderson, *Memoirs*, 176-77; Bennett and Haigh, *History of the Thirty-Sixth Illinois Volunteers*, 166; Bannon Diary, SCL; Voelkner to Family, 18 Mar. 1862, MHS; Maury, "Recollections of the Elkhorn Campaign," 188; *St. Louis Missouri Republican*, 11 July 1885.

78. *New York Herald*, 9 Mar. 1862; *OR*, 8 (ser. 1):310; Maury, "Recollections of the Elkhorn Campaign," 189; Mothershead Journal, 13-14, TSLA; Kavanaugh Memoir, 15, WHMC-SHSM; Bannon Diary, SCL; Smith Memoir, 18, WHMC-SHSM; Anderson, *Memoirs*, 177-78; Payne, "Story of the Battle of Pea Ridge," PRNMP; *St. Louis Missouri Republican*, 28 Nov. 1885; Typescript of Vinson Holman Diary, 37, State Historical Society of Iowa, Iowa City; Johnson and Buel, *Battles and Leaders of the Civil War*, 1:322; Sketch of Benjamin Avery Rives, MHS; Marie Oliver Watkins and Helen Watkins, *Tearin' Through the Wilderness: Missouri Pioneer Episodes and Genealogy of the Watkins Family of Virginia and Missouri* (Charleston: private printing, 1957), 80; Bond, "History of Elkhorn Tavern," 4; *Mobile Register and Advertiser*, 29 Mar. 1862.

79. Boyce 1914 Paper, MHS; Bannon Sketch, CM; Champ Clark Scrapbook, vol. 15, Champ Clark Papers, Western Historical Manuscript Collection, State Historical Society of Missouri; Bannon Diary, SCL; *St. Louis Missouri Republican*, 11 July 1885; Voelkner to Family, 18 Mar. 1862, MHS.

80. *St. Louis Missouri Republican*, 28 Nov. and 11 July 1885; Brauckman Scrapbook, MHS; *OR*, 8 (ser. 1):310; Maury, "Recollections of the Elkhorn Campaign," 188-89; Payne, "Story of the Battle of Pea Ridge," PRNMP; Clark Family Papers, MHS; Eli Hilles Larkin Schoninger to Aunt Sarah, 10 April 1862, William Carr Lane Collection, MHS; *Mobile Register and Advertiser*, 29 and 30 Mar. 1862; Bannon Diary, SCL; Bevier, *History of the First and Second Missouri Confederate Brigades*, 110; Anderson, *Memoirs*, 177-78; Barr, "Confederate Artillery in Arkansas," 248.

81. Bannon Diary, SCL; Brauckman Scrapbook, MHS; *OR*, 8 (ser. 1):310; *St. Louis Missouri Republican*, 11 July and 28 Nov. 1885; *Richmond Enquirer*, 14 Mar. 1862.

82. Bannon Diary, SCL; *OR*, 24 (ser. 1):310-13; Compiled Missouri Service Records, Rolls 110 and 118, NA; *History of Andrew and DeKalb Counties, Missouri* (Chicago: Goodspeed Publishing Co., 1888), 222; Carmeta Robertson, Albany, Missouri, to author, 14 April 1989; Mary Jameson, Albany, Missouri, to author, 4 Mar. 1989.

83. *St. Louis Missouri Republican*, 11 July 1885; Bannon Diary, SCL; Pea Ridge National Military Park Centennial Committee, The Battle of Pea Ridge 1862, 42; *Mobile Register and Advertiser*, 16 Mar. 1862; Bevier, *History of the First and Second Missouri Confederate Brigades*, 111-12; Faye L. Stewart, "Battle of Pea Ridge," *Missouri Historical Review* 22 (January 1928):188.

84. Bannon Diary, SCL; Brauckman Scrapbook, MHS; Vinson Holman Diary, 37, SHSI; Mothershead Journal, 14, TSLA; *St. Louis Missouri Republican*, 11 July and 28 Nov. 1885; *Richmond Enquirer*, 14 Mar. 1862.

85. Bannon Diary, SCL; *St. Louis Missouri Republican*, 11 July and 28 Nov. 1885; Johnson and Buel, *Battles and Leaders of the Civil War*, 1:329.
86. Bannon Diary, SCL; Castel, *General Sterling Price*, 78; *Mobile Register and Advertiser*, 29 Mar. 1862.
87. Bannon Diary, SCL; Mothershead Journal, 13–15, TSLA; Maury, "Recollections of the Elkhorn Campaign," 189; *St. Louis Missouri Republican*, 11 July 1885; *Mobile Register and Advertiser*, 29 Mar. 1862.
88. Johnson and Buel, *Battles and Leaders of the Civil War*, 1:331–34; Brown, "Pea Ridge: Gettysburg of the West," 15–16; Castel, "New View of the Battle of Pea Ridge," 150–51; Maury, "Recollections of the Elkhorn Campaign," 189–90; *Weekly Mississippian*, 5 Mar. 1862; Edwin C. Bearss, *The Fall of Fort Henry, Tennessee* (Dover: Eastern National Park and Monument Association), 3; Stanley F. Horn, *Tennessee's War 1861–1865* (Nashville: Civil War Centennial Commission, 1965), 56–57; Hamilton, *Battle of Fort Donelson*, 338–44; Cooling, *Forts Henry and Donelson*, 209–27.
89. Bannon Diary, SCL; *St. Louis Missouri Republican*, 26 Dec. 1885; *OR*, 8 (ser. 1):312; Anderson, *Memoirs*, 181; Vinson Holman Diary, 38, SHSI; Anne E. Lane to Sarah L. Glasgow, 21 Mar. 1862, William Carr Lane Collection, MHS.
90. Bevier, *History of the First and Second Missouri Confederate Brigades*, 106–107; *The Intelligencer*, Atlanta, Georgia, 11 April 1862.
91. Bannon Diary, SCL; Mothershead Journal, 16–17, TSLA.
92. *Mobile Register and Advertiser*, 30 Mar. 1862; Maury, "Recollections of the Elkhorn Campaign," 190; Castel, *General Sterling Price*, 81–82.
93. Compiled Service Records, NA; Bannon Diary, SCL; Anderson, *Memoirs*, 187–89; *Mobile Register and Advertiser*, 30 Mar. 1862.
94. Bannon Diary, SCL.
95. Ibid.; Boyce 1914 Paper, MHS; James J. Pillar, *The Catholic Church in Mississippi, 1837–1865* (New Orleans: Hauser Printing Co., 1964), 233n.
96. Bannon Diary, SCL; Mothershead Journal, 17–19, TSLA.
97. Mothershead Journal, 18–19, TSLA; Dunlap Diary, 82, WHMC-SHSM; James Lee McDonough, *Shiloh—In Hell before Night* (Knoxville: University of Tennessee Press, 1977), 196–206; *Mobile Register and Advertiser*, 8 and 11 April 1862.
98. Compiled Missouri Service Records, Rolls 92–138, NA; *Richmond Enquirer*, 10 Oct. 1861; Maury, "Recollections of the Elkhorn Campaign," 191; *Dublin Telegraph*, 14 July 1913; Mothershead Journal, 19, TSLA.
99. Bannon Diary, SCL; Mothershead Journal, 19–20, TSLA.

FOUR   Hard Fighting in Mississippi

1. Bannon Diary, SCL; Mothershead Journal, 20–21, TSLA; Anderson, *Memoirs*, 191–92.

2. *Mobile Register and Advertiser*, 7 May 1862; Mothershead Journal, 21, TSLA; Bannon Diary, SCL; Johnson and Buel, *Battles and Leaders of the Civil War*, 2:717–18; John Tyler to William Lowndes Yancey, 15 Oct. 1862, WHMC-SHSM; Ellen Ryan Jolly, *Nuns of the Battlefield* (Philadelphia: Providence Visitor Press, 1897), 250–51, 258–70.

3. George Barton, *Angels of the Battlefield* (Philadelphia: Catholic Art Publishing Co., 1897), 19–21, 53.

4. Bannon Diary, SCL; Little Diary, USAMHI; Mothershead Journal, 22, TSLA.

5. Bannon Diary, SCL; Little Diary, USAMHI; Mothershead Journal, 24–28, TSLA; Johnson and Buel, *Battles and Leaders of the Civil War*, 2:717–19.

6. Bannon Diary, SCL; Wiley, *Life of Johnny Reb*, 174–75; Gardiner H. Shattuck, Jr., *A Shield and Hiding Place: The Religious Life of the Civil War Armies* (Macon: Mercer University Press, 1987), 65–66.

7. Johnson and Buel, *Battles and Leaders of the Civil War*, 2:719; Bannon Diary, SCL; Barton, *Angels of the Battlefield*, 53; Pillar, *Catholic Church in Mississippi*, 223.

8. Bannon Diary, SCL; Mothershead Journal, 24–28, TSLA; Johnson and Buel, *Battles and Leaders of the Civil War*, 2:718–19.

9. Bannon Diary, SCL; Compiled Missouri Service Records, Roll 127, NA; *St. Louis Missouri Republican*, 30 Jan. 1886; George William Warren Diary, George William Warren IV, Montpelier, Va.; Avington Wayne Simpson Diary, Western Historical Manuscript Collection, State Historical Society of Missouri; Kennedy's 1860 St. Louis City Directory, 91.

10. Boyce Scrapbook, MHS; Menra Hopewell, History of the Missouri Volunteer Militia (St. Louis: George Knapp, 1861), 18.

11. Compiled Missouri Service Records, Roll 127, NA; Bannon Diary, SCL; Thomas Hogan letters, Civil War Collection, MHS; *St. Louis Missouri Republican*, 30 Jan. 1886; Albert Carey Danner, Historical Memorandum 1845–1865, Mrs. Dorothy Danner Tribets, Mobile, Ala.

12. Bevier, *History of the First and Second Missouri Confederate Brigades*, 330; Brauckman Scrapbook, MHS.

13. Romero, *The Rebel Chaplain*, 35; Boyce 1914 Paper, MHS; William Barnaby Faherty, St. Louis, to author, 29 June 1990.

14. Hogan letters, MHS; *St. Louis Missouri Republican*, 30 Jan. 1886.

15. Thomas L. Snead to Joseph Boyce, 26 July 1886, Boyce Papers, MHS.

16. Bevier, *History of the First and Second Missouri Confederate Brigades*, 330; Joseph M. Hernon, Jr., "The Irish Nationalists and Southern Secession," *Civil War History* 12 (March 1966):43–44.

17. Shattuck, *A Shield and Hiding Place*, 35–37; Emory M. Thomas, *The Confederacy as a Revolutionary Experience* (Englewood Cliffs: Prentice-Hall, 1971), 116; Towey, "Kerry Patch Revisited," 155; Bannon 1864 Ireland Poster, Washington, D.C., NA; Daisy La Grave Manuscript on Father John Bannon, 187, 190; Charles P. Roland, *The Confederacy* (Chicago: University of Chicago Press, 1960),

NOTES TO PAGES 66–69

160; Bannon Diary, SCL; Thomas L. Connelly and Barbara L. Bellows, *God and General Longstreet: The Lost Cause and the Southern Mind* (Baton Rouge: Louisiana State University Press, 1982), 11–12; John Leavy Journal, 54, Philip Mallinckrodt, Salt Lake City, Utah; Emory M. Thomas, *The Confederate Nation: 1861–1865* (New York: Harper and Row, 1979), 21; Drew Gilpin Faust, *The Creation of Confederate Nationalism: Idealogy and Identity in the Civil War South* (Baton Rouge: Louisiana State University Press, 1988), 22, 26–29, 32; Father Bannon to Yates Snowden, Yates Snowden Collection, South Caroliniana Library, University of South Carolina, Columbia; James W. Silver, *Confederate Morale and Church Propaganda* (Tuscaloosa: Norton and Co., 1957), 25–40; *Weekly Mississippian*, 22 Oct. 1861; Hackey and McCaffrey, *Perspectives on Irish Nationalism*, 9; Jones, Still, Beringer, and Hattaway, *Why the South Lost the Civil War*, 82–83, 91–97, 100–101, 268–69.

18. Little Diary, USAMHI; Bannon Diary, SCL; Johnson and Buel, *Battles and Leaders of the Civil War*, 2:733.

19. Bannon Diary, SCL; Compiled Service Records, NA; Pitts, *Chaplains in Gray*, 6–8; Boyce 1914 Paper, MHS.

20. Compiled Missouri Service Records, Roll 118, NA; Bannon Diary, SCL; Little Diary, USAMHI.

21. Shalhope, *General Sterling Price*, 207–208; William F. Mack to Colonel Cobb, 11 April 1862, Hunter-Dawson Historic Site Archives, New Madrid, Missouri; Johnson and Buel, *Battles and Leaders of the Civil War*, 1:443, and 2:719; Maury, "Recollections of the Elkhorn Campaign," 191; Brauckman Scrapbook, MHS; Bannon Diary, SCL; Mothershead Journal, 25–26, TSLA; *Mobile Register and Advertiser*, 7, 11, 14, 20, and 31 May 1862; *Memphis Daily Appeal*, 20 and 24 May 1862.

22. Thomas, *Confederate Nation*, 245; Faust, *Creation of Confederate Nationalism*, 26; Bannon Diary, SCL; Mothershead Journal, 26–27, TSLA; Roland, *The Confederacy*, 160; Clark Family Papers, MHS; *Weekly Mississippian*, 4 Mar. 1863.

23. Bannon Diary, SCL; Faust, *Creation of Confederate Nationalism*, 22–30; Billon Scrapbook, vol. 2, MHS; Roland, *The Confederacy*, 160; Jones, Still, Beringer, and Hattaway, *Why the South Lost the Civil War*, 82–83, 95–97.

24. Bannon Diary, SCL; William Clark Kennerly, *Persimmon Hill: A Narrative of Old St. Louis and the Far West* (Norman: University of Oklahoma Press, 1948), 178.

25. *Mobile Register and Advertiser*, 14, 24, and 31 May and 3 and 12 June 1862; Bannon Diary, SCL; Johnson and Buel, *Battles and Leaders of the Civil War*, 2:719.

26. Little Diary, USAMHI; Bannon Diary, SCL; Compiled Service Records, NA; Romero, *The Rebel Chaplain*, 35; Wiley, *Life of Johnny Reb*, 188–90; Pitts, *Chaplains in Gray*, 5–15; John C. Moore, *Confederate Military History*, ed. Clement A. Evans (New York: Thomas Yoseloff, 1962), 10:96, 314–15; John F. Walter, "Capsule Histories of Arkansas Military Units," Manuscript, AHC; *The Encyclopedia of the New West* (Marshall: United States Biographical Co., 1881), 113–15.

27. Bannon Diary, SCL; Johnson and Buel, *Battles and Leaders of the Civil War*, 2:719.

28. Bannon Diary, SCL; Little Diary, USAMHI.

29. Bannon Diary, SCL; Little Diary, USAMHI; Kenny and Morrissey, "Father John Bannon, S.J.," 93; Henry Hance to Family, 15 Aug. 1864, Edward C. Robbins Collection, Mercantile Library, St. Louis; Photographic Collections, MHS.

30. Bannon Diary, SCL.

31. Ibid.; Johnson and Buel, *Battles and Leaders of the Civil War*, 2:720; *Mobile Register and Advertiser*, 3 June 1862.

32. Bannon Diary, SCL; Mothershead Journal, 29–31, TSLA; Johnson and Buel, *Battles and Leaders of the Civil War*, 2:719–20; *Mobile Register and Advertiser*, 3 June 1862.

33. Bannon Diary, SCL; *Mobile Register and Advertiser*, 3 and 12 June 1862; Mothershead Journal, 29–34, TSLA; Castel, *General Sterling Price*, 86; Johnson and Buel, *Battles and Leaders of the Civil War*, 2:720; *Memphis Daily Appeal*, 4 and 9 June 1862.

34. Bannon Diary, SCL; Little Diary, USAMHI.

35. Bannon Diary, SCL; Mothershead Journal, 34, TSLA; Johnson and Buel, *Battles and Leaders of the Civil War*, 2:722; *Mobile Register and Advertiser*, 30 July 1862.

36. Little Diary, USAMHI; Bannon Diary, SCL; Johnson and Buel, *Battles and Leaders of the Civil War*, 2:722–26; *OR*, 17 (ser. 1, pt. 2):596; Moore, *Confederate Military History*, ed. Evans, 10:213–15.

37. Bannon Diary, SCL; Little Diary, USAMHI.

38. Warren Diary; Simpson Diary, WHMC-SHSM.

39. Castel, *General Sterling Price*, 87–92.

40. Warren Diary.

41. Anderson, *Memoirs*, ix; Castel, *General Sterling Price*, 139; Romero, *Rebel Chaplain*, 28; Pitts, *Chaplains in Gray*, 2; Bevier, *History of the First and Second Missouri Confederate Brigades*, 21–23; Wiley, *Life of Johnny Reb*, 191; Jones, Still, Beringer, and Hattaway, *Why the South Lost the Civil War*, 95–98, 100–101, 268–69; *Weekly Mississippian*, 17 and 20 Nov. 1862 and 4 Jan. 1863; *Mobile Register and Advertiser*, 9, 19, and 24 Jan. 1864; Roher, "Confederate Generals," 13.

42. Billon Scrapbook, MHS; Bannon Diary, SCL; *Weekly Mississippian*, 5 Mar. 1862.

43. Leavy Journal, 55; Albert C. Danner, "Some Recollections of Bishop Marvin and Others," Albert C. Danner Papers, Dorothy Danner Tribets, Mobile.

44. Bannon Diary, SCL; Warren Diary; Simpson Diary, WHMC-SHSM; Faust, *Creation of Confederate Nationalism*, 14, 15, 21, 26–31; Joseph P. Cullen, *The Peninsula Campaign 1862: McClellan and Lee Struggle For Richmond* (New York: Bonanza Books, n.d.), 159–81; Milo Quaife, *Absalom Grimes: Confederate Mail Runner* (New Haven: Yale University Press, 1926), 63–65; Clifford Dowdey, *The Seven Days: The Emergence of Lee* (Boston: Little, Brown and Co., 1964), 347–59; Jones, Still, Beringer, and Hattaway, *Why the South Lost the Civil War*, 82–83, 90–93, 268.

45. Castel, *General Sterling Price*, 139; Francis Marion Cockrell Scrapbook, MHS; Leavy Journal, 58, 63; *Mobile Daily Advertiser & Register*, 19, 23, and 24 Jan.

1864; Warren Diary; Little Diary, USAMHI; Simpson Diary, WHMC-SHSM; Bannon Diary, SCL.

46. Bannon Diary, SCL; Little Diary, USAMHI.

47. *Mobile Register and Advertiser*, 30 July 1862; Little Diary, USAMHI; Bannon Diary, SCL; Castel, *General Sterling Price*, 93.

48. Castel, *General Sterling Price*, 93; Bannon Diary, SCL.

49. Billon Scrapbook, vol. 2, MHS.

50. *Mobile Register and Advertiser*, 2 Oct. 1862; Warren Diary; Simpson Diary, WHMC-SHSM; Johnson and Buel, *Battles and Leaders of the Civil War*, 2:725–28; Thomas L. Connelly, *Civil War Tennessee: Battles and Leaders* (Knoxville: University of Tennessee Press, 1979), 55–57.

51. Harriet Lane Cates Hardaway, "The Adventures of General Frost and His Wife Lily during the Civil War," *Florissant Valley Historical Society Quarterly* 14 (July 1972):4; Necrologies Scrapbook, vol. 2, MHS; W. A. Mitchell, "The Confederate Mail Carrier," *Confederate Veteran* 22 (1914):529; Compiled Missouri Service Records, Microcopy 322, Roll 4, NA.

52. Thomas Lawrence Connelly, *Army of the Heartland: The Army of Tennessee, 1861–1862* (Baton Rouge: Louisiana State University Press, 1967), 196–201; Douglas Southall Freeman, *Lee's Lieutenants: A Study in Command, Cedar Mountain to Chancellorsville* (New York: Charles Scribner's Sons, 1943), 144–45; Connelly, *Civil War Tennessee*, 54–57; *Mobile Register and Advertiser*, 12 and 14 Sept. 1862; Horn, *Army of Tennessee*, 162–73.

53. Little Diary, USAMHI.

54. Castel, *General Sterling Price*, 93–94; Johnson and Buel, *Battles and Leaders of the Civil War*, 2:730; Dabney H. Maury, "Recollections of Campaign Against Grant in North Mississippi in 1862–1863," *Southern Historical Society Papers* 13 (1885):286–87; *Mobile Register and Advertiser*, 2 Oct. 1862; Horn, *Army of Tennessee*, 172–74.

55. Bannon Diary, SCL.

56. Simpson Diary, WHMC-SHSM; Warren Diary; City of St. Louis Census Records 1860; Compiled Missouri Service Records, Rolls 3, 6, 105, 118, and 130, NA; *OR*, 17 (ser. 1, pt. 1):382; Hogan Letters, MHS; *St. Louis Missouri Republican*, 5 Dec. 1884.

57. Bannon Diary, SCL; Little Diary, USAMHI.

58. *Mobile Register and Advertiser*, 17 Sept. and 2 Oct. 1862; Maury, "Recollections of Campaign Against Grant," 286–87.

59. *Mobile Register and Advertiser*, 17 Sept. 1862; Castel, *General Sterling Price*, 97; Little Diary, USAMHI; *Mobile Register and Advertiser*, 2 Oct. 1862; Horn, *Army of Tennessee*, 172–74.

60. Bannon Diary, SCL; Warren Diary; Little Diary, USAMHI; Castel, *General Sterling Price*, 96–97; Simpson Diary, WHMC-SHSM; *Mobile Register and Adertiser*, 2 Oct. 1862; *Richmond Enquirer*, 7 Oct. 1862; Horn, *Army of Tennessee*, 173.

61. Bannon Diary, SCL; Warren Diary; Pitts, *Chaplains in Gray*, 44; Simpson

Diary, WHMC-SHSM; Bevier, *History of the First and Second Missouri Confederate Brigades*, 337.

62. Warren Diary; Little Diary, USAMHI; Johnson and Buel, *Battles and Leaders of the Civil War*, 2:730; Simpson Diary, WHMC-SHSM; *Richmond Enquirer*, 7 Oct. 1862; *Mobile Register and Advertiser*, 2 Oct. 1862.

63. Bannon Diary, SCL; Little Diary, USAMHI.

64. *Mobile Register and Advertiser*, 17 Sept., 2 Oct., and 5 Nov. 1862; Ulysses S. Grant, *Personal Memoirs of U. S. Grant* (New York: Century Co., 1903), 211; Francis V. Greene, *The Mississippi* (New York: Charles Scribner's Sons, 1882), 38; Bannon Diary, SCL; Anderson, *Memoirs*, 218–19; Warren Diary; Johnson and Buel, *Battles and Leaders of the Civil War*, 2:730–31; Little Diary, USAMHI; *Richmond Enquirer*, 7 Oct. 1862.

65. Bannon Diary, SCL.

66. *Weekly Mississippian*, 12 Nov. 1862; Grant, *Personal Memoirs*, 211–13; Castel, *General Sterling Price*, 98–101; Greene, *The Mississippi*, 38–39; Johnson and Buel, *Battles and Leaders of the Civil War*, 2:731; Ben Earl Kitchens, *Rosecrans Meets Price: The Battle of Iuka, Mississippi* (Florence, Ala.: Thornwood Publishers, 1985), 77; William M. Lamers, *The Edge of Glory: A Biography of General William S. Rosecrans, U.S.A.* (New York: Harcourt, Brace and World, 1961), 100–104; Harvey L. Carter and Norma L. Peterson, eds., "William S. Stewart Letters, January 13, 1861 to December 4, 1862," *Missouri Historical Review* 61 (July 1967), pt. 3: 473.

67. Grant, *Personal Memoirs*, 212–13; Lamers, *Edge of Glory*, 105–106; Warren Diary; Simpson Diary, WHMC-SHSM; Carter and Peterson, "William S. Stewart Letters," 473.

68. Grant, *Personal Memoirs*, 213; Bannon Diary, SCL; Simpson Diary, WHMC-SHSM; Castel, *General Sterling Price*, 99–100; Greene, *The Mississippi*, 39; Lamers, *Edge of Glory*, 106–109; Maury, "Recollections of the Campaign Against Grant," 287; Little Diary, USAMHI; Warren Diary.

69. Greene, *The Mississippi*, 39; Grant, *Personal Memoirs*, 213; Maury, "Recollections of the Campaign Against Grant," 287.

70. Warren Diary; Simpson Diary, WHMC-SHSM.

71. Grant, *Personal Memoirs*, 213; Greene, *The Mississippi*, 39–40; Castel, *General Sterling Price*, 99–101; Johnson and Buel, *Battles and Leaders of the Civil War*, 2:731–32.

72. Castel, *General Sterling Price*, 99–101; Greene, *The Mississippi*, 39–40; *Richmond Enquirer*, 10 Oct. 1861; Grant, *Personal Memoirs*, 213–14.

73. Little Diary, USAMHI; Castel, *General Sterling Price*, 100–101; *Richmond Enquirer*, 7 Oct. 1862; Hyde and Conrad, *Encyclopedia of the History of St. Louis*, 4:2440; Maury, "Recollections of the Campaign Against Grant," 287–88; *OR*, 18 (ser. 1, pt. 1):122; Kenneth P. Williams, *Lincoln Finds a General*, 5 vols. (New York: Macmillan Co., 1949–1959), 3:70.

74. Greene, *The Mississippi*, 40–41; Lamers, *Edge of Glory*, 110; Jack W. Gunn,

"The Battle of Iuka," *Journal of Mississippi History* 24 (July 1962):154–55; *Mobile Register and Advertiser*, 23 Sept. and 2 Oct. 1862.

75. Bannon Diary, SCL.

76. Little Diary, USAMHI; Greene, *The Mississippi*, 40–41; Johnson and Buel, *Battles and Leaders of the Civil War*, 2:732; *Mobile Register and Advertiser*, 23 Sept. 1862.

77. Anderson, *Memoirs*, 221; *OR*, 18 (ser. 1, pt. 1):122.

78. Grant, *Personal Memoirs*, 214; Lamers, *Edge of Glory*, 108–109, 129; Anderson, *Memoirs*, 221; Williams, *Lincoln Finds a General*, 4:79–80; Greene, *The Mississippi*, 40–42; Maury, "Recollections of the Campaign Against Grant," 288–89; *OR*, 18 (ser. 1, pt. 1):122; *Mobile Register and Advertiser*, 23 Sept. 1862.

79. Bannon Diary, SCL; Little Diary, USAMHI; *Mobile Register and Advertiser*, 23 Sept. 1862.

80. *Mobile Register and Advertiser*, 23 Sept. and 2 Oct. 1862; *Richmond Enquirer*, 7 Oct. 1862; Tunnard, *Southern Record*, 187; Lamers, *Edge of Glory*, 110–13; Anderson, *Memoirs*, 221–23; Greene, *The Mississippi*, 40–42; Maury, "Recollections of the Campaign Against Grant," 288–89; Gunn, "Battle of Iuka," 155; *OR*, 18 (ser. 1, pt. 1):132–35.

81. Bannon Diary, SCL; Little Diary, USAMHI; *Richmond Enquirer*, 7 Oct. 1862; *OR*, 18 (ser. 1, pt. 1):122–24; *New Orleans Picayune*, 11 Aug. 1901.

82. *Mobile Register and Advertiser*, 23 Sept. and 2 Oct. 1862; Bannon Diary, SCL; *New Orleans Picayune*, 11 Aug. 1901; *St. Louis Missouri Republican*, 5 June 1886; *Richmond Enquirer*, 7 Oct. 1862; Bevier, *History of the First and Second Missouri Confederate Brigades*, 130, 136; Victor M. Rose, *Ross' Texas Brigade* (Louisville: Courier Journal, 1881), 70; Lyla Merrill McDonald, *Iuka's History Embodying Dudley's Battle of Iuka* (Corinth: Rankin Printery, 1923), 16.

83. Little Diary, USAMHI.

84. Bevier, *History of the First and Second Missouri Confederate Brigades*, 333.

85. Compiled Service Records, NA; Bannon Diary, SCL; Hyde and Conrad, *Encyclopedia of History of St. Louis*, 2:1162; *Carondelet (Missouri) New Era*, 24 Sept. and 15 Oct. 1859.

86. Warren Diary; Johnson and Buel, *Battles and Leaders of the Civil War*, 2:736; Greene, *The Mississippi*, 39–40; *OR*, 18 (ser. 1, pt. 1):122, 125; McDonald, *Iuka's History*, 18; Carter and Peterson, "William S. Stewart Letters," 472–74; *Mobile Register and Advertiser*, 23 Sept. and 2 Oct. 1862.

87. Johnson and Buel, *Battles and Leaders of the Civil War*, 2:733.

88. Bannon Diary, SCL; *New Orleans Picayune*, 11 Aug. 1901.

89. *OR*, 18 (ser. 1, pt. 1):124.

90. *Mobile Register and Advertiser*, 23 Sept. and 2 Oct. 1862; Bannon Diary, SCL; *New Orleans Picayune*, 11 Aug. 1901; Greene, *The Mississippi*, 42; Maury, "Recollections of Campaign Against Grant," 290; *Richmond Enquirer*, 7 Oct. 1862.

91. Bannon Diary, SCL; Little Diary, USAMHI; *New Orleans Picayune*, 11 Aug.

1901; Kitchens, *Rosecrans Meets Price*, 152–53; Hyde and Conrad, *Encyclopedia of the History of St. Louis*, 4:2440.

92. *New Orleans Picayune*, 11 Aug. 1901; Boyce Scrapbook, MHS; Kennerly, *Persimmon Hill*, 136–38; Johnson and Buel, *Battles and Leaders of the Civil War*, 2:733.

93. *New Orleans Picayune*, 11 Aug. 1901; Hyde and Conrad, *Encyclopedia of the History of St. Louis*, 4:2440.

94. *New Orleans Picayune*, 11 Aug. 1901.

95. Bevier, *History of the First and Second Missouri Confederate Brigades*, 333.

96. Warren Diary; *Richmond Enquirer*, 7 Oct. 1862; Johnson and Buel, *Battles and Leaders of the Civil War*, 2:733; *Mobile Register and Advertiser*, 23 Sept. and 2 Oct. 1862.

97. Warren Diary; Bevier, *History of the First and Second Missouri Confederate Brigades*, 333; *OR*, 17 (ser. 1, pt. 2):684.

98. Maury, "Recollections of the Campaign Against Grant," 289.

99. *Mobile Register and Advertiser*, 2 Oct. 1862; Bevier, *History of the First and Second Missouri Confederate Brigades*, 136.

100. Castel, *General Sterling Price*, 139; Cockrell Scrapbook, MHS; Maury, "Recollections of the Campaign Against Grant," 289; *Mobile Advertiser & Register*, 19, 23, and 24 Jan. 1864; Leavy Journal, 139; *Weekly Mississippian*, 17 and 20 Nov. 1862 and 4 Jan. 1863; *Mobile Register and Advertiser*, 9, 19, and 24 Jan. 1864; Roher, "Confederate Generals," 13.

101. Bannon Diary, SCL; Little Diary, USAMHI; Anderson, *Memoirs*, 227.

FIVE   Autumn Fury

1. Grant, *Personal Memoirs*, 214; *Richmond Enquirer*, 18 Oct. 1862; Warren Diary; Johnson and Buel, *Battles and Leaders of the Civil War*, 2:734–35; John Tyler to William L. Yancey, 15 Oct. 1862, Western Historical Manuscript Collection, State Historical Society of Missouri, Columbia.

2. Bannon Diary, SCL.

3. Castel, *General Sterling Price*, 104, 106.

4. Maury, "Recollections of the Campaign Against Grant," 292–93; Tyler to Yancey, 15 Oct. 1862, WHMC-SHSM; Castel, *General Sterling Price*, 106–109.

5. Warren Diary; Bannon Diary, SCL; Tyler to Yancey, 15 Oct. 1862, WHMC-SHSM; Kitchens, *Rosecrans Meets Price*, 155; Johnson and Buel, *Battles and Leaders of the Civil War*, 2:733; Dabney Herndon Maury, *Recollections of a Virginian* (New York: Charles Scribner's Sons, 1894), 173; *Weekly Mississippian*, 17 Nov. 1862.

6. Bannon Diary, SCL; Warren Diary; Calkins, ed., "Elkhorn to Vicksburg," 34; Castel, *General Sterling Price*, 109.

7. Maury, *Recollections of a Virginian*, 173.

8. Bevier, *History of the First and Second Missouri Confederate Brigades*, 337; Castel, *General Sterling Price*, 109; Lamers, *Edge of Glory*, 133.

9. Warren Diary; Bannon Diary, SCL; *Richmond Enquirer*, 18 Oct. 1862.

10. Lamers, *Edge of Glory*, 133–34.

11. Warren Diary.

12. Bannon Diary, SCL.

13. Ibid.

14. Ibid.; Lamers, *Edge of Glory*, 136–38; Tyler to Yancey, 15 Oct. 1862, WHMC-SHSM; *Richmond Enquirer*, 18 Oct. 1862.

15. Tyler to Yancey, 15 Oct. 1862, WHMC-SHSM; Maury, "Recollections of the Campaign Against Grant," 294; *Richmond Enquirer*, 18 Oct. 1862.

16. Bannon Diary, SCL; Bannon Sketch, CM; Samuel Churchill Clark to Aunt, 25 Jan. 1862, MHS; "Diary of Lieut. Col. Hubbell of 3d Regiment Missouri Infantry, C.S.A.," *The Land We Love*, 6:2:100; Necrology Scrapbook 11c, MHS; V. M. Porter, "A History of Battery 'A' of St. Louis," *Missouri Historical Society of Collections* 2 (1900–1906):4–5, 17; John Francis McDermott, "Gold Fever: The Letters of 'Solitaire,' Goldrush Correspondent of '49," *Bulletin of the Missouri Historical Society* 5 (July 1949):218–19 notes; *Mobile Register and Advertiser*, 2 and 20 Nov. 1862 and 23 June 1863.

17. "Diary of Lieut. Col. Hubbell," 100; Bevier, *History of the First and Second Missouri Confederate Brigades*, 337.

18. Bannon Diary, SCL; Compiled Missouri Service Records, Roll 91, NA; "Diary of Lieut. Col. Hubbell," 100; Boyce Scrapbook, MHS; Hyde and Conrad, *Encyclopedia of the History of St. Louis*, 4:2441; Ed Robbins to Family, 16 Oct. 1862, ML; *Richmond Enquirer*, 10 Oct. 1862; Bevier, *History of the First and Second Missouri Confederate Brigades*, 337; *Mobile Register and Advertiser*, 8 and 28 Oct. 1862; *Daily Missouri Democrat*, 12 Dec. 1860.

19. Farrington Family Burial Records, Bellefontaine Cemetery, St. Louis; Hyde and Conrad, *Encyclopedia of the History of St. Louis*, 4:2441; Sebree Collection, MHS.

20. Tyler to Yancey, 15 Oct. 1862, WHMC-SHSM; Williams, *Lincoln Finds a General*, 4:85–92; *Richmond Enquirer*, 18 Oct. 1862.

21. Bannon Diary, SCL.

22. Tyler to Yancey, 15 Oct. 1862, WHMC-SHSM; Hogan to Father, 12 Oct. 1862, MHS; Anderson, *Memoirs*, 233–35.

23. Bannon Diary, SCL; Elliott Journal, 21, TSLA; Compiled Missouri Service Records, NA.

24. *Richmond Enquirer*, 7 Oct. 1862.

25. Johnson and Buel, *Battles and Leaders of the Civil War*, 2:747–48, 759–60.

26. Ibid.; Anderson, *Memoirs*, 234–35; Kavanaugh Memoir, 25, WHMC-SHSM; Lamers, *Edge of Glory*, 145.

27. Bannon Diary, SCL; Hogan to Father, 12 Oct. 1862, MHS; *St. Louis Missouri*

Republican, 5 Dec. 1884; Bannon, "Experiences of a Confederate Army Chaplain," 201–202.

28. Compiled Missouri Service Records, Roll 132, NA; Bannon, "Experiences of a Confederate Army Chaplain," 201–202; Kennedy's 1859 St. Louis City Directory, 495.

29. Compiled Missouri Service Records, Roll 91, NA; Bannon, "Experiences of a Confederate Army Chaplain," 201–202; Anderson, *Memoirs*, 235; Bevier, *History of the First and Second Missouri Confederate Brigades*, 338.

30. Bannon Diary, SCL; Johnson and Buel, *Battles and Leaders of the Civil War*, 2:748–49; *Richmond Enquirer*, 10 and 18 Oct. 1862; Bevier, *History of the First and Second Missouri Confederate Brigades*, 338.

31. Bannon Diary, SCL.

32. Bevier, *History of the First and Second Missouri Confederate Brigades*, 338–39; Kavanaugh Memoir, 26, WHMC-SHSM.

33. Kavanaugh Memoir, 26–27, WHMC-SHSM; Anderson, *Memoirs*, 234, 236; Johnson and Buel, *Battles and Leaders of the Civil War*, 2:750; *Weekly Mississippian*, 26 Nov. 1862; Tyler to Yancey, 15 Oct. 1862, WHMC-SHSM; Greene, *The Mississippi*, 48–50.

34. Castel, *General Sterling Price*, 115–16; Tyler to Yancey, 15 Oct. 1862, WHMC-SHSM; Maury, "Recollections of the Campaign Against Grant," 296; *Mobile Register and Advertiser*, 21 Nov. 1862.

35. Hogan to Father, 12 Oct. 1862, WHMC-SHSM; Bevier, *History of the First and Second Missouri Confederate Brigades*, 340–41; *Richmond Enquirer*, 18 Oct. 1862.

36. Bannon Diary, SCL.

37. Brauckman Scrapbook, MHS; "Rev. John Bannon," 451; Bannon, "Experiences of a Confederate Army Chaplain," 202; Jones, Still, Beringer, and Hattaway, *Why the South Lost the Civil War*, 100.

38. *The Holy Bible* (Cleveland: World Publishing Co., 1962), 174; Compiled Missouri Service Records, Rolls 114 and 118, NA; Brauckman Scrapbook, MHS; Bannon, "Experiences of a Confederate Army Chaplain," 202; Bannon Diary, SCL.

39. *OR*, 17 (ser. 1, pt. 1):382.

40. Maury, "Recollections of Campaign Against Grant," 296; *OR*, 17 (ser. 1, pt. 1):378, 379, 394.

41. Kavanaugh Memoir, 27, WHMC-SHSM.

42. Bannon, "Experiences of a Confederate Army Chaplain," 202.

43. Hogan to Father, 12 Oct. 1862, MHS; Bannon Sketch, CM.

44. Boyce 1914 Paper, MHS; Bannon Diary, SCL; Bannon Sketch, CM.

45. Ed Robbins to Family, 16 Oct. 1862, ML; Bevier, *History of the First and Second Missouri Confederate Brigades*, 153–54; Hogan to Father, 12 Oct. 1862, MHS; Evert A. Duychinck, *National History of the War for the Union*, 3 vols. (New York: Fry and Co., 1861–1865), 2:623–26; William A. Ruyle Memoir, 21, Dee Ruyle,

Bolivar, Missouri; Johnson and Buel, *Battles and Leaders of the Civil War*, 2:749; Tyler to Yancey, 15 Oct. 1862, WHMC-SHSM; Anderson, *Memoirs*, 237; "Diary of Lieut. Col. Hubbell of 3d Regiment Missouri Infantry, C.S.A.," 101; *Mobile Register and Advertiser*, 15 Oct. and 4 Nov. 1862.

46. Tyler to Yancey, 15 Oct. 1862, WHMC-SHSM; Bevier, *History of the First and Second Missouri Confederate Brigades*, 341–42; Ruyle Memoir, 21–22; Anderson, *Memoirs*, 237–38; *Mobile Register and Advertiser*, 8 and 15 Oct. and 5 and 20 Nov. 1862.

47. Bevier, *History of the First and Second Missouri Confederate Brigades*, 341–42.

48. Ruyle Memoir, 21–22; Castel, *General Sterling Price*, 116–19; Tyler to Yancey, 15 Oct. 1862, WHMC-SHSM; Johnson and Buel, *Battles and Leaders of the Civil War*, 2:749; *Mobile Register and Advertiser*, 5 Nov. 1862.

49. Bannon, "Experiences of a Confederate Army Chaplain," 202–203; Pitts, *Chaplains in Gray*, 79; Elliott Journal, 22, TSLA; Bannon Diary, SCL; Johnson and Buel, *Battles and Leaders of the Civil War*, 2:759–60.

50. Bannon Diary, SCL.

51. Williams, *Lincoln Finds a General*, 4:94–95; Castel, *General Sterling Price*, 119; *Richmond Enquirer*, 18 Oct. 1862.

52. Bannon Diary, SCL.

53. Ibid.; Tyler to Yancey, 15 Oct. 1862, WHMC-SHSM.

54. *Mobile Register and Advertiser*, 15 and 23 Oct. and 5 Nov. 1862; Castel, *General Sterling Price*, 120–22; *Richmond Enquirer*, 17 and 18 Oct. 1862; Elliott Journal, 22, TSLA; Maury, "Recollections of the Campaign Against Grant," 302–304.

55. Bannon Diary, SCL; Castel, *General Sterling Price*, 121; Maury, "Recollections of the Campaign Against Grant," 304.

56. Bannon Diary, SCL; Castel, *General Sterling Price*, 121–22; Elliott Journal, 22, TSLA; Anderson, *Memoirs*, 243–44; Maury, "Recollections of the Campaign Against Grant," 304.

57. Bannon Diary, SCL; Maury, "Recollections of the Campaign Against Grant," 304–305; *Mobile Register and Advertiser*, 2 and 14 Nov. 1862.

58. Bannon Diary, SCL; Maury, "Recollections of the Campaign Against Grant," 304–305; *Mobile Register and Advertiser*, 28 Oct. 1862.

59. Connelly, *Civil War Tennessee*, 56–57; *Weekly Mississippian*, 26 Nov. 1862; Allan Nevins, *Ordeal of the Union*, 8 vols. (New York: Charles Scribner's Sons, 1947–1959), 2:225–28, 283–90; Clement Eaton, *A History of the Southern Confederacy* (New York: Macmillan Co., 1954), 186–89; Bruce Catton, *This Hallowed Ground* (New York: Pocket Books, 1971), 197–207, 214–15; *Mobile Register and Advertiser*, 20, 24, and 26 Sept. and 2, 14, 18, 19, and 22 Oct. 1862; James A. Rawley, *Turning Points of the Civil War* (Lincoln: University of Nebraska Press, 1989), 117–43.

60. Maury, "Recollections of the Campaign Against Grant," 304–305.

61. Bannon Diary, SCL; Elliott Journal, 22, TSLA; Dr. J. C. Roberts, "Caring For the Wounded at Iuka," *Confederate Veteran* 2 (November 1894):328.

62. Clifford Dowdey, *Experiment in Rebellion* (New York: Doubleday and Co., 1946), 245; *Weekly Mississippian*, 19 Nov. 1862; Maury, "Recollections of the Campaign Against Grant," 305; *Mobile Register and Advertiser*, 15 Oct. 1862.

63. *Weekly Mississippian*, 20 Nov. 1862.

64. Warren Diary; Bannon Diary, SCL; Compiled Service Records, NA; *Weekly Mississippian*, 14 and 20 Nov. 1862 and 4 Jan. 1863; *Mobile Register and Advertiser*, 2, 14, and 21 Nov. and 18 Dec. 1862, and 9, 19, and 24 Jan. 1864; Roher, "Confederate Generals," 13; Elliott Journal, 33, TSLA; Maury, "Recollections of the Campaign Against Grant," 305; Archer Jones, *Confederate Strategy from Shiloh to Vicksburg* (Baton Rouge: Louisiana State University Press, 1961), 114–15.

65. Bannon Diary, SCL; Roland, *The Confederacy*, 71–73.

66. Warren Diary; Bannon Diary, SCL; Elliott Journal, 35, TSLA.

67. *Mobile Register and Advertiser*, 11 Sept. 1862; Bannon Diary, SCL; Compiled Service Records, NA.

68. Compiled Service Records, NA; Bannon Diary, SCL; Romero, *Rebel Chaplain*, 37; Roland, *The Confederacy*, 27; Norton, *Rebel Religion*, 29; Joseph T. Durkin, *Stephen R. Mallory: Confederate Navy Chief* (Chapel Hill: University of North Carolina Press, 1954), 11, 131–33.

69. Bannon Diary, SCL; Romero, *Rebel Chaplain*, 37; Norton, *Rebel Religion*, 29; John Bannon Chaplain Commission, 12 Feb. 1863, Yates Snowden Collection, South Caroliniana Library, University of South Carolina, Columbia.

70. Bannon Diary, SCL.

71. Pitts, *Chaplains in Gray*, 40–41.

72. Bannon Diary, SCL; Boyce 1914 Paper, MHS.

73. Bannon Diary, SCL; *Richmond Enquirer*, 11 Sept. 1863; Pillar, *Catholic Church in Mississippi*, 106, 132, 191.

74. Little Diary, USAMHI; Bannon Diary, SCL.

75. Compiled Service Records, NA; "Sketch—Gen. Bowen's Life," John Bowen Papers, MHS; Seventh United States Census, Chatham County, Georgia, District 13, 309; *Weekly Mississippian*, 17 Nov. 1862.

76. Compiled Missouri Service Records, Rolls 94 and 101, NA; Kearny-Kennerly Scrapbook, vol. 2, MHS; Carolyn Hewes Toft, *Carondelet: The Ethnic Heritage of an Urban Neighborhood* (St. Louis: Landmarks Association of St. Louis, 1980), 7; *St. Louis Missouri Republican*, 10 Nov. 1883.

SIX   Battleflags Amid the Magnolias

1. Warren Diary; Elliott Journal, 39–40, TSLA.
2. Bannon Diary, SCL; Warren Diary.
3. Bannon Diary, SCL; Pillar, *Catholic Church in Mississippi*, 260.
4. Barton, *Angels of the Battlefield*, 55.

5. Compiled Missouri Service Records, NA; Bannon Diary, SCL; Elliott Journal, 41, TSLA; Warren Diary.

6. Bannon Diary; Pillar, *Catholic Church in Mississippi*, 11, 20, 276.

7. Johnson and Buel, *Battles and Leaders of the Civil War*, 3:493–94; Robert J. Rombauer Order Book, Journals and Diaries, MHS; *Weekly Mississippian*, 5 Mar. and 20 Nov. 1862.

8. Bannon Diary, SCL.

9. Johnson and Buel, *Battles and Leaders of the Civil War*, 3:476, 561–63.

10. Bannon Diary, SCL; Elliott Journal, 43–45, TSLA; *OR*, 24 (ser. 1, pt. 1):469–70; Edwin C. Bearss, "Grand Gulf's Role in the Civil War," *Civil War History* 5 (March 1959):15.

11. Bevier, *History of the First and Second Missouri Confederate Brigades*, 406–407; Elliott Journal, 45, TSLA.

12. Bannon Diary, SCL; Simpson Diary, WHMC-SHSM; Compiled Service Records, NA.

13. Bevier, *History of the First and Second Missouri Confederate Brigades*, 22–23.

14. Jon L. Wakelyn, *Biographical Dictionary of the Confederacy* (Westport: Greenwood Press, 1977), 103; Warner, *Generals in Gray*, 29–30; "Sketch—Gen. Bowen's Life," MHS; John S. Bowen to Col. Humphries, 14 Mar. 1863, John S. Bowen Letter Book, Virginia Historical Society, Richmond; *St. Louis Missouri Republican*, 17 Sept. 1886; Bowen to Major R. W. Memminger, 27 Mar. 1863, VHS.

15. *OR*, 24 (ser. 1, pt. 1):79; *St. Louis Missouri Republican*, 17 Sept. 1886; William C. Wright, *The Confederate Magazine at Fort Wade, Grand Gulf, Mississippi: Excavations, 1980–1981* (Jackson: Mississippi Department of Archives and History and the Grand Gulf State Military Monument, 1982), 9, 15.

16. Alfred H. Guernsey and Henry M. Alden, *Harper's Pictorial History of the Civil War* (New York: Fairfax Press, n.d.), 437n.

17. *OR*, 24 (ser. 1, pt. 1):30–32; *Weekly Mississippian*, 5 Mar. and 20 Nov. 1862.

18. *St. Louis Missouri Republican*, 17 Sept. 1886; Compiled Missouri Service Records, Roll 91, NA; Bowen to Memminger, 1 April 1863, VHS; Bearss, "Grand Gulf's Role in the Civil War," 18.

19. Bannon Diary, SCL; Elliott Journal, 49, TSLA; *Weekly Mississippian*, 4 Mar. 1863.

20. Wiley, *Life of Johnny Reb*, 174–75, 182–83.

21. Bevier, *History of the First and Second Missouri Confederate Brigades*, 22.

22. *Mobile Register and Advertiser*, 24 Mar. 1863; Bearss, "Grand Gulf's Role in the Civil War," 17–18; Wright, *Confederate Magazine at Fort Wade*, 9, 15; *Weekly Mississippian*, 26 Nov. 1862.

23. Bannon Diary, SCL; Mrs. L. G. Mitchell, "Camp Life in the Sixties," *Confederate Veteran* 24 (September 1916):394; Quaife, *Absalom Grimes*, 65, 107–109, 114; Bowen to Memminger, 1 April 1863, TSLA; Elliott Journal, 48, TSLA.

24. Compiled Missouri Service Records, Roll 91, NA; Bowen to Memminger, 1

April 1863, VHS; "The Storey (sic) of 'Guibor's Battery, C.S.A.,' " Box 1, Civil War Papers, MHS.

25. Bowen to Memminger, 1 April 1863, VHS; Bannon Diary, SCL; Mary Emerson Branch, "The Story Behind the Story of the Arkansas and the Carondelet," *Missouri Historical Review* 79 (April 1985):313, 318–19.

26. Bowen to Memminger, 1 April 1863, VHS.

27. Ibid.; Bannon Diary, SCL; Elliott Journal, 49, TSLA.

28. Bowen to Memminger, 1 April 1863, VHS; Bannon Diary, SCL; *St. Louis Missouri Republican*, 17 Sept. 1886; Elliott Journal, 49; Mike Casey to Family, 6 April 1863, Robbins Collection, ML.

29. Mike Casey to Family, 6 April 1863, Robbins Collection, ML; *St. Louis Missouri Republican*, 17 Sept. 1886; Bowen to Memminger, 1 April 1863, VHS; Elliott Journal, 49, TSLA; *OR*, 24 (ser. 1, pt. 1):140, 493; Bearss, "Grand Gulf's Role in the Civil War," 17–18.

30. Bannon Diary, SCL; Elliott Journal, 49, TSLA; *St. Louis Missouri Republican*, 17 Sept. 1886; Bowen to Memminger, 1 April 1863, VHS.

31. Bowen to Memminger, 1 April and 1 April 1863 [different letters], VHS; *St. Louis Missouri Republican*, 17 Sept. 1886; Warren Guibor Papers.

32. Bowen to Memminger, 4 April 1863, VHS; Elliott Journal, 49, TSLA; Boyce 1914 Paper, MHS; David D. Porter, *The Naval History of the Civil War* (New York: Sherman Publishing Co., 1886), 313.

33. Bannon Diary, SCL; Boyce 1914 Paper, MHS; Pillar, *Catholic Church in Mississippi*, 33, 109–12; *St. Louis Missouri Republican*, 17 Sept. 1886; Kennedy's 1860 St. Louis City Directory, 165, 519.

34. Bannon Diary, SCL; Boyce Scrapbook, MHS; Bevier, *History of the First and Second Missouri Confederate Brigades*, 173–74; Maury, "Recollections of the Elkhorn Campaign," 192; William Wade to Governor Robert Stewart, 23 Feb. 1860, WHMC-SHSM.

35. Anne Lane to Sarah Glasgow, 28 Nov. 1851, William Carr Lane Collection, MHS.

36. Partnership Agreement Between Wade, Stille, Osborne, and Daniel M. Frost as Trustee, 9 April 1853, MHS.

37. *St. Louis Missouri Republican*, 15 Aug. 1861.

38. Bevier, *History of the First and Second Missouri Confederate Brigades*, 173–74; Compiled Missouri Service Records, Roll 91, NA.

39. Maury, "Recollections of the Elkhorn Campaign," 192.

40. Bannon Diary, SCL; Boyce 1914 Paper, MHS; Hyde and Conrad, *Encyclopedia of the History of St. Louis*, 3:1505; Compiled Missouri Service Records, Roll 91, NA.

41. Bannon Diary, SCL; Elliott Journal, 50, TSLA; Francis Marion Cockrell to Gen. Samuel Cooper, 12 Sept. 1863, VHS.

42. *Weekly Mississippian*, 11 and 25 Dec. 1861; *OR*, 24 (ser. 1, pt. 1):753–55, 770; Bannon Diary, SCL; Johnson and Buel, *Battles and Leaders of the Civil War*, 3:493–95; Samuel Carter III, *The Final Fortress: The Campaign For Vicksburg 1862–1863* (New York: St. Martin's Press, 1980), 152–54, 181; Earl S. Miers, *The Web of Victory: Grant at Vicksburg* (Baton Rouge: Louisiana State University Press, 1984), 138–39.

43. Miers, *Web of Victory*, 138–40.

44. Bevier, *History of the First and Second Missouri Confederate Brigades*, 406–10; Anderson, *Memoirs*, 281–88; Casey to Family, 6 April 1863, ML; John Appler Diary, 12–14, MHS; Smith Memoir, 26, WHMC-SHSM.

45. Bannon Diary, SCL.

46. Edwin C. Bearss, *The Campaign For Vicksburg: Grant Strikes a Fatal Blow*, 3 vols. (Dayton: Morningside, 1986), 3:258–59.

47. *Savannah (Georgia) Republican*, 6 May 1863.

48. Casey to Family, 6 April 1863, ML; Bannon Diary, SCL; *OR*, 24 (ser. 1, pt. 1):32, 80–81; Bevier, *History of the First and Second Missouri Confederate Brigades*, 414, 418; Emily Crawford to Mrs. Elizabeth Lewis, 11 June 1863, Charles Sullivan, Perkinston, Miss.; Bruce Catton, *Grant Moves South* (Boston: Little, Brown and Co., 1960), 418–24.

49. *OR*, 24 (ser. 1, pt. 1):32, 80, 81.

50. Ibid., 32, 80–82; Elliott Journal, 57, TSLA; *St. Louis Missouri Republican*, 17 Sept. 1886.

51. Rowena Reed, *Combined Operations in the Civil War* (Annapolis: Naval Institute Press, 1978), 254; *St. Louis Missouri Republican*, 6 Sept. 1884 and 17 Sept. 1886; *OR*, 24 (ser. 1, pt. 1):80–82; Elliott Journal, 57, TSLA; Alfred Thayer Mahan, *The Gulf and Inland Waters* (New York: Charles Scribner's Sons, 1905), 160–62; Porter, *Naval History of the Civil War*, 313–15; Bearss, "Grand Gulf's Role in the Civil War," 23–26.

52. Porter, *Naval History of the Civil War*, 314–15; *St. Louis Missouri Republican*, 3 July and 17 Sept. 1886; Bevier, *History of the First and Second Missouri Confederate Brigades*, 411.

53. Anderson, *Memoirs*, 294; Bevier, *History of the First and Second Missouri Confederate Brigades*, 173–74, 411; *St. Louis Missouri Republican*, 3 July and 17 Sept. 1886.

54. W. L. Truman, "Gallant William Wade—His Battery Flag," *Confederate Veteran* 19 (September 1911):419; Hogan to Father, 22 July 1863, MHS; *Savannah Republican*, 1 May 1863; *Missouri Republican*, 6 Sept. 1884.

55. Hogan to Father, 22 July 1863, MHS.

56. Bannon Diary, SCL; Larry J. Daniel, "Bruinsburg: Missed Opportunity or Postwar Rhetoric?" *Civil War History* 32 (September 1986):264.

57. Catton, *Grant Moves South*, 421; *OR*, 24 (ser. 1, pt. 1):32, 48.

58. Bannon Diary, SCL; *St. Louis Missouri Republican*, 6 Sept. 1884.

59. *OR*, 24 (ser. 1, pt. 1):32, 48.

60. *OR*, 24 (ser. 1, pt. 3):792–93; Catton, *Grant Moves South*, 424.

61. *Savannah Republican*, 6 May 1863.

62. Bannon Diary, SCL; Hogan to Father, 22 July 1863, MHS; Truman, "Gallant William Wade," 419.

63. Hogan to Father, 22 July 1863, MHS; *St. Louis Missouri Republican*, 6 Sept. 1884.

64. Bannon Diary, SCL.

65. Ibid.; Boyce 1914 Paper, MHS; Truman, "Gallant William Wade," 419; Boyce, St. Louis Military Organizations, 66; Hyde and Conrad, *Encyclopedia of the History of St. Louis*, 3:1505; Wade Family Burial Records, Bellefontaine Cemetery, St. Louis; *St. Louis Missouri Republican*, 6 Sept. 1884.

66. *Savannah Republican*, 9 May 1863; Johnson and Buel, *Battles and Leaders of the Civil War*, 2:494–96; Catton, *Grant Moves South*, 424–26; Miers, *Web of Victory*, 152–55.

67. Bowen to Memminger, 2 May and 4 June 1863, VHS.

68. Johnson to Buel, *Battles and Leaders of the Civil War*, 2:496–97; Bowen to Memminger, 2 May and 4 June 1863, VHS; Daniel, "Bruinsburg," 256–67; Catton, *Grant Moves South*, 426–28; Miers, *Web of Victory*, 154–55; Carter, *Final Fortress*, 182–83.

69. Bearss, *Grant Strikes a Fatal Blow*, 405, 407; *Savannah Republican*, 9 and 22 May 1863.

70. Bowen to Memminger, 4 June 1863, VHS.

71. Bannon Diary, SCL; Bearss, *Grant Strikes a Fatal Blow*, 367; Bowen to Memminger, 2 May and 4 June 1863, VHS.

72. *OR*, 24 (ser. 1, pt. 1):670–75, 682; Elliott Journal, 57–58, TSLA; Bearss, *Grant Strikes a Fatal Blow*, 370–72, 384, 406–407; Bowen to Memminger, 2 May and 4 June 1863; *Savannah Republican*, 6 May 1863.

73. Hogan to Father, 22 July 1863, MHS; *OR*, 24 (ser. 1, pt. 1):668–69; Bowen to Memminger, 2 May and 4 June 1863, VHS; Kennedy, ed., *Civil War Battlefield Guide*, 138.

74. Bannon Diary, SCL.

75. Bannon Sketch, CM; Burnes, *If These Towers Could Talk*, n.p.

76. *OR*, 24 (ser. 1, pt. 1):668; Bowen to Memminger, 2 May and 4 June 1863, VHS.

77. *Savannah Republican*, 13 May 1863.

78. Ibid.; Bearss, *Grant Strikes a Fatal Blow*, 407; Emily Crawford to Elizabeth Lewis, 11 June 1863.

79. Bannon Diary, SCL; *Savannah Republican*, 6 May 1863; Bevier, *History of the First and Second Missouri Confederate Brigades*, 418; Catton, *Grant Moves South*, 428; Bowen to Memminger, 2 May and 4 June 1863, VHS; Bearss, *Grant Strikes a Fatal Blow*, 405.

80. Bannon Diary, SCL; Bowen to Memminger, 4 June 1863, VHS.

81. Bevier, *History of the First and Second Missouri Confederate Brigades*, 419; Bowen to Memminger, 4 June 1863, VHS; *OR*, 24 (ser. 1, pt. 1):666, 669.

82. Bannon Diary, SCL; Elliott Journal, 58, TSLA; Grant, *Personal Memoirs*, 254–55; *OR*, 24 (ser. 1, pt. 1):666.

83. Bannon Diary, SCL; Elliott Journal, 59, TSLA; *OR*, 24 (ser. 1, pt. 1):666.

84. Anderson, *Memoirs*, 301–303; Elliott Journal, 59, TSLA; *OR*, 24 (ser. 1, pt. 1):666–67.

85. Bannon Diary, SCL; Hyde and Conrad, *Encyclopedia of the History of St. Louis*, 2:1166; Compiled Missouri Service Records, Roll 81, NA.

86. Hogan to Father, 22 July 1863, MHS; Elliott Journal, 59, TSLA.

87. Bannon Diary, SCL; Hogan to Father, 22 July 1863, MHS; Bowen to Memminger, 11 May 1863, VHS; Grant, *Personal Memoirs*, 258–60; Catton, *Grant Moves South*, 428–30.

88. *Savannah Republican*, 22 May 1863.

89. Bannon Diary, SCL; Amos Camden Riley Papers, H. Riley Bock Collection.

90. Compiled Missouri Service Records, Rolls 92–103, NA.

91. Bannon Diary, SCL; Boyce Scrapbook, MHS.

92. Bannon Diary, SCL.

93. Catton, *Grant Moves South*, 432–39.

94. Richard Wheeler, *The Siege of Vicksburg* (New York: Thomas Y. Crowell, 1978), ix, 6–11; *Richmond Enquirer*, 20 May 1863.

95. *Richmond Enquirer*, 20 May 1863.

96. Ibid.

97. *Savannah Republican*, 12 June 1863.

98. *Mobile Register and Advertiser*, 17, 19, and 22 May 1863; Johnson and Buel, *Battles and Leaders of the Civil War*, 3:502–507; Catton, *Grant Moves South*, 438–43; *OR*, 24 (ser. 1, pt. 1):260–61.

99. Bannon Diary, SCL; *OR*, 24 (ser. 1, pt. 1):261–62.

100. *OR*, 24 (ser. 1, pt. 1):261–62; Johnson and Buel, *Battles and Leaders of the Civil War*, 2:508–509.

101. Bannon Diary, SCL; Consolidated Compiled Missouri Service Records, Microcopy 253, Roll 318, NA; Bannon, "Experiences of a Confederate Army Chaplain," 201–203.

102. Bannon, "Experiences of a Confederate Army Chaplain," 201–203; *OR*, 24 (ser. 1, pt. 2):112.

103. *OR*, 24 (ser. 1, pt. 1):262–64; Bearss, *Grant Strikes a Fatal Blow*, 591–606; Johnson and Buel, *Battles and Leaders of the Civil War*, 3:510–11; *St. Louis Missouri Republican*, 5 Dec. 1884.

104. *St. Louis Missouri Republican*, 5 Dec. 1884; *Vicksburg Daily Herald*, 5 Oct. 1902; *OR*, 24 (ser. 1, pt. 1):264.

105. *Daily Herald*, 5 Oct. 1902; *St. Louis Missouri Republican*, 5 Dec. 1884; Elliott Journal, 60, TSLA; *OR*, 24 (ser. 1, pt. 1):110, 264; Champ Clark Scrapbook, vol. 15, Champ Clark Papers, WHMC-SHSM.

106. Theodore D. Fisher Diary, 1, MHS; *St. Louis Missouri Republican*, 5 Dec. 1884; Elliott Journal, 60, TSLA.

107. *OR*, 24 (ser. 1, pt. 2):110–11.

108. Bannon, "Experiences of a Confederate Army Chaplain," 202.

109. Compiled Missouri Service Records, Rolls 98–103, NA.

110. *OR*, 24 (ser. 1, pt. 2):110–12; Bevier, *History of the First and Second Missouri Confederate Brigades*, 424; *St. Louis Missouri Republican*, 5 Dec. 1884.

111. Bannon, "Experiences of a Confederate Army Chaplain," 202–203.

112. *OR*, 24 (ser. 1, pt. 2):110–11; Anderson, *Memoirs*, 312–13; Elliott Journal, 60, TSLA; *St. Louis Missouri Republican*, 5 Dec. 1884; Fisher Diary, 1, MHS; Bearss, *Grant Strikes a Fatal Blow*, 609–15.

113. Bannon, "Experiences of a Confederate Army Chaplain," 202–205.

114. *OR*, 24 (ser. 1, pt. 2):111–12; Bevier, *History of the First and Second Missouri Confederate Brigades*, 192; Elliott Journal, 60, TSLA; Bearss, *Grant Strikes a Fatal Blow*, 609–15; *St. Louis Missouri Republican*, 5 Dec. 1884.

115. *OR*, 24 (ser. 1, pt. 2):111; Boyce 1914 Paper, MHS; *St. Louis Missouri Republican*, 5 Dec. 1884; "Rev. John Bannon," 451; Clark Scrapbook, vol. 15, Clark Papers, WHMC-SHSM.

116. Brauckman Scrapbook, MHS.

117. *OR*, 24 (ser. 1, pt. 2):112; Bevier, *History of the First and Second Missouri Confederate Brigades*, 192.

118. Bannon, "Experiences of a Confederate Army Chaplain," 205.

119. Elliott Journal, 60, TSLA; Bearss, *Grant Strikes a Fatal Blow*, 611–12; Bevier, *History of the First and Second Missouri Confederate Brigades*, 425–26; Anderson, *Memoirs*, 313; *St. Louis Missouri Republican*, 5 Dec. 1884.

120. Bannon Diary, SCL; Brauckman Scrapbook, MHS; Bannon, "Experiences of a Confederate Army Chaplain," 202.

121. Anderson, *Memoirs*, 313; Bevier, *History of the First and Second Missouri Confederate Brigades*, 425–26.

122. *St. Louis Missouri Republican*, 5 Dec 1884; *OR*, 24 (ser. 1, pt. 2):111; Bearss, *Grant Strikes a Fatal Blow*, 621.

123. Anderson, *Memoirs*, 313–14; Bevier, *History of the First and Second Missouri Confederate Brigades*, 424–26; *St. Louis Missouri Republican*, 5 Dec. 1884; Elliott Journal, 60, TSLA; Bearss, *Grant Strikes a Fatal Blow*, 614–17.

124. Hogan to Father, 22 July 1863, MHS; *St. Louis Missouri Republican*, 5 Dec. 1884; *OR*, 24 (ser. 1, pt. 2):44, 111; Bevier, *History of the First and Second Missouri Confederate Brigades*, 426; Anderson, *Memoirs*, 313; S. H. M. Byers, *Fire and Sword* (New York: Neale Publishing Co., 1911), 76–77.

125. Hyde and Conrad, *Encyclopedia of the History of St. Louis*, 2:1166; *St. Louis Missouri Republican*, 5 Dec. 1884; Adjutant General Records of Missouri Confederate Soldiers, Adjutant General's Office, Jefferson City; *OR*, 24 (ser. 1, pt. 2):111.

126. *OR*, 24 (ser. 1, pt. 2):111; Elliott Journal, 60, TSLA; "Storey of 'Guibor's Battery, C.S.A.',", MHS; Boyce 1914 Paper, MHS; *St. Louis Missouri Republican*, 5 Dec. 1884; Clark Scrapbook, vol. 15, Clark Papers, WHMC-SHSM; Boyce Scrapbook, MHS.

127. Clark Scrapbook, vol. 15, Clark Papers, WHMC-SHSM.

128. *OR*, 24 (ser. 1, pt. 2):111; *St. Louis Missouri Republican*, 5 Dec. 1884; Edward C. Robbins, "Landis Battery," Box 1, Civil War Papers, MHS.

129. *OR*, 24 (ser. 1, pt. 2):111–12; Bearss, *Grant Strikes a Fatal Blow*, 637–39; *St. Louis Missouri Republican*, 5 Dec. 1884; Catton, *Grant Moves South*, 445; Elliott Journal, 60, TSLA.

130. *OR*, 24 (ser. 1, pt. 2):111–12; Anderson, *Memoirs*, 313–14; *St. Louis Missouri Republican*, 5 Dec. 1884; Sandie Murdock to John Ross, 8 Oct. 1925, Box 2, Folder 12, William Skaggs Collection, Arkansas History Commission.

131. Bannon Diary, SCL; *OR*, 24 (ser. 1, pt. 2):112–13; *St. Louis Missouri Republican*, 5 Dec. 1884; Elliott Journal, 60, TSLA; Fisher Diary, 1, MHS; Bevier, *History of the First and Second Missouri Confederate Brigades*, 426; *OR*, 24 (ser. 1, pt. 1):266–67.

132. *OR*, 24 (ser. 1, pt. 1):266; Ruyle Memoir, 31; Bannon, "Experiences of a Confederate Army Chaplain," 204.

133. Bannon, "Experiences of a Confederate Army Chaplain," 202.

134. Fisher Diary, 1, MHS; Elliott Journal, 61, TSLA; Anderson, *Memoirs*, 317–20; *OR*, 24 (ser. 1, pt. 2):113–14; *St. Louis Missouri Republican*, 5 Dec. 1884; *OR*, 24 (ser. 1, pt. 1):267–68.

135. Bannon Diary, SCL; *OR*, 24 (ser. 1, pt. 2):414; Johnson and Buel, *Battles and Leaders of the Civil War*, 3:516–17; Fisher Diary, 1, MHS; Porter, *Naval History of the Civil War*, 320; *St. Louis Missouri Republican*, 5 Dec. 1884; Elliott Journal, 61, TSLA.

SEVEN   City on a River

1. *Mobile Register and Advertiser*, 11, 12, and 21 June 1863; Thomas Hawley to Parents, 18 May 1863, MHS; Johnson and Buel, *Battles and Leaders of the Civil War*, 3:483; *Vicksburg and the Opening of the Mississippi River, 1862–1863* (Washington, D.C.: U.S. Dept. of the Interior, 1986), 45–46.

2. Leavy Journal, 21; *OR*, 24 (ser. 1, pt. 2):414; *OR*, 24 (ser. 1, pt. 1):271.

3. Bannon Diary, SCL; *OR*, 24 (ser. 1, pt. 2):414.

4. Bannon Diary, SCL; Pillar, *Catholic Church in Mississippi*, 1, 105–109, 232–33,

287–88; *In and About Vicksburg: An Illustrated Guide Book to the City of Vicksburg, Mississippi; Its History; Its Appearance; Its Business Houses* (Vicksburg: Gibraltar Publishing Co., 1890), 148.

5. Johnson and Buel, *Battles and Leaders of the Civil War*, 3:517; Catton, *Grant Moves South*, 450–52.

6. Rombauer Order Book 1863, MHS; Edwin C. Bearss, *The Campaign For Vicksburg: Unvexed to the Sea* (Dayton: Morningside, 1986), 3:761–73; *OR*, 24 (ser. 1, pt. 2):414–15; *Mobile Register and Advertiser*, 30 May and 12 June 1863.

7. Hogan to Father, 22 July 1863, MHS.

8. Kenneth Trist Urquhart, ed., *Vicksburg: Southern City Under Siege, William Lovelace Foster's Letter Describing the Defense and Surrender of the Confederate Fortress on the Mississippi* (New Orleans: Historic New Orleans Collection, 1980), 8.

9. Bannon Diary, SCL.

10. Miers, *Web of Victory*, 203–205; Carter, *Final Fortress*, 212–14.

11. Bannon Diary, SCL; *OR*, 24 (ser. 1, pt. 2):415.

12. Johnson and Buel, *Battles and Leaders of the Civil War*, 3:518.

13. *Savannah Republican*, 24 May 1863.

14. *Mobile Register and Advertiser*, 12 June 1863; Rombauer Order Book 1863, MHS; Porter, *Naval History of the Civil War*, 321; Johnson and Buel, *Battles and Leaders of the Civil War*, 3:518.

15. *Savannah Republican*, 22 June 1863.

16. Bannon Diary, SCL; Compiled Missouri Service Records, Rolls 92–120, 123–38, NA; *OR*, 24 (ser. 1, pt. 2):415.

17. List of Exchanged Camp Jackson Prisoners; *St. Louis Missouri Republican*, 5 Dec. 1884; Amos Riley to Francis Marion Cockrell, 26 July 1863, H. Riley Bock Collection, New Madrid, Missouri; Fisher Diary, 2, MHS; Joseph Boyce, "The Flag of the First Missouri Confederate Infantry," Civil War Collection, MHS.

18. Bannon Diary, SCL; *St. Louis Post-Dispatch*, 24 Sept. 1917; *Savannah Republican*, 6 June 1863; Compiled Service Records of Union Soldiers Who Served in Organizations From the State of Missouri, Record Group 109, Microcopy 405, Rolls 428–38, 448–58, War Department Collection of Union Records, NA; *OR*, 24 (ser. 1, pt. 2):264–65; Joseph B. Mitchell, *The Badge of Gallantry* (New York: Macmillan Co., 1968), 111–21.

19. Compiled Missouri Service Records, Rolls 92, 98, NA; *St. Louis Missouri Republican*, 5 Dec. 1884.

20. *Mobile Register and Advertiser*, 16 Jan. 1863; Compiled Missouri Service Records, Rolls 448–58, NA; Hogan to Father, 22 July 1863, MHS; *Mobile Register and Advertiser*, 19 July 1863.

21. Catton, *Grant Moves South*, 452–53.

22. Urquhart, *Vicksburg*, 9.

23. Carter, *Final Fortress*, 229, 238–39; Johnson and Buel, *Battles and Leaders of the Civil War*, 3:518.

24. *Savannah Republican*, 3 June 1863.

25. Bannon, "Experiences of a Confederate Army Chaplain," 206.

26. Boyce 1914 Paper, MHS; "Rev. John Bannon," 451.

27. Boyce 1914 Paper, MHS.

28. McLellan to Boyce, 18 May 1919, MHS.

29. Fisher Diary, 2, MHS; Elliott Journal, 63, TSLA; *Mobile Register and Advertiser*, 2 and 20 June 1863.

30. Bannon Diary, SCL.

31. "Brother Fought Against Brother," *Confederate Veteran* 10 (October 1902):463; Emma Balfour, *Vicksburg, A City Under Siege: Diary of Emma Balfour May 16, 1863– June 2, 1863* (Phillip C. Weinberger, 1983), n.p.

32. Bannon Diary, SCL.

33. Johnson and Buel, *Battles and Leaders of the Civil War*, 3:569; Francis A. Lord, *Civil War Collector's Encyclopedia* (New York: Castle Books, 1965), 33, 179.

34. *Savannah Republican*, 7 July 1863; Edwin B. Coddington, *The Gettysburg Campaign: A Study in Command* (New York: Charles Scribner's Sons, 1984), 4–11.

35. Elliott Journal, 70, TSLA.

36. Bannon Diary, SCL; Porter, *Naval History of the Civil War*, 323; *Mobile Register and Advertiser*, 7 and 12 June 1863.

37. Bannon Diary, SCL; Clark Scrapbook, vol. 15, Clark Papers, WHMC-SHSM.

38. Bannon Diary, SCL.

39. Leavy Journal, 49–50; *Mobile Register and Advertiser*, 19 July 1863.

40. Boyce 1914 Paper, MHS; Bannon Diary, SCL; *OR*, 24 (ser. 1, pt. 2):415.

41. Leavy Journal, 27.

42. Bannon Diary, SCL; Pitts, *Chaplains in Gray*, 82–83.

43. Leavy Journal, 22.

44. Ibid., 27; Bannon Diary, SCL; Billon Scrapbook, vol. 2, MHS; Boyce 1914 Paper, MHS; Clark Scrapbook, vol. 15, Clark Papers, WHMC-SHSM.

45. Clark Scrapbook, vol. 15, Clark Papers, WHMC-SHSM.

46. Ibid.; Billon Scrapbook, vol. 2, MHS; Boyce 1914 Paper, MHS; "Rev. John Bannon," 451; Brauckman Scrapbook, MHS; Bannon, "Experiences of a Confederate Army Chaplain," 202.

47. Bevier, *History of the First and Second Missouri Confederate Brigades*, 182; Bannon, "Experiences of a Confederate Army Chaplain," 209.

48. Bannon, "Experiences of a Confederate Army Chaplain," 206–208.

49. Bannon Diary, SCL; *OR*, 24 (ser. 1, pt. 2):415; Leavy Journal, 21; Kenny and Morrissey, "Father John Bannon, S.J.," 94; Balfour, *Vicksburg, A City Under Siege*, n.p.

50. Bannon Diary, SCL; Elliott Journal, 61–66, 70; Boyce 1914 Paper, MHS; *St. Louis Missouri Republican*, 5 Dec. 1884; Anderson, *Memoirs*, 347–51.

51. Compiled Missouri Service Records, Rolls 92–120, 123–38, NA.

52. Bannon Diary, SCL.

53. Ibid.

54. Catton, *Grant Moves South*, 457, 460–61, 465, 469–70.

55. Bannon Diary, SCL; Pillar, *Catholic Church in Mississippi*, 287–88.

56. Compiled Missouri Service Records, Rolls 127, 129, NA; Hogan to Father, 22 July 1863, MHS.

57. Compiled Missouri Service Records, Roll 98, NA; Fisher Diary, 4, MHS; Bearss, *Unvexed to the Sea*, 1261; "Rev. John Bannon," 451; Leavy Journal, 23–24; "Major John Henry Britts," *Confederate Veteran* 18 (January 1910):36; Boyce 1914 Paper, MHS; *Union and Confederate Annals: The Blue and Gray in Friendship Meet, and Heroic Deeds Recite* (St. Louis, 1884), 1:39; Osborn H. Oldroyd, *A Soldier's Story of the Siege of Vicksburg* (Springfield: H. W. Rokker Printer, 1885), app. 1, 156–58.

58. Compiled Missouri Service Records, Roll 98, NA; Boyce 1914 Paper, MHS; *Union and Confederate Annals*, 40–41; *History of Henry and St. Clair Counties, Missouri* (St. Joseph: National Historical Co., 1883), 502–505.

59. Bannon Diary, SCL.

60. Urquhart, *Vicksburg*, 6.

61. Fisher Diary, 2, MHS.

62. Johnson and Buel, *Battles and Leaders of the Civil War*, 3:526–27.

63. *Savannah Republican*, 23 June 1863.

64. Johnson and Buel, *Battles and Leaders of the Civil War*, 3:539–42; *OR*, 24 (ser. 1, pt. 2):200–202, 333, 415; Miers, *Web of Victory*, 279–80.

65. Johnson and Buel, *Battles and Leaders of the Civil War*, 3:542; Fisher Diary, 6, MHS; *Mobile Register and Advertiser*, 19 July 1863; Elliott Journal, 65, TSLA.

66. Bannon Diary, SCL.

67. Boyce 1914 Paper, MHS; Kenny and Morrissey, "Father John Bannon, S.J.," 94.

68. Bannon Diary, SCL.

69. Ibid.; Leavy Journal, 53; Fisher Diary, 7, MHS; Elliott Journal, 66, TSLA; *Weekly Mississippian*, 17 Nov. 1863.

70. Bannon Diary, SCL.

71. Hogan to Father, 22 July 1863, MHS.

72. Tunnard, *Southern Record*, 262.

73. Bannon Diary, SCL.

74. Hogan to Father, 22 July 1863, MHS; Pillar, *Catholic Church in Mississippi*, 258; *Richmond Enquirer*, 14 Aug. 1863; M. J. Mulvihill, *Vicksburg and Warren County, Mississippi, Tunica Indians, Quebec Missionaries, Civil War Veterans* (Vicksburg: Von Norman Printing Co., 1931), 75.

75. Bannon Diary, SCL.

76. Ibid.; Hogan to Father, 22 July 1863, MHS; Boyce 1914 Paper, MHS; "Rev. John Bannon," 451; *Richmond Enquirer*, 14 Aug. 1863; Pillar, *Catholic Church in Mississippi*, 258.

77. Boyce 1914 Paper, MHS; Hogan to Father, 22 July 1863, MHS; "Rev. John Bannon," 451.

78. Virginia Calohan Harrell, *Vicksburg and the River* (Vicksburg: Virginia Calohan Harrell, 1986), 35, 43; Francis Christian Clewell to Mother, 15 Feb. 1863, "Letters From a Southern Soldier," 87, Gertrude Jenkins Papers, 1859–1908, Manuscript Department, William R. Perkins Library, Duke University, Durham, N.C.; Anderson, *Memoirs*, 341; Bannon Diary, SCL; Mother M. Bernard, *The Story of the Sisters of Mercy in Mississippi, 1860–1930* (New York: P. J. Kennedy and Sons, 1931), 7–10; Jolly, *Nuns of the Battlefield*, 258–60, 270.

79. Bannon, "Experiences of a Confederate Army Chaplain," 208–209.

80. Jolly, *Nuns of the Battlefield*, 260–69.

81. Elliott Journal, 66, TSLA; *OR*, 24 (ser. 1, pt. 2):201, 416; Fisher Diary, 7–8, MHS; *Richmond Enquirer*, 14 Aug. 1963.

82. Bannon Diary, SCL; Fisher Diary, 8, MHS; Compiled Missouri Service Records, Roll 110, NA.

83. Bannon Diary, SCL; *St. Louis Missouri Republican*, 5 Dec. 1884.

84. Bannon, "Experiences of a Confederate Army Chaplain," 209–10.

85. Johnson and Buel, *Battles and Leaders of the Civil War*, 3:550; *Richmond Enquirer*, 14 Aug. 1863.

86. Hogan to Father, 22 July 1863, MHS; Bannon, "Experiences of a Confederate Army Chaplain," 206.

87. *Richmond Enquirer*, 14 Aug. 1863.

88. Ibid., 21 July 1863.

89. Ibid.

90. Bannon Diary, SCL.

91. Johnson and Buel, *Battles and Leaders of the Civil War*, 3:549; *OR*, 24 (ser. 1, pt. 1):281–85.

92. Leavy Journal, 47–48; Bannon Diary, SCL.

93. *St. Louis Missouri Republican*, 3 July 1886; *Union and Confederate Annals*, 52; Howard Michael Madaus and Robert D. Needham, *The Battle Flags of the Confederate Army of Tennessee* (Milwaukee: Milwaukee Public Museum, 1976), 86.

94. Elliott Journal, 66, TSLA.

95. Bannon Diary, SCL.

96. Leavy Journal, 47–48, TSLA; Bearss, *Unvexed to the Sea*, 821.

97. Brauckman Scrapbook, MHS.

98. Bannon Diary, SCL.

99. Ibid.; Madaus and Needham, *Battle Flags*, 44; *St. Louis Missouri Republican*, 5 Dec. 1885; Anderson, *Memoirs*, 357.

100. Bearss, *Unvexed to the Sea*, 1312–15; Catton, *Grant Moves South*, 479, 489; *Richmond Enquirer*, 30 May 1863; *Savannah Republican*, 17 June 1863.

101. Parole Records of Confederates Captured at Vicksburg, Vicksburg National Military Park Archives, Vicksburg.

102. *OR*, 24 (ser. 1, pt. 1):282–83; Johnson and Buel, *Battles and Leaders of the Civil War*, 3:530; "Sketch—Gen. Bowen's Life," MHS.

103. Bannon Diary, SCL.

104. Ibid.

105. Boyce, "Flags of the First Missouri Confederate Infantry," MHS; John S. Bowen Family Genealogy, Georgia Historical Society, Savannah; Bannon Diary, SCL; Kearny-Kennerly Scrapbook, vol. 2, MHS; *St. Louis Missouri Republican*, 5 Dec. 1884.

106. Bannon Diary, SCL; Kearny-Kennerly Scrapbook, vol. 2, MHS; Compiled Service Records, NA.

107. Bannon Diary, SCL.

108. Ibid.; Compiled Service Records, NA; *Weekly Mississippian*, 17 Nov. 1862.

109. *St. Louis Missouri Republican*, 5 Dec. 1884.

110. Bannon Diary, SCL.

111. Nathaniel Cheairs Hughes, Jr., *General William J. Hardee: Old Reliable* (Baton Rouge: Louisiana State University Press, 1965), 160–61; Bannon Diary, SCL; Elliott Journal, 67–68, TSLA; Henry Martyn Cheavens Diary, WHMC-SHSM.

112. Bannon Diary, SCL.

113. Hogan to Father, 22 July 1863, MHS.

EIGHT   Diplomatic Mission for the Confederacy

1. Cheavens Journal, WHMC-SHSM; *OR*, 24 (ser. 1, pt. 3):1010; Bannon Diary, SCL; Simpson Diary, WHMC-SHSM; Compiled Missouri Service Records, NA.

2. Compiled Missouri Service Records, NA; Bannon Diary, SCL; Silverman, "Stars, Bars, and Foreigners," 269; John Bannon to Yates Snowden, 20 Feb. 1903, Yates Snowden Collection, South Caroliniana Library, University of South Carolina; Leo Francis Stock, "Catholic Participation in the Diplomacy of the Southern Confederacy," *Catholic Historical Review* 16 (April 1930):5.

3. Bannon to Snowden, 20 Feb. 1903, SCL; Compiled Missouri Service Records, NA.

4. Compiled Missouri Service Records, NA; Warren Diary; Simpson Diary, WHMC-SHSM; *Mobile Register and Advertiser*, 9 Jan. 1864.

5. Frank Von Phul to Joseph Boyce, 5 Dec. 1914, in Boyce Papers, MHS; Francis Marion Cockrell Scrapbook, MHS; *Weekly Mississippian*, 17 and 20 Nov. 1862 and 4 Jan. 1863; *Mobile Register and Advertiser*, 9, 19, and 24 Jan. 1864; Roher, "Confederate Generals," 13.

6. Bannon Diary, SCL.

7. Ibid.; Simpson Diary, WHMC-SHSM.

8. Bannon Diary, SCL; Boyce 1914 Paper, MHS; Benjamin J. Keiley to Yates Snowden, 25 June 1905, Yates Snowden Collection, SCL.

9. Keiley to Snowden, 25 June 1905, SCL.

10. Ibid.

11. Bannon to Snowden, 20 Feb. 1903, SCL.

12. Keiley to Snowden, 25 June 1905, SCL; Charles P. Cullop, *Confederate Propaganda in Europe, 1861–1865* (Coral Gables: University of Miami Press, 1969), 105–10.

13. Bruce Catton and American Heritage editors, *Picture History of the Civil War* (New York: American Heritage, 1960), 414; Joseph M. Hernon, Jr., *Celts, Catholics and Copperheads: Ireland Views the American Civil War* (Columbus: Ohio State University Press, 1968), 23; James M. McPherson, *Battle Cry of Freedom: The Civil War Era* (New York: Oxford University Press, 1988), 606.

14. David H. Donald, ed., *Why the North Won the Civil War* (Baton Rouge: Louisiana State University Press, 1960), 81–82.

15. Robert Douthat Meade, *Judah P. Benjamin: Confederate Statesman* (New York: Oxford University Press, 1943), 296; C. Vann Woodward, ed., *Mary Chesnut's Civil War* (New Haven: Yale University Press, 1981), 417.

16. *Official Records of the Union and Confederate Navies in the War of the Rebellion*, 31 vols. (Washington, D.C.: U.S. Government Printing Office, 1895–1929), 3 (ser. 2):1075, all future *OR* citations from this volume.

17. Cullop, *Confederate Propaganda in Europe*, 100–103; John Bigelow, *Retrospections of an Active Life*, 5 vols. (New York: Baker and Taylor Co., 1909–1913), 1:547; Hernon, *Celts, Catholics and Copperheads*, 23–24.

18. J. E. MacFarland to Judah P. Benjamin, 6 June 1863, 1: Pickett Papers, Division of Manuscripts, Library of Congress, Washington, D.C.; Hernon, *Celts, Catholics and Copperheads*, 23–28.

19. Meade, *Judah P. Benjamin*, 296; Bigelow, *Retrospections*, 1:562–63; Keiley to Snowden, 25 June 1905, SCL; Cullop, *Confederate Propaganda in Europe*, 102–106; Burton J. Hendrick, *Statesmen of the Lost Cause: Jefferson Davis and His Cabinet* (New York: Literary Guild of America, 1939), 153.

20. Cullop, *Confederate Propaganda in Europe*, 102–106; Hernon, *Celts, Catholics and Copperheads*, 28.

21. Ibid., 108; Meade, *Judah P. Benjamin*, 296.

22. Cullop, *Confederate Propaganda in Europe*, 107; Meade, *Judah P. Benjamin*, 296.

23. Bannon Diary, SCL; Leo Francis Stock, "Catholic Participation," 7; Keiley to Snowden, 25 June 1905, SCL; Ignatius L. Ryan, "Confederate Agents in Ireland," *United States Historical Society: Historical Records and Studies* 24 (1936) 68; Bannon to Snowden, 20 Feb. 1903, SCL; Cullop, *Confederate Propaganda in Europe*, 110.

24. Bannon Diary, SCL; Compiled Missouri Service Records, NA; Keiley to Snowden, 25 June 1905, SCL; Samuel J. T. Moore, Jr., *Moore's Complete Civil War Guide to Richmond* (Richmond: Samuel J. T. Moore, 1978), 45–46.

25. Keiley to Snowden, 25 June 1905, SCL; Dowdey, *Experiment in Rebellion*, 108–10; Albert C. Danner, "Some Recollections of Bishop Marvin and Others,"

Manuscript, Dorothy Danner Trabits, Mobile; James D. Richardson, ed., *A Compilation of the Messages and Papers of the Confederacy, Including the Diplomatic Correspondence 1861–1865* (Nashville: United States Publishing Co., 1905), 2:562; John Bannon to Judah Benjamin, 2 Sept. 1863, "Domestic Letters" File, Box 25, September–December 1863, Confederate States of America, Pickett Papers, Manuscript Division, Library of Congress; Eli N. Evans, *Judah P. Benjamin: The Jewish Confederate* (New York: Free Press, 1988), 237–38.

26. Richardson, *Compilation of the Messages and Papers of the Confederacy*, 2:562; Danner, "Recollections of Bishop Marvin," Manuscript; Stock, "Catholic Participation," 15; McPherson, *Battle Cry of Freedom*, 387; Bannon to Benjamin, 2 Sept. 1863, Pickett Papers, LC.

27. *Weekly Mississippian*, 8 Nov. 1862; Bannon to Benjamin, 2 Sept. 1863, Pickett Papers, LC; Hendrick, *Statesmen of the Lost Cause*, 107–109, 114–17.

28. Danner, "Recollections of Bishop Marvin," Manuscript; Richardson, *Compilation of the Messages and Papers of the Confederacy*, 2:562; Hendrick, *Statesmen of the Lost Cause*, 3–11, 156.

29. Donald, *Why the North Won the Civil War*, 72; Stock, "Catholic Participation," 15; Donaldson Jordan and Edwin J. Pratt, *Europe and the American Civil War* (New York: Houghton Mifflin, 1931), 205–13; Bannon to Benjamin, 2 Sept. 1863, Pickett Papers, LC; Hendrick, *Statesmen of the Lost Cause*, 114–15; Woodward, ed., *Mary Chesnut's Civil War*, 88.

30. *Weekly Mississippian*, 5 Nov. 1861; Jordan and Pratt, *Europe and the American Civil War*, 208–13; Bannon to Benjamin, 2 Sept. 1863, Pickett Papers, LC.

31. *Mobile Register and Advertiser*, 19 April 1862.

32. Bannon to Snowden, 20 Feb. 1903, SCL; Danner, "Recollections of Bishop Marvin," Manuscript; Bannon to Benjamin, 2 Sept. 1863, Pickett Papers, LC.

33. *Richmond Enquirer*, 7 Aug. 1863; Bannon Diary, SCL.

34. Compiled Missouri Service Records, NA; Bannon Diary, SCL.

35. Bannon Diary, SCL; Compiled Missouri Service Records, NA; *Richmond Enquirer*, 7 Aug. 1863; "Inspection Report of First Missouri Brigade," 25 Aug. 1864, NA.

36. Bannon Diary, SCL; Compiled Missouri Service Records, NA.

37. Bannon Diary, SCL; Keiley to Snowden, 25 June 1905, SCL; W. Buck Yearns and John G. Barrett, eds., *North Carolina Civil War Documentary* (Chapel Hill: University of North Carolina Press, 1980), 65, 72.

38. Richardson, *Compilation of the Messages and Papers of the Confederacy*, 2:562.

39. *OR*, 3 (ser. 2):894.

40. Bannon Diary, SCL; Stock, "Catholic Participation," 17–18; *OR*, 3 (ser. 2):910–11, 975; John Bannon to Judah P. Benjamin, 2 Sept. 1863 and 9 Mar. 1864, Pickett Papers, LC; Hernon, *Celts, Catholics and Copperheads*, 13.

41. Barton, *Angels of the Battlefield*, 55; Yearns and Barrett, *North Carolina Civil War Documentary*, 73; Francis A. Litz, *Father Tabb: A Study of His Life and Works* (Baltimore: Johns Hopkins University Press, 1923), 15, 19–20.

42. Bannon Diary, SCL; Litz, *Father Tabb*, 1, 15, 32; Yearns and Barrett, *North Carolina Civil War Documentary*, 72.

43. Richardson, *Compilation of the Messages and Papers of the Confederacy*, 2:562; Litz, *Father Tabb*, 20; Barton, *Angels of the Battlefield*, 55; Bannon Diary, SCL; Danner, "Recollections of Bishop Marvin," Manuscript; Keiley to Snowden, 25 June 1905, SCL; Kenny and Morrissey, "Father John Bannon, S.J.," 95.

44. Richardson, *Compilation of the Messages and Papers of the Confederacy*, 2:562; Danner, "Recollections of Bishop Marvin," Manuscript; Yates Snowden to Joseph Boyce, 30 Aug. 1918, Boyce Papers, MHS.

45. Albert C. Danner, "Father Bannon's Secret Mission," *Confederate Veteran* 27 (May 1919):180; Danner, "Recollections of Bishop Marvin," Manuscript; Richardson, *Compilation of the Messages and Papers of the Confederacy*, 2:562; Bannon to Benjamin, 9 Mar. 1864, Pickett Papers, LC; *OR*, 3 (ser. 2):975; Bannon to Benjamin, 2 Sept. 1863, Pickett Papers, LC.

NINE   Confederate Secret Agent in Ireland

1. *OR*, 3 (ser. 2):944; Danner, "Recollections of Bishop Marvin," Manuscript.

2. Kenny and Morrissey, "Father John Bannon, S.J.," 94; John Bannon to Judah P. Benjamin, 17 Nov. 1863, Pickett Papers, LC; *OR*, 3 (ser. 2):963.

3. John Bannon, "Experiences of a Confederate Army Chaplain," 205–206.

4. Ibid., 205.

5. Cullop, *Confederate Propaganda in Europe*, 110; Bannon to Benjamin, 17 Nov. 1863, Pickett Papers, LC; *OR*, 3 (ser. 2):1089.

6. John Bannon to Judah P. Benjamin, 17 and 22 Nov. 1863, Pickett Papers, LC; Cullop, *Confederate Propaganda in Europe*, 106–109, 115; *Vicksburg Daily Whig*, 9 April 1863; *Memphis Daily Appeal*, 20 Dec. 1861, 28 May 1862, and 25 April 1863.

7. Bannon to Benjamin, 17 and 22 Nov. 1863, Pickett Papers, LC; Danner, "Recollections of Bishop Marvin," Manuscript; *Mobile Register and Advertiser*, 3 Mar. 1863; Bannon to Benjamin, 2 Sept. 1863, LC.

8. *OR*, 3 (ser. 2):910–11; Richardson, *Compilation of the Messages and Papers of the Confederacy*, 2:562; Bannon to Benjamin, 2 Sept. 1863, LC.

9. Stock, "Catholic Participation," 16; Ryan, "Confederate Agents in Ireland," 72; Cullop, *Confederate Propaganda in Europe*, 111; *OR*, 3 (ser. 2):949–50.

10. William L. Yancey and A. Dudley Mann to Earl Russell, 14 Aug. 1861, vol. 1, Pickett Papers, LC.

11. Danner, "Recollections of Bishop Marvin," Manuscript.

12. *OR*, 3 (ser. 2):949–50.

13. Ibid., 952–55, 963–64.

14. Leo Francis Stock, "The United States at the Court of Pius IX," *Catholic Historical Review* 3 (April 1923):116.

15. *OR*, 3 (ser. 2):973–75.

16. Ibid.; Danner, "Father Bannon's Secret Mission," 180; Bannon to Benjamin, 9 Mar. 1864, Pickett Papers, LC.

17. *OR*, 3 (ser. 2):1000; *Mobile Register and Advertiser*, 13 Feb. 1864.

18. John Bannon to Judah P. Benjamin, 19 Jan. 1864, Pickett Papers, LC.

19. Ibid.; Bannon to Snowden, 20 Feb. 1903, SCL; Bannon to Benjamin, 17 Nov. and 15 Dec. 1863, Pickett Papers, LC.

20. Bannon to Benjamin, 15 Dec. 1863 and 19 Jan. 1864, Pickett Papers, LC; Bannon Poster, Pickett Papers, LC.

21. *Mobile Register and Advertiser*, 12 April 1863; Paul Jones, *The Irish Brigade* (New York: Robert B. Luce, 1969), 153–59; William L. Burton, *Melting Pot Soldiers: The Union's Ethnic Regiments* (Ames: Iowa State University Press, 1988), 112–25.

22. Bannon to Benjamin, 15 Dec. 1863 and 19 Jan. 1864, Pickett Papers, LC.

23. *Richmond Enquirer*, 21 Nov. 1863.

24. Bannon Poster, LC.

25. Danner, "Recollections of Bishop Marvin," Manuscript; John Bannon to Judah P. Benjamin, 15 Dec. 1863 and 17 Feb. 1864, Pickett Papers, LC; Bannon to Snowden, 20 Feb. 1903, SCL.

26. Bannon to Snowden, 20 Feb. 1903, SCL; Bannon to Benjamin, 15 Dec. 1863, 19 and 17 Jan. and 9 Mar. 1864, Pickett Papers, LC; Stock, "Catholic Participation," 8; Joseph M. Hernon, Jr., "Irish Religious Opinion on the American Civil War," *Catholic Historical Review* 49 (January 1964):508.

27. Bannon to Benjamin, 15 Dec. 1863 and 19 Jan. 1864, Pickett Papers, LC.

28. Ibid.; Keiley to Snowden, 25 June 1903, SCL; Cullop, *Confederate Propaganda in Europe*, 112; Stock, "United States at the Court of Pius IX," 119–20; Hernon, "Irish Religious Opinion on the American Civil War," 508.

29. Arthur J. L. Freemantle, *Three Months in the Southern States: April–June 1863* (New York: John Bradburn Publishers, 1864), 100; *Richmond Enquirer*, 11 Sept. 1863; Bannon to Benjamin, 19 Jan. 1864, Pickett Papers, LC; *Mobile Register and Advertiser*, 19 May 1863.

30. Stock, "Catholic Participation," 12; Bannon to Benjamin, 17 Feb., 9 Mar., and 9 April 1864, Pickett Papers, LC; Ryan, "Confederate Agents in Ireland," 78; Keiley to Snowden, 25 June 1905, SCL; Stock, "United States at the Court of Pius IX," 119–20; Cullop, *Confederate Propaganda in Europe*, 112; Hernon, *Celts, Catholics and Copperheads*, 15–18, 105–108; Hernon, "Irish Religious Opinion on the American Civil War," 513, 516.

31. Henry Hotze to Judah P. Benjamin, 12 Mar. 1864, Pickett Papers, LC.

32. Keiley to Snowden, 25 June 1905, SCL; Ryan, "Confederate Agents in Ireland," 78; *OR*, 3 (ser. 2):1098; Cullop, *Confederate Propaganda in Europe*, 112; Bannon to Benjamin, 17 Feb. 1864, Pickett Papers, LC; Stock, "United States at the Court of Pius IX," 119–20; Hernon, *Celts, Catholics and Copperheads*, 15–18, 105–108; Hernon, "Irish Religious Opinion on the American Civil War," 512–13, 516.

33. Stock, "Catholic Participation," 2; Bannon to Benjamin, 17 Feb. and 9 Mar.

1864, Pickett Papers, LC; Hernon, "Irish Religious Opinion on the American Civil War," 508, 513, 516; Bannon to Benjamin, 2 Sept. 1863, Pickett Papers, LC.

34. Cullop, *Confederate Propaganda in Europe*, 112–15; Stock, "United States at the Court of Pius IX," 119–20; Ryan, "Confederate Agents in Ireland," 78–80; Stock, "Catholic Participation," 8; Bannon to Benjamin, 17 Feb., 9 Mar., and 9 April 1864, Pickett Papers, LC; Hernon, *Celts, Catholics and Copperheads*, 107–108; Hernon, "Irish Religious Opinion on the American Civil War," 508, 516; Faherty Collection.

35. Bannon to Benjamin, 17 Feb. and 9 Mar. 1864, Pickett Papers, LC; Keiley to Snowden, 25 June 1905.

36. Keiley to Snowden, 25 June 1905, SCL; Bannon to Benjamin, 17 Feb. and 9 Mar. 1864, Pickett Papers, LC; Ryan, "Confederate Agents in Ireland," 78–79; Cullop, *Confederate Propaganda in Europe*, 112–13, 115; Stock, "United States at the Court of Pius IX," 119–20; Hernon, *Celts, Catholics and Copperheads*, 107–108; Hernon, "Irish Religious Opinion on the American Civil War," 516.

37. Bannon to Benjamin, 9 Mar. 1864, Pickett Papers, LC; Hernon, *Celts, Catholics and Copperheads*, 107–108; Hernon, "Irish Religious Opinion on the American Civil War," 516.

38. Stock, "United States at the Court of Pius IX," 119–20; Hernon, "Irish Religious Opinion on the American Civil War," 511, 516.

39. Bannon to Benjamin, 9 Mar. 1864, Pickett Papers, LC.

40. Bannon to Benjamin, 17 Feb., 9 Mar., and 9 April 1864, Pickett Papers, LC; Compiled Missouri Service Records, NA; Thomas, *The Confederate Nation*, 261–62.

41. Bannon to Benjamin, 17 Feb., 9 Mar., and 9 April 1864, Pickett Papers, LC.

42. Ibid.; Bannon to Benjamin, 9 April and 28 May 1864, Pickett Papers, LC; Hernon, *Celts, Catholics and Copperheads*, 33.

43. Bannon to Benjamin, 9 April and 28 May 1864, Pickett Papers, LC; Hernon, "Irish Religious Opinion on the American Civil War," 516; Hendrick, *Statesmen of the Lost Cause*, 144–47.

44. *OR*, 3 (ser. 2):1140–47; Keiley to Snowden, 25 June 1905, SCL; Stock, "Catholic Participation," 17–18; Cullop, *Confederate Propaganda in Europe*, 112; Stock, "United States at the Court of Pius IX," 120; Bannon to Benjamin, 9 April 1864, Pickett Papers, LC; Rawley, *Turning Points of the Civil War*, 140–43.

45. Kenny and Morrissey, "Father John Bannon, S.J.," 93, 96; Bannon Obituary, *Dublin Telegraph*, 14 July 1913; Danner, "Recollections of Bishop Marvin," Manuscript; Bannon to Snowden, 20 Feb. 1903, SCL; Danner, "Father Bannon's Secret Mission," 180.

46. Boyce 1914 Paper, MHS; Danner, "Father Bannon's Secret Mission," 180; Father William Barnaby Faherty to author, 29 June 1990.

47. Bannon Obituary, *Dublin Telegraph*, 14 July 1913; Fergus O'Donoughue to author, 9 Mar. 1990; William and Sarah Fetherston, County Dublin, Collection; Faherty to author, 29 June 1990.

48. Kenny and Morrissey, "John Bannon, S.J.," 93–94.

49. Boyce 1914 Paper, MHS; Boyce Scrapbook, MHS.

50. Danner, "Recollections of Bishop Marvin," Manuscript; Boyce Scrapbook, MHS; John Bannon to William Barlow, 2 Aug. 1895, Boyce Papers, MHS.

51. Boyce Scrapbook, MHS.

52. Ibid.; Danner, "Recollections of Bishop Marvin," Manuscript.

53. Boyce Scrapbook, MHS; Danner, "Recollections of Bishop Marvin," Manuscript; Bannon Obituary, *Dublin Telegraph*, 14 July 1913; Blied, *Catholics and the Civil War*, 91; Kenny and Morrissey, "Father John Bannon, S.J.," 95.

54. *St. Louis Republican*, 1 and 13 Aug. 1913; Kenny and Morrissey, "Father John Bannon, S.J.," 97; Faherty to author, 29 June 1990; Boyce Scrapbook, MHS.

BIBLIOGRAPHY

MANUSCRIPT COLLECTIONS

Adjutant General Records of Confederate Soldiers of Missouri. Adjutant General's Office, Jefferson City.

Appler, John. Diary. Missouri Historical Society, St. Louis.

Babcock Scrapbook. Missouri Historical Society, St. Louis.

Bannon, John. Sketch. Confederate Museum, Richmond, Virginia.

Bannon, John. Diary. Yates Snowden Collection, South Caroliniana Library, University of South Carolina, Columbia, South Carolina.

Billon Scrapbook. Missouri Historical Society, St. Louis.

Boyce, Joseph. Papers. Missouri Historical Society, St. Louis.

Boyce, Joseph. "Rev. John Bannon-Chaplain Price's Missouri Confederate Division: Paper Read 8 Mar. 1914 at Confederate Veteran Meeting, Camp 731, St. Louis, Missouri, United Confederate Veterans." Missouri Historical Society, St. Louis.

Boyce, Joseph. Scrapbook. Missouri Historical Society, St. Louis.

Boyce, Joseph. "St. Louis Military Organizations." Missouri Historical Society, St. Louis.

Bowen, John S. Papers. Missouri Historical Society, St. Louis.

Bowen, John S. Genealogy. Georgia Historical Society, Savannah.

Bowen, John S. Letter-Book. Virginia Historical Society, Richmond.

Brauckman Scrapbook. Missouri Historical Society, St. Louis.

Breckenridge, William Clark. Papers. Missouri Historical Society, St. Louis.

Breckenridge Scrapbooks. Missouri Historical Society, St. Louis.

Burbridge, H. C. Papers. Jacksonville, Florida.

Camp Jackson Clippings. Missouri Historical Society, St. Louis.

Camp Jackson Papers. Missouri Historical Society, St. Louis.

Census Records of the Eighth Census of the United States, Fifth Ward. City of St. Louis, Missouri, 1860.

Cheavens, Henry Martyn. Diary. Historical Manuscript Collection, State Historical Society of Missouri, Columbia.

Civil War Collection. Missouri Historical Society, St. Louis.

Civil War Papers. Missouri Historical Society, St. Louis.

Clark, Champ. Papers. Western Historical Manuscript Collection, State Historical Society of Missouri, Columbia.

Clark, Champ. Scrapbooks. Western Historical Manuscript Collection, State Historical Society of Missouri, Columbia.

Clark Family. Papers. Missouri Historical Society, St. Louis.

Cockrell, Francis M. Scrapbook. Missouri Historical Society, St. Louis.

Crawford, Emily, to Mrs. Elizabeth Lewis, 11 June 1863. Charles Sullivan Collection, Perkinston, Mississippi.

Danner, Albert Carey. Papers. Mrs. Dorothy Danner Tribets, Mobile.

Dunlap, Samuel Baldwin. Diary. Western Historical Manuscript Collection, State Historical Society of Missouri, Columbia.

Elliott, George. Journal. Tennessee State Library and Archives, Nashville.

Elliot, William G., Jr. Papers. Missouri Historical Society, St. Louis.

Faherty, William B. Collection of John Bannon Material. St. Louis.

Farrington Family Burial Records. Bellefontaine Cemetery Archives, St. Louis.

Fetherston, William and Sarah, County Dublin, Ireland. Collection of John Bannon Material.

Fisher, Theodore D. Diary. Missouri Historical Society, St. Louis.

Frost, Daniel. Papers. Missouri Historical Society, St. Louis.

Gamble, Hamilton R. Papers. Missouri Historical Society, St. Louis.

Garesche Family. Papers. Missouri Historical Society, St. Louis.

Greene, H. P. Diary. Washington County, Arkansas Historical Society, Fayetteville.

Guibor, Warren R. Guibor Family Papers. Manchester, Missouri.

Hawley to Parents, 18 May 1863. Missouri Historical Society, St. Louis.

Herndon, Dallas T. "Traditions of the Battle of Pea Ridge and Elkhorn Tavern." Arkansas History Commission, Little Rock.

Historic Homes of Missouri Scrapbooks. Missouri Historical Society, St. Louis.

Hogan, Thomas. Letters. Missouri Historical Society, St. Louis.

Holman, Vincent. Diary typescript. State Historical Society of Iowa, Iowa City.

Hubble, Richard M. "Personal Reminiscences and Fragments of Old Settlers." Missouri Historical Society, St. Louis.

Isaac, Deborah. "Confederate Days in St. Louis." Newspaper clippings, Missouri Historical Society, St. Louis.

Jenkins, Gertrude. Papers, 1859–1908. Manuscript Department, William R. Perkins Library, Duke University, Durham, North Carolina.

Kavanaugh, William. Memoirs and Papers. Western Historical Manuscript Collection, State Historical Society of Missouri, Columbia.

Kearny-Kennerly Scrapbooks. Missouri Historical Society, St. Louis.

Kennedy's St. Louis Directory, 1859 and 1860.

LaGrave, Daisy E. "The Artist Unknown and a Missing Diary: A Report Presenting Certain Selected Data in the History of St. John's Church, St. Louis, Missouri, October 1960." St. John's Church Archives, St. Louis.

Lane, William Carr. Collection. Missouri Historical Society, St. Louis.

Leavy, John. Journal. Philip Mallinckrodt, Salt Lake City, Utah.

Little, Henry. Biographical Sketch. Maryland Historical Society, Baltimore.

Little, Henry. Diary. United States Army Military History Institute, Carlisle Barracks, Pennsylvania.

Love, James E. Papers. Missouri Historical Society, St. Louis.

Mack, William F., to Colonel Cobb, 11 April 1862. Hunter-Dawson Historical Site Archives, New Madrid, Missouri.

McLellan, Alden, to Albert Danner, 18 May 1919. Missouri Historical Society, St. Louis.

Map, topographical. Pea Ridge Quadrangle. United States Department of the Interior, Geological Survey.

Maryland General Assembly Laws, 1849–1850. Resolution 15. Maryland State Archives, Annapolis.

Mesker Collection. Missouri Historical Society, St. Louis.

Missouri Militia Collection. Missouri Historical Society, St. Louis.

Mothershead, Joseph R. 1862 Journal. Tennessee State Library and Archives, Nashville.

National Archives. Bannon, John. 1864 Ireland Poster. Washington, D.C.

National Archives. Compiled Service Records of Confederate Soldiers Who Served in Organizations From the State of Missouri, Record Group 109.

National Archives. Compiled Service Records of Union Soldiers Who Served in Organizations From the State of Missouri, Record Group 109.

National Archives. Compiled Service Records of Confederate General and Staff Officers and Nonregimental Enlisted Men.

Necrologies Scrapbook. Missouri Historical Society, St. Louis.

Neuman, Dorothy Breen. "Kerry Patch." Undated typescript. Missouri Historical Society, St. Louis.

O'Hare, Frank. Papers. Missouri Historical Society, St. Louis.

O'Neil, Horton. "The Story of Joseph O'Neil, 1817–1893." Manuscript. Missouri Historical Society, St. Louis.

Parole Records of Confederates Captured at Vicksburg, Mississippi. Vicksburg National Military Park Archives, Vicksburg.

Parsons, Monroe Mosby. Papers. Missouri Historical Society, St. Louis.

Partnership Agreement Between Wade, Stille, Osborne, and Frost as Trustee, 9 April 1853. Missouri Historical Society, St. Louis.

Payne, Asa M. "Story of the Battle of Pea Ridge." Pea Ridge National Military Park Archives, Pea Ridge, Arkansas.

Pickett Papers. Division of Manuscripts, Library of Congress, Washington, D.C.

Riley, Amos Camden. Papers. H. Riley Bock Collection, New Madrid, Missouri.

Rives, Benjamin Avery. Sketch. Missouri Historical Society, St. Louis.

Robbins, Edward C. Papers. Mercantile Library, St. Louis.

Rombauer Order Book, Journals, and Diaries. Missouri Historical Society, St. Louis.

Ruyle, William A. Memoir. Dee Ruyle, Bolivar, Missouri.

Sebree Collection. Missouri Historical Society, St. Louis.

Simpson, Avington Wayne. Diary. Western Historical Manuscript Collection, State Historical Society of Missouri, Columbia.

Skaggs, William. Collection of Confederate Veteran Letters, Arkansas History Commission, Little Rock.

Smith, Isaac Vincent. Memoir. Western Historical Manuscript Collection, State Historical Society of Missouri, Columbia.

Soulard, Antoine P. Papers. Missouri Historical Society, St. Louis.

St. John's Church Archives Records. St. Louis.

Tyler, John, to William Yancey, 15 Oct. 1862. Western Historical Manuscript Collection, State Historical Society of Missouri, Columbia.

Voelkner, Henry, to Family, 18 Mar. 1862. Missouri Historical Society, St. Louis.

Wade, William, to Governor Robert M. Stewart, 23 Feb. 1860. Western Historical Manuscript Collection, State Historical Society of Missouri, Columbia.

Wade Family Burial Records. Bellefontaine Cemetery Archives, St. Louis.

Walter, John F. "Capsule Histories of Arkansas Military Units." Manuscript. Arkansas History Commission, Little Rock.

Warren, George William. Diary. George Warren IV, Montpelier, Virginia.

INTERVIEW

Evans, Marjorie. Lincoln County Historical Society, Missouri, to author, Troy, Missouri, 20 Nov. 1990.

PUBLISHED SOURCES

Adamson, Hans Christian. *Rebellion in Missouri 1861*. New York: Chilton Co., 1961.

Anderson, Ephraim McDowell. *Memoirs: Historical and Personal; Including the Cam-*

paigns of the First Missouri Confederate Brigade. Ed. Edwin Cole Bearss. 1868; reprint ed., Dayton: Morningside, 1972.

Anderson, Galusha. *The Story of a Border City during the Civil War.* Boston: Little, Brown and Co., 1908.

Balfour, Emma. *Vicksburg, A City Under Siege: Diary of Emma Balfour May 16, 1863–June 2, 1863.* Phillip C. Weinberger, 1983.

Bannon, John. "Experiences of a Confederate Army Chaplain." *Letters and Notices of the English Jesuit Province* 34 (1866–1868): 201–210.

Barr, Alwyn. "Confederate Artillery in Arkansas." *Arkansas Historical Quarterly* 22:3 (Autumn 1963): 238–49.

Barton, George. *Angels of the Battlefield.* Philadelphia: Catholic Art Publishing Co., 1897.

Battlefield of Pea Ridge, Arkansas, Battlefield Folklore. Fayetteville: Washington County Historical Society, 1958.

Battle of Pea Ridge, The. Rogers: Pea Ridge National Military Centennial Committee, 1963.

Battle of Pea Ridge, The. Pea Ridge National Park Association.

Baxter, William. *Pea Ridge and Prairie Grove or Scenes and Incidents of the War in Arkansas.* Cincinnati: Poe and Hitchcock, 1864.

Bearss, Edwin C. *The Fall of Fort Henry, Tennessee.* Dover: Eastern National Park and Monument Association, n.d.

————. *The Campaign For Vicksburg: Grant Strikes a Fatal Blow.* 3 vols. Dayton: Morningside, 1986.

————. *The Campaign For Vicksburg: Unvexed to the Sea.* Dayton: Morningside, 1986.

————. "From Rolla to Fayetteville with General Curtis." *Arkansas Historical Quarterly* 19:3 (Autumn 1960): 225–59.

————. "The Battle of Pea Ridge." *Arkansas Historical Quarterly* 20:1 (Spring 1961): 89–93.

————. "The First Day at Pea Ridge." *Arkansas Historical Quarterly* 17:1 (Spring 1958): 132–54.

————. "Grand Gulf's Role in the Civil War." *Civil War History* 5:1 (March 1959): 5–29.

————. "The Battle of Pea Ridge." *Annals of Iowa* 36:8 (Spring 1963): 569–89.

————. "The Battle of Pea Ridge." *Annals of Iowa* 37:1 (Summer 1963): 9–37.

————. "The Battle of Pea Ridge." *Annals of Iowa* 37:2 (Fall 1963).

————. "The Battle of Pea Ridge." *Annals of Iowa* 37:3 (Winter 1964): 207–39.

————. "The Battle of Pea Ridge." *Annals of Iowa* 37:4 (Spring 1964): 201–10.

Bennett, L. G., and William M. Haigh. *History of the Thirty-Sixth Regiment Illinois Volunteers: During the War of the Rebellion.* Aurora: Knickerbocker and Hodder, 1876.

Bernard, Mother M. *The Story of the Sisters of Mercy in Mississippi, 1860–1930*. New York: P. J. Kennedy and Sons, 1931.

Bevier, Robert S. *History of the First and Second Missouri Confederate Brigades, 1861–1865 and From Wakarusa to Appomattox, A Military Anagraph*. St. Louis: Bryan, Brand and Co., 1879.

Bigelow, John. *Retrospections of an Active Life*. 5 vols. New York: Baker and Taylor Co., 1909–1913.

Blied, Reverend Benjamin J. *Catholics and the Civil War*. Milwaukee: private printing, 1945.

Bond, John W. "The History of Elkhorn Tavern." *Arkansas Historical Quarterly* 21:1 (Spring 1962): 3–15.

Branch, Mary Emerson. "The Story Behind the Story of the Arkansas and the Carondelet." *Missouri Historical Review* 79:3 (April 1985): 313–31.

Britton, Wiley. *The Civil War on the Border*. 2 vols. New York: G. P. Putnam's Sons, 1899.

"Brother Fought Against Brother." *Confederate Veteran* 10:10 (October 1902): 463.

Brown, Walter L. "Pea Ridge: Gettysburg of the West." *Arkansas Historical Quarterly* 15:1 (Spring 1956): 3–16.

Browne, Junius Henri. *Four Years in Secessia*. Hartford: O. D. Case and Co., 1865.

Burnes, Brian P. *If These Towers Could Talk*. St. Louis: private printing, 1947.

Burton, William L. *Melting Pot Soldiers: The Union's Ethnic Regiments*. Ames: Iowa State University Press, 1988.

Byers, S. H. M. *Fire and Sword*. New York: Neale Publishing Co., 1911.

Calkins, Homer L., ed. "Elkhorn to Vicksburg: James H. Fauntleroy's Diary for the Year 1862." *Civil War History* 2:1 (January 1956): 7–43.

Carson, William G. B. "Secesh." *Bulletin of the Missouri Historical Society* 23:2 (January 1967): 119–31.

Carter, Harvey L., and Norma L. Peterson, eds. "William S. Stewart Letters, January 13, 1861 to December 4, 1862." *Missouri Historical Review* 61:4 (July 1967): 463–88.

Carter, Samuel III. *The Final Fortress: The Campaign For Vicksburg, 1862–1863*. New York: St. Martin's Press, 1980.

Castel, Albert. *General Sterling Price and the Civil War in the West*. Baton Rouge: Louisiana State University Press, 1968.

———. "A New View of the Battle of Pea Ridge." *Missouri Historical Review* 62:2 (January 1968): 136–51.

Catton, Bruce. *Grant Moves South*. Boston: Little, Brown and Co., 1960.

———. *Picture History of the Civil War*. New York: American Heritage Publishing Co., 1960.

———. *This Hallowed Ground*. New York: Pocket Books, 1971.

Coddington, Edwin B. *The Gettysburg Campaign: A Study in Command*. New York: Charles Scribner's Sons, 1984.

Cole, Franklin P. Introduction to *The Preached Liberty*. Indianapolis: Liberty Press, n.d.

Comerford, R. V. "Nation, Nationalism, and the Irish Language," in Thomas H. Hackey and Lawrence J. McCaffrey, eds., *Perspectives on Irish Nationalism*. Lexington: University of Kentucky Press, 1989.

Connelly, Thomas L. *Civil War Tennessee: Battles and Leaders*. Knoxville: University of Tennessee, 1979.

———. *Army of the Heartland: The Army of Tennessee, 1861–1862*. Baton Rouge: Louisiana State University Press, 1967.

Connelly, Thomas L., and Barbara L. Bellows. *God and General Longstreet: The Lost Cause and the Southern Mind*. Baton Rouge: Louisiana State University Press, 1982.

Cooling, Benjamin Franklin. *Forts Henry and Donelson: The Key to the Confederate Heartland*. Knoxville: University of Tennessee Press, 1987.

Covington, James W. "The Camp Jackson Affair: 1861." *Missouri Historical Review* 55:3 (April 1961): 197–212.

Cullen, Joseph P. *The Peninsula Campaign 1862: McClellan and Lee Struggle For Richmond*. New York: Bonanza Books, n.d.

Cullop, Charles P. *Confederate Propaganda in Europe, 1861–1865*. Coral Gables: University of Miami Press, 1969.

Daniel, Larry J. "Bruinsburg: Missed Opportunity or Postwar Rhetoric?" *Civil War History* 32:3 (September 1986): 256–67.

Danner, Albert C. "Father Bannon's Secret Mission." *Confederate Veteran* 27:5 (May 1919): 180–81.

Davis, Richard. *The Young Ireland Movement*. Dublin: Gill and Macmillan, 1987.

Depp, Thomas. "Personal Experiences at Pea Ridge." *Confederate Veteran* 20:1 (January 1912): 17–20.

"Diary of Lieut. Col. Hubbell of 3d Regiment Missouri Infantry, C.S.A." *The Land We Love* 6:2 (1868–69).

Donald, David H., ed. *Why the North Won the Civil War*. Baton Rouge: Louisiana State University Press, 1960.

Dowdey, Clifford. *Experiment in Rebellion*. New York: Doubleday and Co., 1946.

———. *The Seven Days: The Emergence of Lee*. Boston: Little, Brown and Co., 1964.

Duke, Basil. *Reminiscences of General Basil W. Duke*. Garden City: Doubleday, Page and Co., 1911.

Durkin, Joseph T. *Stephen R. Mallory: Confederate Navy Chief*. Chapel Hill: University of North Carolina Press, 1954.

Duychinck, Evert A. *National History of the War for the Union*. 3 vols. New York: Fry and Co., 1861–1865.

Eaton, Clement. *A History of the Southern Confederacy*. New York: Macmillan Co., 1954.

Encyclopedia of the New West, The. Marshall: United States Biographical Publishing Co., 1881.

Evans, Eli N. *Judah P. Benjamin: The Jewish Confederate*. New York: Free Press, 1988.

Faherty, William Barnaby. *The Catholic Ancestry of Saint Louis*. St. Louis: Bureau of Information, Archdiocese of Saint Louis, 1965.

————. *Better the Dream, Saint Louis: University and Community 1818–1968*. St. Louis: St. Louis University, 1968.

————. *Rebels or Reformers? Dissenting Priests in American Life*. Chicago: Loyola University Press, 1987.

————. *Dream by the River: Two Centuries of Saint Louis Catholicism, 1766–1967*. St. Louis: Piraeus Publishers, 1973.

Faust, Drew Gilpin. *The Creation of Confederate Nationalism: Ideology and Identity in the Civil War South*. Baton Rouge: Louisiana State University Press, 1988.

Fellman, Michael. *Inside War: The Guerrilla Conflict in Missouri During the American Civil War*. New York: Oxford University Press, 1989.

Freeman, Douglas Southall. *Lee's Lieutenants: A Study in Command, Cedar Mountain to Chancellorsville*. 3 vols. New York: Charles Scribner's Sons, 1943.

Fremantle, Arthur J. L. *Three Months in the Southern States: April–June 1863*. New York: John Bradburn Publishers, 1864.

From Kerry Patch to Little Paderborn: A Visit in the Irish-German Communities of Nineteenth Century St. Louis. St. Louis: Landmarks Association of St. Louis, 1966.

Gerber, John. "Mark Twain's Private Campaign." *Civil War History* 1:1 (March 1955): 37–60.

Grant, Ulysses S. *Personal Memoirs of U. S. Grant*. New York: Century Co., 1903.

Greene, Francis V. *The Mississippi*. New York: Charles Scribner's Sons, 1882.

Guernsey, Alfred H., and Henry M. Alden. *Harper's Pictorial History of the Civil War*. New York: Fairfax Press, n.d.

Gunn, Jack W. "The Battle of Iuka." *Journal of Mississippi History* 24:3 (July 1962): 142–57.

Hamilton, James J. *The Battle of Fort Donelson*. New York: Thomas Yoseloff, 1968.

Hanley, Thomas O'Brien. *The American Revolution and Religion, Maryland 1770–1800*. Washington, D.C.: Catholic University of America Press, 1971.

Hardaway, Harriet Lane Cates. "The Adventures of General Frost and His Wife Lily during the Civil War." *Florissant Valley Historical Society Quarterly* 14:2 (July 1972): 1–10.

Harrell, Virginia Calohan. *Vicksburg and the River*. Vicksburg: Virginia C. Harrell, 1986.

Hartje, Robert G. *Van Dorn: The Life and Times of a Confederate General*. Nashville: Vanderbilt University Press, 1967.

Harwood, Nathan C. *The Pea Ridge Campaign, Civil War Sketches and Incidents Read Before the Nebraska Commandery, Nebraska Military Order of the Loyal Legion*. Omaha: Ackerman Brothers and Heintze Printers, 1887.

Hendrick, Burton J. *Statesmen of the Lost Cause: Jefferson Davis and His Cabinet*. New York: Literary Guild of America, 1939.

Hernon, Joseph M., Jr. *Celts, Catholics and Copperheads: Ireland Views the American Civil War*. Columbus: Ohio State University Press, 1968.

————. "The Irish Nationalists and Southern Secession." *Civil War History* 12:1 (March 1966): 43–53.

————. "Irish Religious Opinion on the American Civil War." *Catholic Historical Review* 49:4 (January 1964): 508–23.

History of Andrew and DeKalb Counties, Missouri. Chicago: Goodspeed Publishing Co., 1888.

History of Henry and St. Clair Counties, Missouri. St. Joseph: National Historical Co., 1883.

History of Lincoln County, Missouri. Chicago: Goodspeed Publishing Co., 1881.

Holcombe, R. I., and F. W. Adams. *An Account of the Battle of Wilson's Creek, or Oak Hills*. Springfield: Dow and Adams, 1883.

Holland, Dorthy Garesche. *The Garesche, De Bauduy and Des Chapelles Families: History and Genealogy*. St. Louis: Schneider Printing Co., 1963.

Hopewell, Menra. *History of the Missouri Volunteer Militia*. St. Louis: George Knapp, 1861.

Horn, Stanley F. *Tennessee's War 1861–1865*. Nashville: Civil War Centennial Commission, 1965.

————. *The Army of Tennessee*. Norman: University of Oklahoma Press, 1952.

Howe, Henry. *The Times of the Rebellion in the West*. Cincinnati: private printing, 1867.

Hughes, Michael. "The Battle of Pea Ridge or Elkhorn Tavern." *Blue & Gray Magazine* 5:3 (January 1988): 1–50.

Hughes, Nathaniel Cheairs, Jr. *General William J. Hardee: Old Reliable*. Baton Rouge: Louisiana State University Press, 1965.

Hyde, William, and Howard L. Conrad. *Encyclopedia of the History of St. Louis*. 4 vols. St. Louis: Southern Historical Co., 1899.

In and About Vicksburg: An Illustrated Guide Book to the City of Vicksburg, Mississippi; Its History; Its Appearance; Its Business Houses. Vicksburg: Gibralter Publishing Co., 1890.

Johnson, J. B. *History of Vernon County, Missouri*. 2 vols. Chicago: C. F. Cooper, 1911.

Johnson, Robert V., and C. C. Buel, eds. *Battles and Leaders of the Civil War*. 4 vols. New York: Thomas Yoseloff, 1956.

Jolly, Ellen Ryan. *Nuns of the Battlefield*. Philadelphia: Providence Visitor Press, 1897.

Jones, Archer. *Confederate Strategy from Shiloh to Vicksburg*. Baton Rouge: Louisiana State University Press, 1961.

Jones, Archer, William N. Still, Richard Beringer, and Herman Hattaway. *Why the South Lost the Civil War*. Athens: University of Georgia Press, 1986.

Jones, Paul. *The Irish Brigade*. New York: Robert B. Luce, 1969.

Jordan, Donaldson, and Edwin J. Pratt. *Europe and the American Civil War*. New York: Houghton Mifflin, 1931.

Kennedy, Frances H., ed. *The Civil War Battlefield Guide*. Boston: Houghton Mifflin, 1990.

Kennerly, William Clark. *Persimmon Hill: A Narrative of Old St. Louis and the Far West*. Norman: University of Oklahoma Press, 1948.

Kenny, Rev. Laurence J., and Joseph P. Morrissey. "Father John Bannon, S.J." *Historical Records and Studies of the United States Historical Society* 26 (1936): 92–98.

King, James T. *A Life of General Eugene A. Carr*. Lincoln: University of Nebraska Press, 1963.

Kirkpatrick, Arthur Roy. "Missouri in the Early Months of the Civil War." *Missouri Historical Review* 55:3 (April 1961): 235–66.

Kirschten, Ernest. *Catfish and Crystal*. New York: Doubleday, 1960.

Kitchens, Ben Earl. *Rosecrans Meets Price: The Battle of Iuka, Mississippi*. Florence, Ala.: Thornwood Publishers, 1985.

Knox, Thomas W. *Camp-Fire and Cotton-Field: Southern Adventure in Time of War*. Philadelphia: Jones Brothers, 1865.

Lamers, William M. *The Edge of Glory: A Biography of Gen. William S. Rosecrans, U.S.A.* New York: Harcourt, Brace and World, 1961.

Litz, Francis A. *Father Tabb: A Study of His Life and Works*. Baltimore: Johns Hopkins University Press, 1923.

Lord, Francis A. *Civil War Collector's Encyclopedia*. New York: Castle Books, 1965.

Lyon, William H. "Claiborne Fox Jackson and the Secession Crisis in Missouri." *Missouri Historical Review* 58:4 (July 1964): 422–41.

McDermott, John Francis. "Gold Fever: The Letters of 'Solitarie,' Goldrush Correspondent of '49." *Bulletin of the Missouri Historical Society* 5:3 (July 1949).

McDonald, Lyla Merrill. *Iuka's History Embodying Dudley's Battle of Iuka*. Corinth: Ranking Printery, 1923.

McDonough, James Lee. *Shiloh—In Hell before Night*. Knoxville: University of Tennessee Press, 1977.

McDonough, James Lee, and Thomas L. Connelly. *Five Tragic Hours: The Battle of Franklin*. Knoxville: University of Tennessee Press, 1983.

McElroy, John. *The Struggle for Missouri*. Washington, D.C.: National Tribune Co., 1909.

McPherson, James M. *Battle Cry of Freedom: The Civil War Era*. New York: Oxford University Press, 1988.

Madaus, Howard Michael, and Robert D. Needham. *The Battle Flags of the Confederate Army of Tennessee*. Milwaukee: Milwaukee Public Museum, 1976.

Mahan, Alfred Thayer. *The Gulf and Inland Waters*. New York: Charles Scribner's Sons, 1905.

"Major John Henry Britts." *Confederate Veteran* 18:1 (January 1910): 36.

Maury, Dabney Herndon. *Recollections of a Virginian*. New York: Charles Scribner's Sons, 1894.

———. "Recollections of the Elkhorn Campaign." *Southern Historical Society Papers* 2 (Jan.–Dec. 1876): 180–92.

———. "Recollections of the Campaign Against Grant in North Mississippi in 1862–1863." *Southern Historical Society Papers* 13 (Jan.–Feb. 1885): 285–311.

Meade, Robert Douthat. *Judah P. Benjamin: Confederate Statesman*. New York: Oxford University Press, 1943.

Meagher, Timothy J., ed. *From Paddy to Studs: Irish-American Communities in the Turn of the Century Era*. Westport, Conn.: Greenwood Press, 1986.

Miers, Earl S. *The Web of Victory: Grant at Vicksburg*. Baton Rouge: Louisiana State University Press, 1984.

Mitchell, Joseph B. *The Badge of Gallantry*. New York: Macmillan Co., 1968.

Mitchell, Mrs. L. G. "Camp Life in the Sixties." *Confederate Veteran* 24:9 (September 1916): 394–97.

Mitchell, W. A. "The Confederate Mail Carrier." *Confederate Veteran* 22:12 (December 1914): 529.

Monaghan, Jay. *Civil War on the Western Border 1854–1865*. New York: Bonanza Books, n.d.

Moody, Claire N. *Battle of Pea Ridge or Elkhorn Tavern*. Little Rock: Arkansas Valley Printing Co., 1956.

Moody, Theodore William, and F. Martin, eds. *The Course of Irish History*. Cork: Mercier Press, 1967.

Moore, John C. *Confederate Military History*, ed. Clement A. Evans. 12 vols. New York: Thomas Yoseloff, 1962.

Moore, Samuel J. T., Jr. *Moore's Complete Civil War Guide to Richmond*. Richmond: Samuel J. T. Moore, 1978.

Mullins, Michael A. *The Fremont Rifles: A History of the 37th Illinois Veteran Volunteer Infantry*. Wilmington: Broadfoot Publishing Co., 1990.

Mulvihill, M. J. *Vicksburg and Warren County, Mississippi, Tunica Indians, Quebec Missionaries, Civil War Veterans*. Vicksburg: Von Norman Printing Co., 1931.

Musser, Richard H. "The War in Missouri." *Southern Bivouac* 2 (1886): 745–52.

Nevins, Allan. *Ordeal of the Union*. 8 vols. New York: Charles Scribner's Sons, 1947–1959.

Norman, Edward. *A History of Modern Ireland*. London: Allen Lane, 1971.

O'Hanlon, John. *Life and Scenery in Missouri: Reminiscence of a Missionary*. Dublin: J. Duffy and Co., 1890.

Oldroyd, Osborn H. *A Soldier's Story of the Siege of Vicksburg*. Springfield: H. W. Rokker Printer, 1885.

O'Neil, Daniel J. *Three Perennial Themes of Anti-Colonialism: The Irish Case*. Denver: University of Denver Press, 1976.

Organization and Status of Missouri Troops in Service During the Civil War. Washington, D.C.: U.S. Government Printing Office, 1902.

O'Tuathaigh, Gearold. *Ireland Before the Famine 1798–1848*. Dublin: Gill and Macmillan, 1972.

Payne, James E. "The Test of Missourians." *Confederate Veteran* 37:2 (February 1929): 64–65, 101–104.

Phillips, Christopher. *Damned Yankee: The Life of General Nathaniel Lyon*. Columbia: University of Missouri Press, 1990.

Pillar, James J. *The Catholic Church in Mississippi, 1837–1865*. New Orleans: Hauser Printing Co., 1964.

Pitts, Charles F. *Chaplains in Gray: The Confederate Chaplains' Story*. Nashville: Broadman Press, 1957.

Pollard, Edward A. *Southern History of the War: The First Year of the War*. 2 vols. London: Philip and Son, 1863.

Porter, David D. *The Naval History of the Civil War*. New York: Sherman Publishing Co., 1886.

Porter, V. M. "A History of Battery 'A' of St. Louis." *Missouri Historical Society Collections* 2:4 (1900–1906).

Prentis, Noble L. *Kansas Miscellanies*. Topeka: Kansas Publishing Co., 1889.

Primm, James Neal. *Lion of the Valley: St. Louis, Missouri*. Boulder: Pruett Publishing Co., 1981.

Primm, James Neal, and Steven Rowan, eds. *Germans for a Free Missouri: Translations from the St. Louis Radical Press 1857–1862*. Columbia: University of Missouri Press, 1983.

Quaife, Milo. *Absalom Grimes: Confederate Mail Runner*. New Haven: Yale University Press, 1926.

Rawley, James A. *Turning Points of the Civil War*. Lincoln: University of Nebraska Press, 1989.

Reed, Rowena. *Combined Operations in the Civil War*. Annapolis: Naval Institute Press, 1978.

Reports on the Historic Marker Program, March 10, 1963. Rogers: Pea Ridge Memorial Association, 1963.

"Restoration of St. John's, The." *Bulletin of the Missouri Historical Society* 13:3 (April 1957).

"Rev. John Bannon." *Confederate Veteran* 21:9 (September 1913): 451.

Richardson, James D., ed. *A Compilation of the Messages and Papers of the Confederacy, Including the Diplomatic Correspondence 1861–1865*. Nashville: United States Publishing Co., 1905.

Roberts, Dr. J. C. "Caring For the Wounded at Iuka." *Confederate Veteran* 2:11 (November 1894): 328.

Roher, Walter A. "Confederate Generals: The View from Below." *Civil War Times Illustrated* (July 1979): 13–14.

Roland, Charles P. *The Confederacy*. Chicago: University of Chicago Press, 1960.

Rombauer, Robert J. *The Union Cause in St. Louis in 1861*. St. Louis: Nixon-Jones Printing Co., 1909.

Romero, Sidney J. *The Rebel Chaplain: Religion in the Rebel Ranks.* Lanham, Md.: University Press of America, 1983.

————. "The Confederate Chaplain." *Civil War History* 1:2 (June 1955): 127–40.

Rose, Victor M. *Ross' Texas Brigade.* Louisville: Courier Journal, 1881.

Rothensteiner, John. *History of the Archdiocese of St. Louis.* 2 vols. St. Louis: Press of Blackwell Wielandy Co., 1928.

Ruyle, Walter Harrington. *Missouri: Union or Secession.* Nashville: George Peabody College for Teaching, 1931.

Ryan, Ignatius L. "Confederate Agents in Ireland." *United States Historical Society: Historical Records and Studies* 26 (1936).

St. Peters, Robert. *Memorial Volume of the Diamond Jubilee of St. Louis University, 1829–1904.* St. Louis: St. Louis University Press, 1904.

Scharf, John T. *History of St. Louis City and County from the Earliest Period to the Present Day.* 2 vols. Philadelphia: Louis H. Everts and Co., 1883.

Schneider, John C. "Riot and Reaction in St. Louis." *Missouri Historical Review* 68:2 (January 1974): 171–85.

Schroeder, L. E. "The Battle of Wilson's Creek and Its Effect upon Missouri." *Missouri Historical Review* 71:2 (January 1977): 156–73.

Shalhope, Robert E. *Sterling Price: Portrait of a Southerner.* Columbia: University of Missouri Press, 1971.

Shattuck, Gardiner H., Jr. *A Shield and Hiding Place: The Religious Life of the Civil War Armies.* Macon: Mercer University Press, 1987.

Silver, James W. *Confederate Morale and Church Propaganda.* Tuscaloosa: Norton and Co., 1957.

Silverman, Jason H. "Stars, Bars, and Foreigners: The Immigrant and the Making of the Confederacy." *Journal of Confederate History* 1:2 (Fall 1988): 265–85.

Stanley, Lois, George F. Wilson, and Mary Helen Wilson, eds. *Death Records from Missouri Newspapers: The Civil War Years, January 1861–December 1865.* Decorah: Anundsen Printing Co., 1983.

Stevens, Walter. *St. Louis, The Fourth City.* 3 vols. St. Louis: S. J. Clarke, 1909.

Stewart, Faye L. "Battle of Pea Ridge." *Missouri Historical Review* 22:2 (January 1928): 187–92.

Stock, Leo Francis. "Catholic Participation in the Diplomacy of the Southern Confederacy." *Catholic Historical Review* 16:1 (April 1930): 1–18.

————. "The United States at the Court of Pius IX." *Catholic Historical Review* 3:1 (April 1923).

Strauss, Erich. *Irish Nationalism and British Democracy.* New York: Columbia University Press, 1951.

Sunderland Glenn W. *Five Days to Glory.* New York: A. S. Barnes, 1970.

Switzler, William F. *Switzler's Illustrated History of Missouri from 1541 to 1877.* St. Louis: C. R. Barns, 1879.

Thomas, Emory M. *The Confederate Nation: 1861–1865.* New York: Harper and Row, 1979.

————. *The Confederacy as a Revolutionary Experience*. Engelwood Cliffs: Prentice-Hall, 1971.

Toft, Carolyn Hewes. *Carondelet: The Ethnic Heritage of an Urban Neighborhood*. St. Louis: Landmarks Association of St. Louis, 1980.

Towey, Martin G., and Margaret L. Sullivan. "The Knights of Father Mathew: Parallel Ethnic Reform." *Missouri Historical Review* 75:2 (January 1981): 168–83.

Truman, W. L. "Gallant William Wade—His Battery Flag." *Confederate Veteran* 19:9 (September 1911): 419.

Tunnard, William H. *A Southern Record: The History of the Third Regiment Louisiana Infantry*. Dayton: Morningside repr., 1970.

Union and Confederate Annals: The Blue and Gray in Friendship Meet, and Heroic Deeds Recite 1:1 (St. Louis, 1884).

United States Department of the Interior. *Vicksburg and the Opening of the Mississippi River, 1862–1863*. Washington, D.C.: U.S. Government Printing Office, 1986.

Urquhart, Kenneth Trist, ed. and introduction to *Vicksburg: Southern City Under Siege, William Lovelace Foster's Letter Describing the Defense and Surrender of the Confederate Fortress on the Mississippi*. New Orleans: Historic New Orleans Collection, 1980.

Wakelyn, Jon L. *Biographical Dictionary of the Confederacy*. Westport: Greenwood Press, 1977.

Warner, Ezra J. *Generals in Gray: Lives of the Confederate Commanders*. Baton Rouge: Louisiana State University Press, 1959.

War of the Rebellion, The: A Compilation of the Official Records of the Union and Confederate Armies. 130 vols. Washington, D.C.: U.S. Government Printing Office, 1880–1901.

War of the Rebellion, The: A Compilation of the Official Records of the Union and Confederate Navies. 31 vols. Washington, D.C.: U.S. Government Printing Office, 1895–1929.

Watkins, Marie Oliver, and Helen Watkins. *Tearin' Through the Wilderness: Missouri Pioneer Episodes and Genealogy of the Watkins Family of Virginia and Missouri*. Charleston: private printing, 1957.

Wheeler, Richard. *The Siege of Vicksburg*. New York: Thomas Y. Crowell, 1978.

Wickersham, John T. *The Gray and the Blue*. Berkeley: John T. Wickersham, 1915.

Wiley, Bell Irvin. *The Life of Johnny Reb: The Common Soldier in the Confederacy*. Baton Rouge: Louisiana State University Press, 1978.

Williams, Kenneth P. *Lincoln Finds a General*. 5 vols. New York: Macmillan Co., 1959.

Williams, Walter. *History of Northeast Missouri*. 3 vols. Chicago: Lewis Publishing Co., 1913.

Woodward, C. Vann, ed. *Mary Chesnut's Civil War*. New Haven: Yale University Press, 1981.

Wright, William C. *The Confederate Magazine at Fort Wade, Grand Gulf, Mississippi:*

Excavations, 1980–1981. Jackson: Mississippi Department of Archives and History and the Grand Gulf State Military Monument, 1982.

Wyman, Mark. *Immigrants in the Valley: Irish, Germans, and Americans in the Upper Mississippi Country, 1830–1860.* Chicago: Nelson Hall, 1983.

Yearns, W. Buck, and John G. Barrett, eds. *North Carolina Civil War Documentary.* Chapel Hill: University of North Carolina Press, 1980.

INDEX

ABOUT THE AUTHOR

PHILLIP THOMAS TUCKER is a United States Air Force Historian at Edwards Air Force Base, California. He received his B.S. and M.A. degrees from Central Missouri State University and his Ph.D. from St. Louis University.